THE LAND OF THE GURKHAS OR THE HIMALAYAN KINGDOM OF NEPAL

Ojaswi Rajanya, Projjwal Nepal Tara, Ati Pravala Gorkha Dakshina Bahu Prithuladheesha,
HIS HIGHNESS MAHARAJA JOODHA SHUMSHERE JUNG BAHADUR RANA,
G.C.L.H., G.C.L., G.C.S.I., G.C.SS.M.L., G.C.I.E.,
Yi Teng Pao Ting Shun Chian, Luh Chuan Shang Chang;
Honorary Lieutenant-General in the British Army,
Honorary Colonel of All the Gurkha Rifle Regiments in the Indian Army;

Prime Minister and Supreme Commander-in-Chief
OF NEPAL.

THE LAND OF THE GURKHAS OR THE HIMALAYAN KINGDOM OF NEPAL

W. BROOK NORTHEY

WITH A CHAPTER BY
BRIGADIER-GENERAL THE HON. C. G. BRUCE

GYAN

Published by

GYAN

Gyan Publishing House
5, Ansari Road
Daryaganj, New Delhi-110002
Phone: 011-47034999, 9811692060
E-mail: books@gyanbooks.com

Distribution Network
gyanbooks.com
India, USA, Canada, UK, Australia, France

ISBN : 978-81-212-3681-2 (PB)
First Published, London, 1937

2nd Impression 2020

Printed at: Gyan Press, Delhi.

The Land of the Gurkhas or The Himalayan Kingdom of Nepal
Author: W. Brook Northey

The LAND of the GURKHAS

OR

The Himalayan Kingdom of NEPAL

by Major W. BROOK NORTHEY, M.C.

(Order of the Star of Nepal); late 1st K.G.O. Gurkha Rifles

With a Chapter by

Brigadier-General the Hon. C. G. Bruce, C.B., M.V.O.

late 5th Royal Gurkha Rifles and 6th Gurkha Rifles

CAMBRIDGE

W. HEFFER & SONS LTD

Preface

In writing this book, undertaken at the suggestion of many friends, I have tried to steer a middle course between those accounts of Nepal, inevitably cursory and incomplete, that are to be found in ordinary works of travel whose authors have paid merely brief visits to that little-known country, and the more elaborate and exhaustive works written by those who from their close connection, official or non-official, with the country, can claim to be actual experts on the subject.

This claim I cannot make for myself, although I hope that, as the result of my twenty years' experience in a Gurkha Regiment, which included such work as training the Nepal Escort in Kathmandu in 1910, service with the Nepalese Contingent on the Indian Frontier during the Great War and the post of Recruiting Officer for five years (during which I was kindly permitted by H.H. the late Sir Chandra Shumshere to visit parts of the country usually inaccessible to Europeans) I can count myself not wholly unqualified for the task which I have undertaken.

Something more than mere knowledge of the subject is, however, necessary when the writing of a book is involved, and for such literary shortcomings as my work may disclose I can only ask the indulgence of my readers and plead in extenuation the interest of my theme, in the shape of one of the most picturesque and fascinating countries in the world.

To the various earlier works on Nepal, particularly those by such eminent authorities as the late Professor Sylvain Levi, the late Mr. Percival Landon and Mr. Percy Brown, upon which I have drawn heavily from time to time, I have made due acknowledgments in the text. To Brig.-Gen. The Hon. C. G. Bruce, C.B., M.V.O., I am most grateful for his valuable chapter and much kind help and suggestions throughout.

Of the many other kind friends who have helped me with information and advice I am specially indebted to Dr. R. L. Turner, M.C., Director of the School of Oriental Studies, London, for assistance in the writing of chapter X; to Mr. Douglas Smythe Osborne, of Soom Tea Estate, Mr. Basil Crees, of Lopchu Tea Estate and Mr. E. C. Partridge, late of Gielle T.E., for their help in the chapters on Darjeeling; to Sir Frederick O'Connor, K.C.S.I., C.I.E., C.V.O., Major C. J. Morris, late 3rd Q.A.O. Gurkha Rifles, Major R. A. Briggs, 5th (Royal) Gurkha Rifles, and Mrs. Kilburn, for the photographs they have kindly placed at my disposal; to Mr. Stanley M. Ballance, A.R.P.S., F.R.Met.S., F.R.A.S., for the excellent reproductions made from my own negatives and to Lieut.-Col. Alan Latham, D.S.O., of my own regiment, for reading and generally criticising the MS.

Lastly, my warmest thanks are due to His Excellency The Nepalese Minister in London, Lieut.-General Krishna Shumshere Jung Bahadur Rana, without whose help and personal assistance this book could never have been completed.

The map has been drawn from the most recent survey of Nepal and I am indebted to His Highness the Maharaja and to the Surveyor-General in India for permission to reproduce it.

Contents

		PAGE
PREFACE		v
LIST OF ILLUSTRATIONS		viii
I.	A GENERAL SURVEY OF NEPAL, BY BRIG.-GEN. THE HON. C. G. BRUCE, C.B., M.V.O.	1
II.	THE LIE OF THE LAND. The Hill Territory	17
III.	THE LIE OF THE LAND (*contd.*). The Valley and the Terai	23
IV.	THE EARLY HISTORY OF NEPAL	31
V.	RISE OF THE GURKHAS	42
VI.	TURBULENT YEARS	51
VII.	JUNG BAHADUR AND HIS DAYS	63
VIII.	EVENTFUL TIMES	71
IX.	NEPAL IN MODERN DAYS	79
X.	THE GURKHA AS HE IS	92
XI.	CUSTOMS AND CHARACTERISTICS	103
XII.	SPORTS AND DIVERSIONS	115
XIII.	THE HIGH ROAD TO KATHMANDU	127
XIV.	THE CAPITAL OF NEPAL	141
XV.	TEMPLES AND SHRINES	149
XVI.	PATAN	161
XVII.	BHATGAON AND NAWAKOT	168
XVIII.	CENTRAL NEPAL	180
XIX.	THE WESTERN BORDER	193
XX.	THE EASTERN BORDER	201
XXI.	DARJEELING AND ITS SURROUNDINGS	210
XXII.	DARJEELING TO-DAY	218
BIBLIOGRAPHY		231
INDEX		233

List of Illustrations

His Highness Sir Joodha Shumshere Jung Bahadur Rana, Maharaja and Prime Minister of Nepal *Frontispiece*

Facing pages

A Temple in the Indian Style. Nepal Valley 10

Temple of Akas Bhairab, Kathmandu 11

Temple on the Banks of the Baghmati 24

A Village. Nepal Valley 25

Entrance Gateway at Bhatgaon 44

Entrance Gateway at Patan 48

Temples in Bhatgaon 49

Hitaura Village near Churia Pass.. 58

Bhim Sen Temple at Patan 59

A Village Scene. Nepal Valley 70

His Highness Sir Chandra Shumshere and his Sons .. 83

Commanding General Sir Baber Shumshere Jung Bahadur Rana, G.B.E., K.C.S.I., K.C.I.E. 89

Gurkha Rifleman (Magar) in Uniform 94

Gurkha Rifleman (Gurung) in Mufti 94

Lalsing (Gurung) and his Wife 104

Men of the Magar and Gurung Tribes 104

Gurkha Women (Magar Tribe) 105

Women Weaving. Palpa District 111

Moving up into Position at a Tiger Shoot 116

A Fine Trophy 117

Returning to Camp 120

On the Road to Kathmandu 132

The Road near Chitlong 133

Ascending the Chandragiri Pass 137

Kathmandu Street Scene. (Figure of Kal Bhairab in Foreground) 141

Facing pages

Street Scene in Kathmandu 142
A Jemadar—Purano Gorakh Regiment, Nepalese Army .. 143
Approach to Darbar Square. Kathmandu 146
A Corner of Swayambhunath 150
Shrines at Swayambhunath 151
The Buddhist Temple of Bodhnath 152
The Temple of Pashupatinath 153
In Pashupatinath 154
Shrines near Changu Narayan. Nepal Valley 155
Column in the Village of Temi, near Kathmandu .. 156
A Temple Entrance. Kathmandu 157
The Darbar Square. Patan 161
The Darbar Square. Patan 162
A Temple at Patan 163
In the Darbar Square at Bhatgaon 168
Temples in Bhatgaon .. .. *following page* 168
The Temple of the Five Stages. (Nyat Pola) .. „ 168
Street Scene in Bhatgaon 169
The Junction of the Tadi and Tirsul Rivers at Devighat 174
Street Scene after Earthquake 175
Repairing a Temple 175
Destruction in the Darbar Square. Patan 176
Darbar Square, Bhatgaon, under Repair 176
Column of Bhimsen, after the Earthquake 177
Fissures on the Thuni Khel 177
Damage to H.M. the King's Palace 178
Entrance to Singha Darbar 178
Near Patan, after the Earthquake 179
Wreckage in Bhatgaon 179
Recruits at the Recruiting Depôt, Gorakhpur .. 180
Family Pensioners at Gorakhpur 180
On the Way to Batauli (Butwal) 181

Facing pages

Bridge over the Dobhan River. Palpa District .. 186
Customs House at Morek 187
A Powa or Rest-House. Palpa District 188
View from Massiang Ridge, looking towards Tansing .. 189
Village of Massiang. Palpa District 190
Palpa Landscape. Central Nepal 191
Gurkha Line-Boys 196
Gurkha Line-Girls 196
The Western Boundary of Nepal—The Kali River .. 197
Village of Simalghat. Western Nepal 197
The Temple of Baramdeo 198
Darjeeling 210
Kangchenjunga, from Eastern Nepal 211
Bridge over the Mai Khola, near Ingla, Eastern Nepal 214
A Village in Eastern Nepal 215
Escort and Village Headman (Brahman). Eastern Nepal 216
Limbu Women of Eastern Nepal 217
Darjeeling Bazaar on a Festival Day 222
Havildar Dhansar, Manbahadur and Saila 223
Map 248

CHAPTER I

A General Survey of Nepal

By Brig.-Gen. The Hon. C. G. Bruce, C.B., M.V.O.

Notwithstanding a hundred years of ceaseless effort on the part of the Indian Survey Department and fifty years of mountain exploration by various parties from England and the Continent of Europe, it may be said that, so far as the British public is concerned, it was the various attempts to scale Mount Everest which first definitely brought the Himalayas from Asia into Europe. These expeditions made the public of the British Isles and also of the continent realise what the great Himalaya really meant, and from the commencement of those expeditions an immense stimulus has been given to exploration and to climbing expeditions of every kind in the great mountain system of which the Himalaya itself forms but a part, though the most important part.

Infrequent as these pioneering expeditions, as one might almost call them, have been until lately, one even begins to hear already among mountaineering purists the fear expressed that the Himalaya may be vulgarised. Such a remark might, with more or less correctness, be made of the Alps, as they have become an international playground, and such centres as Chamonix or the Little Scheidegg are almost Alpine scandals.

But even the intrusion of funicular railways in the centre of the Alps, while it may familiarise, cannot vulgarise. It is indeed largely a matter of the eyes that look at the country rather than the appeal made to the trippering public. Certainly such an idea as that of vulgarising the Himalayas is beyond conception. But it still pleases me to think that, notwithstanding the familiarity at present gained of many portions of the Himalaya, there are still great sections of that chain untouched, unknown and almost unseen, covering many miles of its length and containing populations representing primitive and ancient civilisations, ancient customs and ancient methods of life, unaffected by contact with what is known as the civilised world; and it is from this particular aspect that I want to write a little about the 500 miles of the Himalaya contained in the kingdom of Nepal, a portion of the Himalaya which contains mountain scenery of all kinds unsurpassed by any portion of the range. It must, in fact, be so.

There are such wonderful great groups cut through by deep gorges and through a country which we know by analogy and by information received to be well wooded, with fine pastures and containing everything in its boundaries which makes for magnificence. Owing to the enterprise of the Government of Nepal, with the help of the India Survey Department, almost the whole of the mountain country has been efficiently mapped, thus not only increasing our knowledge of the country itself but confirming the belief that it contains capacities in the way of beauty and interest comparable with any other known part of the chain.

The kingdom of Nepal, though 500 miles in length, is extraordinarily narrow—wherefore it had been possible to fix on the maps the great centres of elevation visible from the low level of the plains in British India.

We knew in the old days, therefore, to a great extent, before the country was fully mapped, what to expect. We also knew from reports many of the main routes traversing the country and many of the passes which lead into Tibet north of the range. Those too who have had the privilege of an invitation to visit Kathmandu, if they have had the luck of clear weather, have obtained from the passes leading into the valley that most glorious view of the Dhaulagiri massif and the central chain and have had their admiration and curiosity suitably stimulated. On second thoughts, though, considering how the most hidden parts of the world are now being opened up, one really is thankful that there remain, and are likely to remain, glorious countries still in some distant future to be explored, for so far the whole of this great mountain country has never been viewed by a single European with a discerning eye and an appreciative mind from close range.

Naturally the history of the country and its inhabitants has been tremendously modified by its mountainous character. Even under the present enlightened government of Nepal communications east and west throughout the country are rather primitive, for Nepal, as is quite easy to understand, cannot under any conditions have a great deal of finance to spare for the opening of roadways through such a gigantic and complicated mountain area.

To trace the line of the great mountains from a westerly to any easterly direction we leave on the west one of the most beautiful of all the Himalayan centres, dominated by the group of Nanda Devi, pass along its crest to Nanda Kote and the five Cooking Places (Panch Chulia) and then over the border into Nepal. The Himalaya here tends slightly to the south and has its dominating summit the Peak of Nampa, overlooking the Karnali, but all along this portion of western Nepal the main chain has no very outstanding centre of great altitude, but keep a rough altitude of 20,000 feet or so with just a few points exceeding that mark, such as the last-mentioned Nampa and a peak called Api, a little over 23,000 feet.

But it is magnificent mountain country, very broken and deep cut, forming the basin and catchment of the Karnali River and its tributaries. Then following due east we come to some of the most interesting parts of the entire Himalaya, the portion where the great Kali River, which takes its rise high up in Tibet, cuts through the main axis of the range on its journey down to join the Tirsuli River or Narayani, flowing through one of the greatest centres of altitude east or west—the great massifs of Dhaulagiri, Maccha Pucchar and Annapurna. One day we hope it will be accorded to some favoured individual to be allowed to illustrate, if such a thing is possible, the magnificent gorges and scenery of these very, very wonderful groups.

At least four of them exceed 27,000 feet, backed up by a whole host of supporters. We know, too, that the altitude at which the river flows cannot be more than from 5,000 to 7,000 feet from any portion of the gorge and that as it is so near the plains the forest scenery must be equal almost to the mountain scenery and that it should be in a way analogous to that of the Nanda Devi group.

There is, too, almost underlying this great centre, a town and a great mart which has always attracted my curiosity almost beyond any other town in Nepal. No one has been there, no one has seen it, but we know that its climate is almost tropical, that it cannot be more than 2,500 feet in altitude, that it is on the banks of a great lake and that it is in an open valley and lies almost immediately at the foot of these magnificent giants. Phewa Tal is the name of the lake and Pokhra that of the town. Some day and from somewhere someone will arise who will do adequate justice to what must be one of the most impressive and beautiful sights to be found in any mountain country.

Up to this point the main chain lies in Nepal territory, but from now to the Sikkim border it forms the boundary between Nepal and Tibet. And indeed the Nepal district of Mustang is purely Tibetan in character and contains marts and places of interest and inhabitants definitely Tibetan and Mongolian in origin.

The range now forms, as I have said, the actual border between Tibet and Nepal, and from now on we pass to the great group containing the highest summits in the whole chain. For lying due east of the Kali river we come to the Holy Mountain of Gosainthan, in whose neighbourhood is held one of the great annual pilgrimages, and then passing the Jib Jibhia group we approach the magnificent Everest country—a country which I may say has probably been more mapped and photographed on its northern side than any other great mountain area in the world. This, of course, is on account of the many expeditions to Everest, to which it may be added that even the southern face has within recent years been made sufficiently familiar also, thanks to the photographs taken by the air expedition which actually flew over the summit of the mountain.

From west to east of this great mass of mountain country innumerable ridges descend in a southerly direction, and naturally communications between the different valleys have always been poor and tended consequently to isolate the peoples. In fact, the only communications which keep the different parts of the country in touch are the main great roads through the foothills connecting the hill country with the centre of Government in Kathmandu, which is described elsewhere in this volume.

The Valley of Nepal it is, with Kathmandu as its capital, which contains all the ancient civilisation and, in fact, gives its name to the whole Nepal Kingdom, and it should be realised that in old days the only civilised part of the present kingdom was contained in this self-same valley until the time when the Gurkha invasion subdued the ancient kingdoms situated in it and made the whole country by degrees subject to the ancestors of the present rulers.

Besides these great east-to-west roads there are communications leading to certain centres and also to the passes which lead into Tibet, and through which a certain amount of trade has always been carried on. From time immemorial indeed there has been intercourse not only with Tibet but also with China, and that intercourse and accompanying trade has been carried out under difficulties via the great river gorges. Though the great passes of the Himalaya used to be regarded as almost impracticable, many of them in point of fact are not unduly difficult to traverse, and are quite suitable for animal transport. The real difficulty has always lain in the fact that the lines of communications follow the rivers with their deep gorges and in the want of properly constituted roads, and that probably continues to this day to a great extent.

The narratives of the Capuchin and Franciscan monks who traversed this country in the early eighteenth century gives one undoubtedly an exaggerated idea of these same difficulties, because we hear later, after the Gurkhas were repulsed from their invasion of Tibet, of a Chinese and Tibetan army of very great strength pouring down over the Kuti and Kyirong passes and remaining for quite a long time within two marches of the Nepal valley. Considering that they must also have been supplied with food and transport, this could not possibly have been done if the condition of the roads had been such as is described in the early narratives. At the same time, the hasty treaty made by the Chinese with the Nepalese and the easy terms on which that treaty was arranged, evidently showed their anxiety to be back through this difficult country before they could be caught by the snows of winter and to get from the wet country with its heavy snowfalls into dry Tibet in which the snowfall is almost negligible.

The rise and origin of the present ruling clans in Nepal, who are themselves hill men, have been described carefully in this book, but it might be worth while just to glance for a time at the many military and other Mongolian clans which are found more or less buried in the great valleys and cut off so much one from the other, for they raise very interesting questions concerning the ethnology and anthropology of this country.

Before doing so, however, it would be as well to describe how the country is divided. Of course, from the point of view of the Indian Army, the country and valleys which supply us with the bulk of our Gurkha soldiery are those in which we take the greatest interest, because it is from the character of this country and from the life which the people lead there that they derive their essential military value. This would sound for the moment as if it applied to the entire hill country, for the western area of Nepal is very much the same in its physical features as the rest of the country—that is, exceedingly mountainous and with very poor and hard-working inhabitants. In fact, however, the latter, known as Dotiwals, differ considerably both in appearance and in character from the better class military tribes of Nepal and are of not much military value. In addition to farming in very precipitous and rather barren country they earn their living largely by taking contracts as load carriers and porters of all kinds across the western border of Nepal in the British district of Kumaon. Many thousands come for work every year and are utilised in the transport of supplies, provisions and private luggage in the hill stations of Kumaon, and notably in the summer hill station of the United Province, Naini Tal. They live in a country which is drained by the Karnali river and its great tributaries Bheri Ganga and the Seti. The Karnali is a magnificent river and one of the greatest in all Nepal, and is of interest as it rises fairly near to the great Man lakes in Tibet where the Indus, the Sutlej and the Brahmaputra have their source—(these lakes are usually called Mansarowar Lakes, but "sarowar" itself means "lake"). The Karnali is also one of the many great rivers which cut directly through the main axis of the Himalaya.

This part of the country has lately received a great number of immigrants from the Central Nepal, especially those belonging to the Magar clan, and the inhabitants tend more and more to resemble those of Central Nepal.

The next division is the great mass of mountain country drained by the systems of the Gandak river and its tributaries. The whole of this great system is known in Nepal as the Sapt Gandakis, that is to say, the country drained by the seven Gandaks, and it contains the real heart of true Gurkha history, for in its boundaries lies the little kingdom of Gurkha as it used to be known in the old days, the name town and origin of the Gurkha race and the Janam Bhumi or birthplace of the reigning house and of the ruling families.

It contains also the most characteristic part of the whole hill country—magnificent groups of mountains on both sides of the great Kali river, Dhaulagiri, Annapurna and that wonderful peak, the Fish Tail or Maccha Pucchar, so well known in native songs. It is almost certainly in this district that the finest scenery in all Nepal is to be found, and in the head waters of at least the Kali and the Tirsuli there are passes leading into Tibet. Between the great groups of Maccha Pucchar and

Dhaulagiri lies that marvellous gorge where the Kali river breaks through the mountains descending from the most northerly Province of Mastang. Surely there is not such another to be found on the world's surface.

It also contains districts from which the great part of our Gurkha troops are drawn, whether they belong to the clans representing the ruling classes, that is to say the true Hindu clans, the Chetriya clans, or the Mongolian military clans, the Magar and Gurung. Here, too, inside this district existed in the old days, before Prithwi Narain rose as a conquering chief, the twenty-four little kingdoms known as the Chaubisia Raj ruled, with the exception of one, by representatives of the present ruling clans, the one exception being the most populous probably of all, the Magar kingdom of Palpa, which did not submit to the Gurkha Raj until 1800.

This great country is drained by rivers all well known in Nepal history and song, and all of them tributaries of the great Tirsuli river which, when it arrives in India, is known as the Gandak. Here are their names—the Bartijai, Narayani, Seti Gandaki, Marsiangdi, Daramdi, Gandi and Tirsuli—no one can write of this country without mentioning them. The above-mentioned Kali river, rising away up in the Nepal Tibet, that is the district of Mastang, and not joining the Gandak until it arrives actually on the borders of Hindustan, and then the almost equally well known Seti Khola which flows from what must be one of the most interesting and most beautifully situated little towns in the world, the before-mentioned Pokhra, a settlement and lake lying directly at the foot of the great mountain passes and at certainly no greater altitude than 2,000 feet above the sea. Lucky will be the man who first visits and paints or photographs or describes with an adequate eye and pen this magnificent country.

Then the Marsiangdi, the Buria Gandak, the Chaépi and the Tirsuli itself, near the head water of which lies Nilam and the route over the Kuti Pass, and down which the invading army of Chinese poured in 1783 and poured back again in their hurry to escape the snows of the southern slopes before being overtaken by winter.

This is the country *par excellence* of the military tribes, the Magar and the Gurung, although it is also very largely inhabited by great numbers naturally of the ruling classes living much the same life as farmers and hard working peasants, but distinct in respect of their superior position which they hold in the Hindu hierarchy.

North of Pokhra lies the district of Ghandrung with its little capital of Siklis, the birthplace and place of origin of the Gurung tribe. There one finds the Gurung as near as possible as he used to be, speaking his own language as distinct from the Nepal language, the lingua franca used throughout the whole kingdom, and although he has been obliged during the course of time to submit to the Hindu ceremonial laws he has not altogether lost interest in or repudiated his former Lamaistic Buddhistic rites. But where did he come from? And where originally, and at what time, did he cross over from Tibet—for his Mongolian origin is perfectly clear? We do not know. Nor are we certain even of the correctness of the divisions of his clans as laid down in our official classification. There still remains an immense amount of anthropological work to be done as regards all these hill clans, and among the most interesting matters to be determined must be that of the origin and customs of this race. Some of its own special rites belong entirely and exclusively to themselves. There is, for instance, a certain religious ceremony which every superior Gurung who belongs to the four clans or the Charjat will never forego if it is possible. These rites are known as the *Arghun*, and have to do with some form of funeral purification, and they are, I believe, peculiar to the Gurungs, as I have never heard of anything of the same kind in connection with any other clan inhabiting Nepal.

Several details of these rites are very curious and require elucidating—the production, for instance, by the officiating lama of a gilded bull's head which is specially kept and treasured for these occasions, and also the feeding of presentation goats and sheep which are finally sacrificed. These goats and sheep are fed on every kind of food—rice, curry, grain, etc.—and, curiously enough, when killed are alleged to contain nothing but fresh grass. I wonder from where this very ancient rite came? I have never heard of it in Tibetan monasteries nor have I heard of it, as I have said before, among other Nepali tribes. But there must be among so interesting and isolated a people still an immense amount to discover.

There is one interesting story told of how a Ghale became a Gyabring. I must, however, explain first that the Gurung tribe is divided into a superior caste called the Charjat, abovementioned, and a lower division called the Solajat or sixteen clans. It is related that a Ghale, a priest of the Charjat, was travelling with a Kamara or hereditary slave, and that while asleep the Kamara, who had some grudge against the priest, put spirits and buffalo flesh into his mouth, both of which are forbidden to the Ghale. When he woke up he discovered what had been done, and considering himself polluted became a Gyabring or priest of the Solahjat, thus accounting for the fact that the much-respected Gyabring priest of the Solajat was once a man of far greater respectability.

The next division we come to is the valley of Nepal, the heart, brain and centre of the whole hill country. It is perfectly wonderful to think that the present government of Nepal, known as the Gurkha Government, has only been in existence say, 150 years or so, and that before that time the whole hill country was in such an utterly primitive condition. True it was connected already with the Nepal valley by the same roadways as at the present time, but otherwise without organisation or coherence until Prithwi Narain arose, organised his own wild people and began his career of conquest.

Nepal, however, has had an intensely interesting and very ancient civilisation and has been the centre of religious and artistic culture for quite 2,000 years. The Nepal valley itself, locally known as the "country inside the four passes," is about fifteen miles long and ten broad and within that very small

A TEMPLE IN THE INDIAN STYLE. NEPAL VALLEY.

TEMPLE OF AKAS BHAIRAB, KATHMANDU.

space was preserved for hundreds and hundreds of years one of the most interesting hidden civilisations of the world, connected with India by rough tracks over the hills, the scene of innumerable pilgrimages, but from its very position cut off entirely from ordinary contact from Hindustan. How ancient was that culture it is difficult to say, but it is almost certain that the valley was visited by Gautama Buddha himself about 550 B.C., and it is believed that even at that very remote period Hinduism was thoroughly established in the valley.

By far the most important of the early visitors from India was the Emperor Asoka, who was one of the greatest missionaries that ever lived, and who may be described as being the St. Paul of Buddhism, for it was he who carried Buddhism throughout the length and breadth of India. He was, naturally, as a great missionary, also a great traveller and master builder, and wherever he went he left monuments of his work. He visited Nepal 250 B.C., and although Kathmandu was even at that period already established as a city, it was in the city of Pātăn that he built five great stupas and other Buddhistic temples which, at a period later than this were used by both Hindus and Buddhists. From the time of his visit it is curious to see that in this part of India, and in this part alone, Buddhism and Hinduism flourished side by side without any apparent enmity; and to-day, although Hinduism is the state religion of the whole country, yet the valley still remains a centre for pilgrims both from Tibet and other Buddhistic countries.

From that time on the culture of the valley continued more or less unhindered, and right up to the time of the invasion of Nepal in the middle of the eighteenth century it had its own very distinctive civilisation. Is it not strange, indeed, to think how this little valley, buried in the middle of the Himalayas for centuries, kept up its cultural communications with India, while the hill country on both sides of it remained almost in a state of barbarism? It took the Gurkhas the best part of twenty years really to establish themselves, and so great was the opposition put up by the numerous kinglets who fought the Gurkha King

Prithwi Narain for the possession of their valley, and so fierce were the feelings in those days, that when the Gurkha Government had finally overcome all opposition and had given the title of Gurkhali to all its followers, the inhabitants of the Nepal valley itself, belonging to the Newar race, were never allowed that title, and to this day are known as Newars and Newars only. One exception was however made, the circumstances of which are rather curious. The Newars, besides representing all the culture of the land, are also the merchants and bankers of the country, and the particular Newars who had set themselves up and even so employed in the little kingdom of Gurkha at the time when Prithwi Narain invaded Nepal, were allowed the title of Gurkhali.

After the Gurkhas had consolidated themselves in the valley of Nepal their ambition was to spread their power both east and west. Having finished with the west, they set out to bring under their sway the wild tribes of the hill country lying to the east of the valley.

And now we enter the third great division—that terrific mountain country known as the Sapt Kosi, which includes the highest mountain in the world, none other than Everest itself, and is drained both north and south by the tributaries of the great Kosi river. Just as Central Nepal is drained by the tributaries of the Tirsuli, so is the eastern portion of the kingdom drained by the tributaries of the Kosi.

But where the east differs from the central is, in being considerably more humid, as it is more exposed to the action of that branch of the monsoon currents which advance up the Bay of Bengal. It is connected with the capital by one great east-west road which traverses the foothills from Kathmandu to the eastern towns of Dhankuta and Ilam, but even to-day it is by no means easy to traverse, and in fact very often officials find it better to descend from the hills and to take the railway that runs through northern Bengal and the United Provinces when they are journeying to Kathmandu.

The principal rivers of the Sapt Kosi are the Milamchi,

Sun Kosi, Tama Kosi, Dudh Kosi, Arun, Tambar and certain other great tributaries which drain the whole of the south face of the great Everest massif, and even our old friend of the geography book, known as Gauri Sankar, that splendid impostor which intervenes between Everest and Nepal, and has always been taken, when viewed from Nepal, to be the crown of the mountains itself, whereas it is only a little insignificant fellow of not quite 24,000 feet!

We are now among the greatest giants of the world's surface—Everest and Makalu and other great supporters—and so continue to the Sikkim border, and the third, if not the second, highest summit of the world, Kangchengjunga, and the regiment of subordinates which surround it.

Now this country has four special clans, all of whom can be classed as belonging to the Mongolian military tribes—first a rather inferior type known as Murmis or Tamangs, and the more interesting Sunwars, whose habitat is on the banks of the Sun Kosi river and who appear to be closely affiliated to the Central Nepal tribes and the two great races—the Rais representatives of the very ancient Kirantis, and the Limbus, whose country is known as the Limbuhang.

The Kirantis have a history of their own, and claim in the old days to have had representative kings who actually governed the valley of Nepal itself, but the Limbus are a wilder people, very Mongolian in appearance, having strange customs of their own, who are believed by ethnologists to have entered Nepal by way of the valley of the Brahmaputra, coming down from the upper waters of that river. At any rate, their habitat and customs are entirely different from those of any other of the neighbouring races, and it was not until the Gurkhas had completely subdued them, somewhere about 1790, that they submitted to the Hindu ceremonial laws, and actually gave up the greatest of all Hindu crimes, that of cow eating.

They had in their religion, up to that date, certain traces of Lamaistic Buddhism, but even these were very slight, for they had their own particular kind of priest and their own special rites. They might easily be classed as animistic in their religious attitude, and to this day they mix up in the most extraordinary manner animistic rites and a very inferior type of Buddhism with the Hinduism which has been engrafted in them by the ruling classes, although they keep, as far as it is possible for them to do, the Hindu ceremonial laws. Their religion is, in fact, in every way a strange mixture, and it is curious to observe that in their dealings with all these wild people, ruling classes, in order to establish their position, allowed proselytism, although Hinduism in itself is not a proselytising religion.

But all the tribes I have mentioned are, from our point of view, very valuable and very interesting, as they furnish most excellent soldiers for our army, although it is curious that at the present time they are not enlisted in the very large Nepali army itself or, if they are, only to a very minor extent, with the exception of the Murmi tribes who are utilised as gun carriers and in other rather menial services.

I am afraid I have said very little concerning the true Gurkhas, the Chetriya classes of Nepal, but that subject has been very adequately dealt with elsewhere. It must, however, be fully understood that they constitute far and away the most representative classes of the whole country. They have far greater influence and far greater cultivation than any others, and in their hands lies the government of the country.

Besides the major tribes I have mentioned, there are a number of smaller ones in every part of the country more or less unclassified. As the Gurkhas conquered the whole country it was found necessary to codify and simplify the national laws, military, religious and civil, and so you find the laws of Nepal based on the ancient code of Manu, containing all that is required for the purposes of religious, military and civil discipline and government.

The state may be said to be run on purely militaristic lines—a very simple form which appears to be thoroughly suited to the needs of the case, and makes for a fairly easy discipline understandable by the people themselves. But this same military outlook pervades every class of society throughout the country.

It is pleasant also to note the sympathy and good feeling prevailing between all classes of the population. Their lives are very simple and very hard-working, and money is but little used, barter in the innumerable fairs which take place weekly being as much employed as the actual exchange of coin. The life, owing to the want of transport animals and of communications and the difficulty of the country, is also particularly strenuous. Thus nearly all the commerce of the country is carried on by means of human transport, and almost the whole of the interchange of commodities in the country fairs is effected in the same way. It is to these fairs and marts, I may add, that one must go if one wants to see the life of the people, nor is there any difficulty in doing this, since at the junction of every river away up on the mountains there is a fair once a week or a market day, where the hillmen pour down to exchange their goods for the luxuries and necessities of life. And even if one has not had the advantage of travelling away back in Nepal, one sees practically the same type of life in the neighbouring valleys of Sikkim.

These people have very few of the resources in the way of entertainments which are now common in the more sophisticated towns in the plains of India, and in consequence have to make their own amusements. Singing, dancing and drinking their native beer and light spirits, form in consequence a very large part of their entertainment, and who would grudge such a desperately hard-working people a little relaxation even if they do go a little too far on occasion? They are a great people too, for proverbs and riddles, and all the little sayings and beliefs common among mountain peoples. Naturally, as the whole Himalaya is looked upon as the abode of the gods, there is fine scope for their fancies, and just as in Switzerland in the old days dragons, ghosts and devils of every description were abundant, so in the far more superstitious East bhuts and devils in the rivers, wild men in the jungles, wizards and witches in the villages are still in existence, and the terror of the great mountains is almost as highly developed as it is in Tibet, although the inhabitants of the mountains here may be divine instead of diabolical.

Many of their proverbs have a peculiarly European sound, and on hearing some of them it is difficult not to think that our own versions must have come originally from the East, as do many of our fairy stories. Here is one, for instance, which sounds extremely familiar—"The fish that gets away is always the biggest." Others are:

"One falls into the pit that one digs for oneself."

"Don't talk knowingly of heaven in the presence of God"—or rather, of Indra, who is the king of heaven.

"Look at the size of your throat before you swallow the bone."

"The frog in the well is always the frog"—in other words—"The leopard cannot change his spots."

"A slippery face shows a wicked heart."

And then a purely English one—"While there's life there's hope"; and a most pleasant one—"In whosesoever house the mice weep that shows it is the house of a millionaire"—and "One January doesn't make a Winter"—very familiar and decidedly English in sound.

Characteristic is, "If the forest is burning, all can see it, but the fire that consumes one's mind is seen by nobody"; while another of the same type is, "The tiger in the jungle may or may not eat you up, but the tiger in one's own mind may tear you to bits," and there are many others of a like nature.

It would be extremely interesting if an adequately instructed Nepali pundit would set to work and collect the folk-lore of his own country, and in doing so would give attention not only to that of his own classes, but would study also that of the more out of the way tribes. Certainly there is a vast amount still to be brought to light in this way which would be of the greatest interest to anthropologists throughout the world.

Let him follow up and add still further to the immense amount of information collected by the sage Brian Hodgson, and not forgetting, please, dear Pandit, in any such researches, those true relics of a bygone age, the Chepang and Kusunda tribes.

CHAPTER II

The Lie of the Land

The Hill Territory

Extending along the southern slopes of the Himalayas for a length of about 500 miles lies a small, and, as far as Europeans are concerned, practically unknown and unexplored tract of country—the kingdom of Nepal. Along its northern boundary it adjoins Tibet; on the east it is bounded by the native state of Sikkim and the district of Darjeeling; on the west by Kumaon and the river Kali; and on the south by Bengal, Behar and the United Provinces.

Thus it is contiguous on three sides to British territory. Lying between the 80th and 88th degrees of east longitude, it is, in shape, long and narrow, varying in breadth from 90 to 100 miles, while its area is estimated at 54,000 square miles. Of its northern frontier very little is known, for formed as it is by the eternal snows of the Himalayas, except at the accessible points of the passes leading into Tibet, where Chinese and Nepalese frontier-posts and custom-houses are established, this frontier is probably not very strictly defined.

In the matter of physical conformation the country can best be described as consisting of four distinct zones running successively upwards and from east to west. (1) The Terai, a narrow belt of country, chiefly grass and sal jungle, lying but little above sea-level and varying in width from 10 to 30 miles. (2) The sandstone range which, separating the sal forests from the second zone, runs practically without break along the whole length of the country and is a continuation of the range known as the Siwaliks. In certain places such as the western part of the southern frontier this sandstone range actually forms the boundary of Nepal. Where however the boundary line is not identical with the range, but runs to the south of it, it is the tract of lowland intervening between the outermost hills and the British frontier that constitutes the aforesaid Terai. (3) The hill country varying in height from 4,000 to 10,000 feet above sea-level, beginning roughly where the main range of the Himalayas rises to the north and mounting in ridge upon ridge of hills ever-increasing in height until they culminate in the vast snowy range that extends grandly and majestically along the entire northern frontier of Nepal. (4) The mountain region, for the most part inaccessible and unexplored, that lies beyond the hill country to which I have just referred.

Although this region contains some of the highest peaks in the world, including Mount Everest (29,002 feet) and above the lower slopes presents a rugged broken wall of rock, it is, nevertheless, traversed by several passes leading into Tibet, which, however, owing to their great elevation, are only open to travellers during a very short period in the hottest months of the year. A certain amount of trade between Nepal and Tibet still passes over these routes, but as communication with British India becomes easier it has a tendency to become less and less, many of the old trade routes to the east of eastern Nepal having, in fact, fallen into complete disuse nowadays.

Of these passes leading into Tibet the most important are the Takla Pass, midway between the peaks of Nanda Devi and Dhaulagiri; the Mustang Pass, 40 miles to the east of Dhaulagiri and chiefly important for its being the route to the well-known village of Muktinath which is much visited by pilgrims as well as by traders in Tibetan salt; the Kyirong and Kuti passes, which, being the passes nearest to the capital are most frequented by the Tibetan pilgrims and traders who come in large numbers to the valley of Nepal during the cold months of the year; the Hatia Pass, about 50 miles east of the Kuti; and lastly, the Wallang or Wallanchen Pass, which lies in the eastern extremity of the Nepal Himalayas, and but a little to the west of Kangchenjunga. From the fact that the main route to Lhasa runs over it, the traffic over the Kuti Pass is greater than that on any of the others, and this although the track is extremely difficult for any form of animal transport. The Kyirong Pass on the other hand is passable for ponies.

As Nepal is a closed land so far as Europeans are concerned, the number of those who have traversed this Kuti-Lhasa route is very small. They have in fact been confined to the very rare travellers of more distant days, usually missionaries, such as Father Ippolito Desideri, of Pistoia, who made the journey in the beginning of the eighteenth century, and the Jesuit missionaries Father Grueber and Father Dorville, who visited Nepal about the year 1662. There is record also of three Augustinians, Fathers Georgi, Marc and Cassion who, in the middle of the eighteenth century, used this route in the course of what must have been a remarkable journey from Calcutta to Lhassa.

Most of these have left some record which, though liable to error in matters of detail, yet leaves no room for doubt as to the tremendous difficulties encountered and the general character of the route. Thus Father Cassion—whose account of this journey has been translated by Professor Sylvain Levi—describes how at one place they had to traverse a prominent rock about sixteen feet in length and with a surface slippery as ice that sloped downwards over an abyss. There were holes hacked out on the rock to serve as footholds, but even these apparently did but little to reduce the terrors of the passage.

Even more striking is Father Marc's description of the crossing of some of the chain bridges which had to be negotiated. For he tells of travellers being bound to a plank and then manœuvred across blindfolded, to spare them the sight of the sheer precipices below them, with the water foaming and roaring at the bottom. Not to be outdone by the good fathers, an Indian traveller of later days describes the route as passing in one place through a fearful gorge where the path crossed the river no fewer than fifteen times. "At one point," he records, "the rocky sides of the gigantic chasm were so close that a bridge of twenty-four paces spanned it. At another a path is supported along the perpendicular wall of rock on iron pegs let into the face of the rock. The path, of stone slabs covered with earth, is only eighteen inches wide, one-third of a mile long, and one thousand five hundred feet high above the roaring torrent." From all of which one gathers that the Kuti Pass route is decidedly not a pleasant one.

Although Nepalese subjects, the inhabitants of the loftily-situated villages that lie near the Tibetan border in this district are usually of Tibetan origin and invariably speak a modified form of that tongue. Further, as they may represent eight or nine different races and all insist upon speaking their own particular dialects, cases arise where in some villages the tenants of neighbouring huts or houses are actually unable to converse with or even understand each other. The adoption of an official and universal language for use throughout the country by the Nepalese Govenmernt is gradually improving matters in this respect, but it is necessarily a slow business in the case of such primitive folk as those concerned.

It is to Sir Joseph Hooker and Sarat Chandra Das that we are chiefly indebted for our knowledge of the Wallanchen Pass into Tibet from north-eastern Nepal. In the winter of 1848 the former was permitted, at the urgent request of the Indian Government, to ascend the Kosi river in eastern Nepal to its confluence with the Tamor, whence he made his way to the Yangma river and crossed the Wallanchen and Yangma passes. Although he mentions that the scenery was of the wildest and grandest description, and that towards the summit of the Wallanchen Pass the snow lay very deep, the walls of snow being breast-high on each side of the course of a small stream that served as path, Hooker does not seem to have had quite such terrifying experiences as the travellers on the Kuti Pass, though the whole party were affected by giddiness, difficulty of breathing, and general lassitude due to the altitude—the top of the pass being nearly 17,000 feet high.

Sarat Chandra Das on his journey from Darjeeling to Lhasa in 1881 similarly attempted to get into Tibet by the Wallanchen Pass, but was advised against doing so by villagers, on the ground that it was too late in the season—although as a matter of fact Hooker had accomplished it in the same month (November) thirty years before. So Das ascended the Yangma river and crossed into Tibet by the Kanglachen Pass, a little to the east of the Wallanchen. And of the hardships he suffered on this occasion he writes, "how exhausted we were, how overcome by the rarefaction of the air and the intensity of the cold is not easy to describe," while, talking of a night spent in Kanglachen itself, he described himself and his party as being "placed as if in the grim jaws of death, in the bleak and drear regions of snow where death alone dwells."

Thus, in the matter of hardships to endure and difficulties to overcome, there would seem to be little to choose in the case of these high Himalayan passes that lead from Nepal into Tibet.

In this part of the world, besides Tibetans and Nepalese, are to be found a race known as Sherpas. These deserve special mention from the fact that it is from them that the porters for the Mount Everest expeditions are mainly drawn. Their particular stronghold is a place called Solakhambu, situated in north-eastern Nepal and quite near the Tibetan frontier. Although originally of pure Tibetan stock, and in their own homes wholly Tibetan in their manners and customs, yet through mixing with local inhabitants they now not only speak Nepali well, but are exceedingly proud of their Nepalese nationality. While they cannot be said to be wholly free from some of the bad characteristics of the Tibetans—such as a tendency to laziness and gambling—the Sherpas have certainly performed prodigious feats of endurance as humble members of the various climbing expeditions, and in this capacity have won unlimited praise for their loyal and faithful service.

Having thus attempted to give some idea of the wild, inhospitable regions through which, little known and probably not too clearly defined, the northern boundary runs, I will now turn to a brief description of the remaining chief geographical features of Nepal.

To get the hang of these it should be understood that the

territory of Nepal, within the hills, that is from Kumaon on the west to Sikkim on the east, is divided into three large natural divisions by four lofty ridges which, standing out at right angles from the central axis of the Himalayas, run parallel to each other, nearly due south to the plains. These ridges take off from the high peaks of Nanda Devi (25,700 feet), Dhaulagiri (26,826 feet), Gossainthan (26,305 feet) and Kangchenjunga (28,156 feet). Mount Everest (29,002 feet), the highest mountain in the world, lies roughly midway, and somewhat behind the last two, its southern face only being situated in Nepal while the bulk is in Tibetan territory.

Mountain barriers wall in each of these three natural divisions on all four sides; on the north, the snowy range; on the south, the sandstone hills to which I have already referred; on the west and on the east, one or other of the ranges just named. And each of these divisions which, thus walled in, forms a kind of large mountain basin, receives its name from the river by which it is drained; namely, the western division, or mountain basin of the Karnali, or Gogra; the central division, or mountain basin of the Gandak; the eastern division, or basin of the Kosi.

As General Bruce has devoted considerable space to them in his introductory chapter, it is unnecessary to say any more here about these three large natural divisions which may be said to constitute the hill territory of Nepal. There remain, however, two other geographical divisions, namely the Nepal valley, in which is situated Kathmandu, the capital of the country and centre of government, and the Terai, the portion of low-lying land which intervenes between the British frontier and the outermost hills of Nepal.

CHAPTER III

The Lie of the Land

(continued)

THE VALLEY AND THE TERAI

ALTHOUGH of comparatively limited extent, yet containing as it does the capital of the kingdom, the valley of Nepal is historically and economically the most important of all the geographical divisions; it is, further, the only part of Nepal to which Europeans are admitted.

The district lies to the south of the Gosainthan mountain, and consists of an elevated plateau surrounded by hills, and of triangular shape. Separated by the Tirsulganga river from the province of Gurkha on the west, and by the Milamchi river from the Sapt Kosi country on the east, it is best described as lying between the country of the seven Gandaks and the seven Kosis. A range of small hills which lies to the north of the valley and district of Makwanpur forms the base of the triangle.

Lying around the large central valley, and separated from it by an intermediate range of hills, are smaller valleys, such as the Chitlong valley to the south-west, the Nawakot valley to the north, and the valley of Banepa to the east. These may also be said to lie within the district known as Nepal. The valley itself is in the form of a gently undulating plain of nearly oval shape averaging fifteen miles in length and thirteen in breadth while it covers about 250 square miles. Although it lies some 4,700 feet above the sea, it can be unpleasantly hot at times during the summer months, and there is a small bungalow on the Kakani ridge, north of the valley, which the British Envoy usually occupies at these times.

The valley is abundantly drained and watered by a small river, the Baghmati, which rises on the northern slopes of Sheopuri, as the high mountain forming its northern limit is called.

In its course through the valley the Baghmati is joined by a number of small streams, the most important of which is the Bishnumati, and the united waters leave the valley by a narrow gorge called Pharping—the only break in the enclosing circle of mountains. According to ancient Hindu traditions, what is now the valley of Nepal was at one time a large and deep lake, the draining of which was caused by the bursting of one of the barriers. It is quite impossible to say when this event actually occurred, yet from the geological evidence that is available, the theory certainly appears to be correct.

The chain of hills that surrounds the valley of Nepal proper varies in height from five hundred to three thousand feet above the surface of the valley, or from five thousand to eight thousand feet above sea-level. The highest of the mountains by which the valley is enclosed is Mount Sheopuri which bounds it on the north, the pointed summit of which, thickly wooded with sal and oak trees, stands fully eight thousand feet above the sea. Flanking Sheopuri west and east respectively are Kakani and Manichur, each of which is about seven thousand feet in elevation, while joined to Manichur by a lower range of hills is Mount Mahadeo Pokhri, the eastern boundary of the valley six thousand seven hundred feet high.

Other prominent mountains in the chain are Phulchok with its rocky peak overshadowed by fine oaks and about eight thousand feet in elevation on the south-east; Chandragiri on the south-west, known to European visitors to the Nepal valley for its pass, over which the track runs six thousand six hundred feet high; Nagarjun, on the north-west, boldly formed and densely wooded, seven thousand feet high.

Overlooking the valley from the north-west, but not forming part of its immediate boundaries are two mountains, Bhirbandi and Kumhara, of which the former is the loftiest mountain in the district of Nepal proper, for its rounded summit, known as Kaulia peak, and covered with brushwood jungle of hollyoak and rhododendron, is nearly nine thousand feet high.

The six mountains, Kumhara, Bhirbandi, Kakani, Sheopuri,

Temple on the Banks of the Baghmati.

A Village. Nepal Valley.

Manichur and Mahadeo Pokhri, stretch as a continuous range from the banks of the Tirsulganga river on the west to the Milamchi river in the country of the Kosis on the east, thus forming the northern boundary to the district of Nepal proper. Directly opposite this range rises the rugged mass of Mount Jibjibia, which stands as a barrier between the cultivated, populous valleys lying at its base and the snowy peaks of Mount Gosainthan which rise in its rear.

The rounded hill, Mount Indra Than, that forms the western boundary of the valley, is not more than one thousand five hundred feet above the level of the valley, while on the south, the western extremity of Mount Mahabharat forms one side of the pass through which the Baghmati river leaves the valley of Nepal—the only break that occurs in the encircling chain.

I have thought it worth while to give more than a passing reference to these mountains of the Nepal valley so that readers may have a better idea of the geographical character of the only part of Nepal accessible to Europeans, and to but few at that.

We now come to the last geographical division, the Terai. The Terai extends along practically the whole length of the southern boundary of Nepal, from the Sarda or Kali in the west to the Mechi in the east, the portion east of the Kosi river being known as the Morang. This tract of country, which nowhere exceeds thirty miles in breadth and averages about ten, can be divided into two very distinct portions; the open ground under cultivation to which the name Terai, in its strictest sense, should be restricted, and the primaeval jungle, known as the Bhabar. This last varies much in character, but consists for the most part of dense forests of sal trees, intermixed with shisham, semal or cotton trees, and nearer the hills, firs. In places, this jungle in absolutely impenetrable, so thick is the undergrowth and so dense the tangle of giant creepers which swing from tree to tree.

Here and there stretches of prairie land where the grass is ten or fifteen feet high break into the monotony of the forest; in other parts, where the ground is low-lying and swampy, tracts of "elephant grass," in places so dense that not even an elephant can work its way through, are not infrequently found. This is most marked in the eastern Terai where the timber has been swept away by successive floods.

Apart from these swampy patches, however, the actual sal forest area is as dry as a bone. The Terai proper, on the other hand, where the soil of black loam, clay and sand seems to be eminently suitable for growing poppy, sugar cane and tobacco, is distinctly wet. It is indeed to the excessive moisture and swamps, the low site and the rills that percolate through the gravel and sand of the Bhabar, that the Terai owes its evil reputation as one of the most malarious districts in the world. Yet while much of it is still very unhealthy during certain times of the year, the Nepalese Government has in recent years made great efforts to make at any rate certain parts of it more habitable, particularly in the Morang, where large stretches have been cleared and made suitable for human habitation.

One tribe alone, the Tharus, an indigenous race of the Terai, employed chiefly as dak runners, carters and mahouts, are immune from the malarial fever, or awal as it is commonly known, that rages from April to the beginning of October, though, curiously enough, they are said to be just as susceptible as anyone else if they remove themselves elsewhere. Although not to be compared with the Nepalese who live in the hills in the matter of physique, the Tharus are by no means "puny, badly developed and miserable-looking," as one writer, at least, has represented them to be, and the fact that during the hot and rainy season they are employed in the exceedingly difficult and dangerous task of catching wild elephants shows that they possess stamina and energy that their appearance may belie. Darker-skinned and less stockily built than the hill dwellers, the Tharus alone amongst the people of the Terai have the strong Mongolian appearance that characterises people of Nepalese race, the other differing little if at all from those in the contiguous Indian plains.

If the Terai is, generally speaking, owing to its deadly climate, an unattractive country for human beings, it is the home of wild animals in such quantities that it would hardly be going too far, I think, to describe it as the finest big-game preserve in all Asia. In another chapter, where I describe the big shooting camps which are held in the winter season, and at which distinguished guests are entertained on a lavish scale, it will be seen how the Terai has maintained its reputation in this respect to the present day.

The sandstone range of hills to which I have already referred, and which in places forms actually part of the southern boundary of Nepal, really extends under different names along nearly the whole length of the Himalayas. The part of it in Nepal, for instance, which extends from the pass of the Gandak river in the west to the Kosi river in the east, is called the Churyaghati range, the western part of this last again being called the Someswar ridge. It is, in fact, the lowest and outermost of all the mountain ranges, and as such immediately overlooks the plains of India. Varying in height from two to three thousand feet above sea-level, it is traversed by passes in several places, through which the rivers that rise on the southern face of the Himalayas find their way into the Indian plains. Throughout the whole of its extent in Nepal both the northern and southern slopes of this sandstone range are covered with a dense forest chiefly of sal trees.

With regard to communications in Nepal, there is only one short stretch of railway, and only two roads of any real importance, the others consisting of nothing more than a network of hill tracks which, though for the most part of the roughest description, serve their purpose well enough at present. The one railway, a "light" railway made by a Calcutta firm, runs from Raxaul, a small station on a branch line of the Bengal and North-Western Railway, as far as Amlekhganj on the further side of the Terai—a distance of forty miles on the main route from the British frontier to the Nepal valley. From Amlekhganj, a road that is practicable even for motors save during periods of exceptionally heavy rain, takes the traveller another twenty-seven miles as far as Bhimphedi. Here the road becomes impracticable for any form of wheeled traffic until one reaches Thankot, on the further side of the Chandragiri Pass and the first village in the Nepal valley, whence there is a good carriage road for the last eight miles into Kathmandu.

The only other road of any importance in the country is the one which connects the frontier station of Nautanwa, some fifty miles north of Gorakhpur, with the important town of Butwal or Batauli, at the far side of the western Terai. A regular motor service is operated on this road, which is fit for the heaviest motor traffic throughout the year.

The mountainous character of the whole region is, of course, chiefly responsible for the fact that the roads throughout Nepal are in general so poor, though the configuration of the country is another contributory cause. The roads running east and west, for instance, have to be carried right across the natural drainage of the country which is from north to south, and in consequence involve incessant climbing, descending and—worst of all—crossing of rivers. It is indeed the rivers rather than the roads which are chiefly responsible for the slow and tedious character of internal transit in Nepal, though a good deal has been done by the Nepal Government to improve matters in this respect during recent years by providing better bridges in place of the old rope ones, formerly universal.

Of the roads in the hills, the greatest and most important is the one which traverses the entire length of the country from east to west leading from Darjeeling to Pithoragarh in Kumaon, a distance of more than five hundred miles.

No European eye has ever seen more than a twentieth part of this long route, and accordingly the only available information about it has been gleaned from Nepalese, from whom it is difficult to obtain any very illuminating particulars as a rule. There is no doubt, however, that for a large part of the way the going is very difficult, the route being obstructed by many steep ascents and descents, while during flood time it is practically impassable in many places. As it runs during its entire length through the under-features of the Himalayas—under-features which would be considered quite important mountains in any other country —the pace is necessarily extremely slow. Hence the road is for the most part used merely for local purposes, it being easier and quicker for a Nepalese who wishes to travel any distance in his own country to make his way to the nearest railway station on the Indian border—Darjeeling, Raxaul, Bridgmanganj, Bilauri or Jogbani, for example—and make the journey east or west, as the case may be, by rail.

Outside the valley there are but few towns in Nepal that can be called important centres. Some, like Ilam, Dhankuta, Jumla and Salyana, enjoy a certain amount of local prestige as chief towns and civil headquarters of districts, as others, like Silgarhi, Daelekh and Baitadi, do in virtue of their being military stations, while the shrines at Riri and Muktinath attract large numbers of pilgrims from India and Tibet; but that is all that can be said. In fact, of the provincial towns, perhaps only Butwal, Palpa Tansing and Pokhra can with any justice be called important. Not only are all three big administrative centres, but they alone of towns outside the valley have the advantage of possessing flat cultivable land, while from the fact that the old high road between India and Tibet passed through them, they still retain a certain amount of commercial prosperity.

Of Butwal and Palpa I will say more later on. The first I have visited several times, while I have at any rate been lucky enough to see Palpa, even if it was only from a hill a few miles away. Pokhra I have never seen, but from all accounts it must be one of the most attractive places in Nepal. With a population of some ten thousand inhabitants, and lying in a wide flat plain encircled by hills, it is the most important place outside the towns of the valley—Kathmandu, Patan and Bhatgaon. It is both a centre of administration and a military cantonment, while its fertile soil, its size and its position on the road, that runs from east to west through the centre of Nepal, all combine to make it a town that is likely to play a large part in the industrial development of the country.

Pokhra can further claim the distinction of possessing the only real lakes in Nepal. Bordered with trees, and of considerable size, they must add greatly to the general picturesqueness of the place. In summer and the rainy season, however, they can hardly be pleasant from a climatic point of view, for the valley of Pokhra in which they lie is said to be not much higher than the Terai.

So much, therefore, for the geography of Nepal—with which, I may add, I regret that I have not been able to deal to better purpose. But for this a certain amount of excuse may perhaps be pleaded. For, owing to the Nepalese policy of isolation—a policy which, it may be noted, is warmly supported by the British Government—save for the high road that leads from India to Kathmandu, the Terai, the valley of Kathmandu itself, and a few valleys beyond the chain of hills which encircles the central plateau, the kingdom of Nepal is completely closed to Europeans, thus making any accurate or detailed description of the interior of the country practically impossible.

It was the fact that Sir Chandra Shumshere as a special favour kindly permitted me to wander in places a little beyond the beaten tracks and visit certain portions of the country on the eastern and western frontiers, usually unknown to Europeans, that really prompted, in the first instance, the writing of this book.

CHAPTER IV

The Early History of Nepal

[*Note.*—The complicated and involved history of Nepal is a subject that has invariably severely taxed the skill of every writer who has included it in a book on the country.

So vague and obscure in the earlier parts as to be of little real value for the student, even from the time of the rise of the Gurkhas in the middle of the eighteenth century up to modern days, it makes, it is to be feared, at any rate, in places, somewhat dull and tedious reading.

Nevertheless, to avoid omitting anything that might prove of interest to those readers who do wish to learn something of the story of Nepal, I have deemed it inadvisable to condense this section of the book more than I have done here. In any case, where the general reader is concerned, Chapter IV can be omitted in its entirety.]

THE first known "document" to contain any reference to Nepal is the panegyric of the Emperor Samudra Gupta on the pillar at Allahabad, where the king of Nepal is mentioned as being one of those who "paid tribute to and obeyed the orders of the Imperial Master"—as the powerful monarch then dominating India was termed. His name is found between those of two other princes, the kings of Katrapura and Kamarupa. The former name is untraceable elsewhere, but that of Kamarupa occurs not infrequently in ancient literature in connection with Nepal, and refers to the tract of country in north-west Assam bordering on the little independent state of Bhutan.

The date when Nepal may thus be said to enter into positive and authentic history is the fourth century of the Christian era. Early literature, whether Hindu or Buddhist, is so vague where Nepal is concerned, that its remote past is completely shrouded in a fog of doubt and uncertainty. Its name does not even occur in either of the great epic poems, the Mahabharat and the Ramayan, although the Himalayas are frequently mentioned not only in these, but also in many legends and stories of those times. It is true that the word Kamarupa is frequently found in those religious narratives, but the existence of Nepal is merely suggested as the legendary home of a race of uncouth barbarians, inaccessible in their mountains, and both despised and dreaded by the people of the plains.

Buddhist literature is hardly more helpful, for though the word Nepal is certainly mentioned, the dates which are given concerning it are too obviously vague and unreliable. It does, however, record that during the fifth or sixth century B.C. a celebrated ascetic, named Vasubandhu, visited Nepal accompanied by some five hundred disciples, and that he founded religious schools in the country, whose members, as they increased, spread religion throughout the land. Vasubandhu may, therefore, be said to have been the first authentic person from elsewhere to have come into contact with that mysterious country.

Yet veiled in mystery as is the early history of Nepal, there appears little doubt, as previously stated, that the valley, as is not uncommon with similar geographical formations in other parts of the Himalayas, was at one time a lake. Its subsequent transformation into the fertile valley that it is to-day is accounted for in the early Hindu and Buddhist legends by the story that their respective deities Vishnu and Manjusri made a pass through the mountains which encircled the valley with one cut of a sword, thus allowing the water to escape.

More convincing if less picturesque, is the evidence of geologists who, while agreeing with the lake theory, attribute it to some torrential upheaval, or to the constant erosion of the outlet through the southern barrier, thus causing the waters to be drained off and the land reclaimed. Whatever the agency, the valley of Nepal, thus raised from under the surface of the waters, has always possessed a soil of exceptional fertility, and it is fairly safe to assume that its inhabitants have always been pastoral and agricultural in character.

Inscriptions found in and near Kathmandu have enabled Sanskrit scholars such as Professor Sylvain Levi to discover evidence by which certain periods at any rate are fairly well documented, though the fact that they have been unable to pursue these archaeological researches outside the confines of the valley has limited their value to a great extent.

Speaking generally however, the Vamshavali, or Chronicle of Nepal, affords almost the only information about the earlier history of the country and is the source to which all students of that history must necessarily turn, untrustworthy though much of it is. Although it does not date further back than the sixteenth century, it contains the legends and traditions of a much earlier period. Otherwise it is really more in the nature of a genealogical chronicle than a record of historical events, and, further, one in which, as often as not, purely fanciful genealogical descents of the princes of Nepal are recorded. In fact, it presents little more than a series of unhistorical legends and impossible genealogies until the reign of the Malla dynasty in the thirteenth century A.D.

Two illustrations alone will suffice to show the untrustworthiness of the Nepalese Vamshavali, although such instances could be multiplied a hundred-fold. Thus in one case the Nepalese chroniclers in a patriotic attempt to find a sufficiently ancient and famous origin for a ruling line have placed the date of a certain king, Amsu Varman, seven hundred years earlier than the right one. In another, connected with the same king, after stating that the Thakuris (whose dynasty he founded), ruled for 225 years, the chronicle naively adds, "but as they were very numerous, their names have not been recorded."

Yet, even if it cannot be accepted too implicitly, this chronicle can hardly be dismissed altogether. In particular, the notes which accompany the data are of undeniable interest, though they are often inconsistent and exaggerated. In the words of Mr. Percival Landon, "the Vamshavali is a book that must be read with healthy scepticism, with perpetual sympathy, and with an understanding of local credulity and local prejudices. It is a chronicle that should be approached from the right point of view."

And so, although its history begins to take a more coherent form towards the middle of the fourteenth century, it is not really until the rise to power of the Gurkha King Prithwi Narayan Sah as late as A.D. 1769, that we really begin to get any accurate picture of past events in Nepal.

Nevertheless, amongst the almost impenetrable tangle of fact and fiction that obscures early Nepalese history, there stand out certain incidents and events that can hardly be ignored in writing on the country, more particularly those relating to neighbouring lands like Tibet, India and China, and so I have thought it worth while to recall in the briefest manner some of the most important and interesting of these events, in the hope that readers will thereby be better able to understand any historical illusions I may have to make in later chapters.

Although its exact origin is unknown, the word "Nepal" is popularly derived from one Ne Muni, the patron saint of the country. Living at the confluence of the Baghmati and Kesavati rivers, where he expounded his doctrines, it was Ne Muni, who, in selecting a pious cowherd to be the first of a long line of kings, known as the Gopala or Cowherd Dynasty, established the first king of any recognised dynasty in Nepal. Hence, "pala" meaning cherished, or looked after, it is not unreasonable to suppose that the word Nepal meant in the first instance "The country looked after by Ne."

An important event in its early history was the vist to Nepal of Asoka, the fourteenth king of the Sthunko dynasty, about the year 250 B.C. Asoka's capital was at Pataliputra, the modern Patna, and his dominion at that time comprised the whole of northern India, including Kashmir and—although the extent of his practical authority in it is somewhat uncertain—Nepal.

Being a zealous Buddhist and responsible for many edicts inscribed on rocks and pillars in different parts of India, Asoka is always associated with the alleged visit of Buddha himself to Nepal. For, in the firm conviction that Gautama had at some time visited the valley, he built four great stupas, or Buddhist mound temples, at each corner of the city of Patan, which can be seen, almost unchanged, to-day. The erection of these monuments conferred for ever a distinction upon the valley, which became from that time onwards a place of pilgrimage, and, despite the complicated problem introduced by the subsequent intermingling of Buddhism and Hinduism throughout the country, has continued to attract pilgrims from the countries which lie to the north of Nepal right down to the present day.

A reference to Nepal in the seventh century is found in the chronicles of the well-known Chinese traveller Hiuen Tsang, who is definitely known to have visited the country in the year A.D. 637. His comments on the character of the inhabitants are often none too flattering, but his account is interesting as showing them to have possessed, even in those days, considerable artistic skill, while the curious mixture of the two religions to which I have just referred also seems to have made an impression on him. To quote his own words: "The inhabitants of Ni-po-lo are all of a hard and savage nature; to them neither good faith nor justice nor literature appeals, but they are gifted with considerable skill in the arts." Later again he says: "Among them there are both true believers and heretics. Buddhist convents and the temples of the Hindu gods touch each other."

By his frequent references to him, Hiuen Tsang has further enabled modern historians to come to a more correct estimate of the date of the reign of the King Amsu Varman which, as I have already said, had been faked by the Nepalese chroniclers. And whatever his opinion of the inhabitants, he has at any rate nothing but good to say of their king, for he describes Amsu Varman as encouraging learning and respecting virtue, and one whose reputation was spread far and wide.

Further light has been thrown on conditions in Nepal during the seventh century by the discovery of inscriptions which refer to the interchange of visits by Chinese and Nepalese missions a few years after the report on the country by Hiuen Tsang. In the year A.D. 643 the first Chinese mission visited Nepal, and was hospitably received by Narendra Deva, who ruled at that time. A second mission a few years later came to grief through being attacked by followers of the Emperor of India, through whose dominions it had to pass, and only escaped being cut to pieces by invoking the aid of China's allies, Nepal and Tibet. Friendly relations between the two countries had however been established, and in later years Nepal in her turn sent missions to China taking with them presents and messages of goodwill to the Celestial Empire.

From evidence obtained from Chinese documents it appears that such was its prosperity and so great the advance of civilisation during the reign of Narendra Deva that in the year A.D. 650 Nepal could be compared with the best administered states of India at that time. Further, it is said that during this epoch the country was continually visited by Chinese pilgrims, attracted both by its intimate connection with Buddha and by the reputation for piety which it enjoyed.

It was about the beginning of the seventh century also that a new nation had arisen on the high plateau to the north of the Himalaya, under whose sphere of influence Nepal was to pass for a considerable time. These were the Tibetans, for in these snowy solitudes lay a country known in the vernacular as Bhot, and to Europeans as Tibet. From the primitive people who formed its inhabitants an army had been former, numbering, it is said, in the early part of the seventh century 100,000 men, which threatened the peace of India and China.

The founder of the Tibetan Empire, a king on whom the traditions of his country have bestowed the name Namri Srong Btsan, was a man of energy and determination, whose power extended as far as the country of the Brahmans, or India as we now know it. His glory was, however, completely eclipsed by that of his son, Srong Btsan Sgam Po, who was destined to become the Alexander of Tibet. Under him the empire expanded until in course of time it covered the whole of present-day Tibet, while his ministers entered into relations with the Chinese on the east, Hindustan to the south and Nepal to the west. Not content with this, he determined to consolidate his power by means of a suitable alliance, and, according to available records, is said to have despatched an emissary to the court of Nepal to demand the hand of a princess of that country.

As he was reluctant to refuse the demand of so powerful a neighbour, Amsu Varman granted the Tibetan monarch his daughter Princess Bri-btsun in marriage, with the result that, according to the writings of Chinese historians, by the beginning of the eighth century Nepal had become almost a dependent state of the Tibetan Empire. But Nepal exerted in turn a great influence on the life of Lhasa, the new Tibetan capital, which lost no time in assimilating not only the art and literature, but also to some extent the crafts and industries of Nepal. Indeed, the fact that Tibetan arts and crafts have remained Indian rather than Chinese in character can probably be ascribed to Princess Bri-btsun's influence at this time.

During the eighth and ninth centuries the history of the valley is obscure to a degree almost more impenetrable than at any other period, and only from time to time is Nepal mentioned vaguely as a vassal of Tibet.

In the eleventh century, however, the record becomes clearer again, and in the early part of that period a Rajput from the Dekkan, Nanya Deva, is said to have conquered the whole of Nepal, and after establishing his own court at Bhatgaon, to have ruled over the other two capital cities of the valley, Patan and Kathmandu, from the former place. He further established a colony of soldiers who had accompanied him from the Nair country in the Malabar district of southern India, and it is from these that the Newars, who form the bulk of the inhabitants of the Nepal valley nowadays, try to trace their descent. Although the attempt to identify "Newar" with "Nair" is somewhat far-fetched, the link between Nepal and the extreme south of India should not be lost sight of, for the connection is continually reappearing in early Nepalese history. It may have been purely religious in character, but it seems at any rate to have left a distinct influence upon the manners and customs of the mountain state.

To India also can be definitely traced the origin of the Malla dynasty that was destined to play an important part in the later history of Nepal. The name Malla appears from very early days among the tribes of India, although save for the fact that they belonged to a clan of hereditary landowners in India, and that they come from the border country between Oudh and Nepal, not much is known of their origin. Some of the early kings of India however had been given the title of Malla long before it was known in Nepal, and here again recurs a link with the south. For, by a curious coincidence, one of the first of the Indian kings to assume the name Malla was the ruler of Conjecvram in the extreme south of India, a fact which has led Nepalese historians to proclaim that country as the home of one of the first known kings of Nepal, King Dharma Datta.

That the Mallas figured prominently in the history of the valley between the tenth and the sixteenth centuries is at any rate certain. Towards the middle of the thirteenth century they were established both in Kathmandu and Patan, and one of their kings, Ananda Malla, is said to have founded Bhatgaon.

It was about this time that the Khas, a mountain tribe from whom comes the word Khaskura, "the language of the Khas," as Nepali is commonly known, also appeared on the scene. They are said to have come from the west in large numbers during the reign of Ananda Malla and settled in Nepal. The Khas are frequently mentioned as a race in ancient legends and traditions. Some of these refer to a country between Kashmir and the Nepal valley as "the land of the Khas," while a race of Hindus called Khas was known to have inhabited the country lying round Palpa and the southern part of Nepal. To-day, the Khas are more generally known as Chetris, the word Chetri being a corrupt form of the Sanskrit word

Kshatriya, which means literally a fighting man, or one of the fighting caste. Whatever the origin of the Khas, they are at any rate now known to have existed as a separate nation long before the Brahmans penetrated Nepal in the twelfth century, when they, together with multitudes of other Indians, were fleeing before the Moslem invasion.

Yet the Mahommedan invasions were to play an all-important part in the story of the Nepalese nation, for the influx of many foreigners of superior caste, intelligence and breeding could not fail to influence greatly the lives of the illiterate mountaineers, and thus we read in Oldfield: "The progress of Muhammadinism daily drove fresh refugees to the Nepalese mountains. The 'Khas tribes' availed themselves of the superior knowledge of the strangers to subdue the neighbouring aboriginal tribes. They were uniformly successful; and in such a career, continued for ages, they gradually merged the greater part of their own ideas, habits and language (but not physiognomy) in those of the Hindus. The Khas language became, and still is, a corrupt dialect of Hindi, retaining not many traces of primitive barbarism."[1]

Thus the Brahman refugees found many willing converts in their new mountain homes, and to the earliest and most distinguished of these they are believed to have given the rank and honour of the Khattri order. This order they subsequently bestowed on the offspring of Brahmans and the local hill women, and it is from this mixture of the two peoples that the present powerful tribe of Chetris, who hold the dominating influence in Nepal to-day, has sprung.

Nothing of outstanding interest or importance emerges from the fog which obscures Nepalese history during the twelfth and thirteenth centuries. It was an age of constant feudal warfare between the rival rulers of the valley towns, and although the highway from India to Tibet passed through Nepal, it is unlikely that the authorities of those two countries attached any importance to the collection of small kingships that were

[1] *Sketches from Nepal*, Vol. I, Ch. XIII, p. 170.

continually establishing themselves and disappearing again in and around the valley.

From the fourteenth century however the record begins again to assume a somewhat more coherent form, and thus most historians agree that about the year 1326 Harisinha Deva, King of Simraun, conquered Nepal and mounted the throne. Simraun, as the old and strongly fortified capital of what is now known as Tirhut was called, had until then stood out against the tide of the great Mohammedan invasion which had submerged the Brahmanical Empire that surrounded Tirhut. But the advance of the new Emperor of Delhi, Gheyas-ud-din Tughlak, could not be resisted, and Harisinha, rather than submit to Moslem domination, took refuge in Nepal. He did not himself remain long in the country, but his descendants continued to rule until they were displaced by Prithwi Narayan.

Amongst the kings of the fifteenth century, the name of Yaksha Malla can hardly be passed by. Originally entrusted by his father with the government of Bhatgaon, he not only completely subdued the refractory Rajas of Patan and Kathmandu, but, if Kirkpatrick is to be believed, annexed Morang, Tirhur and Gaya in the south, conquered Gurkha in the west, and even extended his territory as far as Shekkar Dzong in Tibet. Before his death, Yaksha Malla divided his country into four kingdoms, Kathmandu, Patan, Bhatgaon and Banepa. To his elder son he gave Bhatgaon; he gave Kathmandu, to which was later added the rule of Banepa, to his younger son; while Patan—although it did not, in point of fact, form a separate kingdom until the seventeenth century—was destined for his daughter.

In thus dividing up the valley of Nepal into small and bitterly-jealous principalities, Yakhsha Malla committed an error that was to prove the ultimate ruin of the Mallas. For a king of Gurkha—a name ever associated with menace to the valley—had already been mentioned in the Nepalese chronicles, and it is a curious fact, and one that argues much for the lack of enterprise and cohesion among the valley's more virile mountain neighbours, that it was not until the middle of the eighteenth century, or three hundred years later, that the Gurkhas, seeking to profit by the numerous petty quarrels of these three principalities, invaded the valley of Nepal.

The first of the Gurkha invaders was Narbhupal Sah, the ninth king of that house, and the date of the invasion 1736. On this occasion, however, the Gurkha arms met with disaster, for the King of Kathmandu, Jaya Prakasha, proved more than a match for them, and the invaders were forced to beat an ignominious retreat. On the death of Narbhupal Sah, in 1742, his son, Prithwi Narayan Sah, became King of Gurkha. He was then twelve years old.

The events, disjointed and vague for the most part, it is true, that I have described so far, have been almost entirely connected with the history of the actual valley of Nepal, which, as will have been gathered, consisted by now of the three small principalities of Kathmandu, Patan and Bhatgaon.

With the accession of Prithwi Narayan, a foreign king who hailed from beyond the boundaries of the valley, the history of Nepal enters upon a new and, it must be added, more coherent phase. From now on, it is the story of the Gurkhas' rise to power and their eventual domination of, not only the valley but the whole of Nepal.

CHAPTER V

Rise of the Gurkhas

THE Gurkhas owe their name as now received to a simple fact. The small kingdom of Gurkha, governed by a member of a leading Chetri family, gave the title of Gurkhali, i.e. follower of the King of Gurkha, to all his subjects, but the Gurkhali *pur sang* as one might say, were the aristocratic Chetris, to which great race, partially descended from the best Sesodhia Rajput blood, the King of Gurkha belonged.

The period during which this fine race was being built up is not historically clear, but when Prithwi Narayan established his rule, all the neighbouring small kingdoms known as the Chaubisia Raj were ruled by representatives of it, as indeed were all the other small states almost up to the Kashmir border.

As to the origin of the Gurkhas, the ultimate conquerors of Nepal, little is known of them prior to their first invasion of the valley in 1736. They are said to have come originally from Rajputana whence they had been driven by the steam-roller of the Mohammedan invasion, and both ancient legends and the early history of India testify to the fact that their royal family was descended from the Rajput princes of Udaipur. The capture of Chitor by Ata-ud-din Khilji early in the fourteenth century drove many Rajputs to seek in the mountains of Nepal the shelter that had been denied them in the plains. They seem also to have arrived there about the time Harisinha Deva fled before the Moslem invaders to Tirhut, but whereas Harisinha, apparently invaded the valley of Kathmandu to the east, the Rajputs from Chitor advanced upon Gurkha to the west.

They seem to have had no difficulty in securing the place from which their descendants took their name, and for several generations they were content to consolidate their interests in this comparatively narrow sphere, for Gurkha of to-day is little more than a village, showing traces of a small princely residence and the ruins of a fort. Nothing is known of the history of the Gurkha princes during this period, but it is said that they intermarried with the upper castes of Central Nepal and that special dispensations were granted them enabling their descendants to be recognised as members of the Kshatriya or Rajput caste.

At the time that Prithwi Narayan Sah came to the throne of Gurkha, it was one of the twenty-four small states in the country of the seven Gandaks, the central province of what is now the kingdom of Nepal. The inhabitants of these states were of Mongolian origin, and, generally speaking, of hardier stock and more warlike than the inhabitants of the valley, the Newars. They too, like the Newars, had been greatly influenced by the Brahman and Rajput immigrants, although the Brahman infiltration had been less orthodox than in the case of the Newars. Thus, although the earlier and more eager converts were admitted as Kshatriyas, as were also the offspring of the irregular unions between Brahmans and hill women, Hinduism sat but lightly on the original Gurkhas and the people of the other hill states, and was in fact chiefly confined to respect for the Brahman and reverence for the cow. The tribes of the Brahmans and Kshatriya orders however enjoyed, as they do to-day, an authority and a prestige denied to other classes, and it was they who provided the main support of the Gurkha Government at the time when Prithwi Narayan came to the throne.

Such then were the people who were in time to become masters of the whole country and whose tiny municipality gave the name to the ruling race by which it is known to-day.

Before continuing their story, however, it is worth while giving attention for a moment to the valley of Nepal and to what was happening within its boundaries at this time. It is known that in the middle of the fourteenth century—the time when Nepalese history assumes a more coherent form—the valley was mainly inhabited by a people of great artistic power known as Newars. As in the case of every Nepalese tribe, no researches have as yet succeeded in determining exactly whence they came, nor when they first settled in the valley. I have already mentioned how in their eagerness to claim an orthodox pedigree they profess to be the descendants of the Nairs of southern India, but their language, customs and physical traits all indicate some north Himalayan origin. The one thing definitely known about the Newars is that in the matter of their religion they were profoundly influenced first by the Buddhist and then by the Hindu refugees who sought refuge in Nepal from the Moslem invaders of India. They were ruled by a succession of dynasties hailing from India, and became in consequence slowly Indianised until not only did they take their political development from their Hindu masters, but saw the introduction of the Brahman predominance that prevails in Nepal to-day.

The valley, as we have already seen, had been divided by Yaksha Malla in the middle of the fifteenth century into three principalities with capitals at Kathmandu, Bhatgaon and Patan, all being within a radius of only seven miles. So the three rulers lived cheek by jowl in the small valley, exercising a kind of suzerainty over states and tribes to east, west and south. And the suzerainty was generally shifting and unstable at that, for the principalities lacked regular frontiers, and none of the three rulers ever ruled over a definite kingdom with definite boundaries.

During the period of three hundred years that elapsed between the division of the valley by Yaksha Malla and the Gurkha invasion in the middle of the eighteenth century, the Newars developed a characteristic style of architecture and great proficiency in manual arts and crafts, and I shall describe in a later chapter how skilfully and effectively they embellished the towns, temples and holy places that are to be found dotted about in the valley. The period was in fact one of great prosperity both in the artistic and commercial senses. Politically, however, it was less happy, the story of this time being one of unceasing internal dissensions and constantly quarrelling chiefs. And it was as a consequence of this that the strength and security of

ENTRANCE GATEWAY AT BHATGAON.

the valley principalities were being slowly but surely sapped at the time when Prithwi Narayan came to the throne in the year 1742.

The causes of the quarrels were as often as not trivial in the extreme. Thus the pretext that they were too vain of their personal appearance was sufficient for the chief of Bhatgaon to imprison some visitors from Kathmandu. The prince of the latter city retaliated by imprisoning in his turn Bhatgaon citizens who had come to Kathmandu to worship, only releasing them after payment of heavy ransoms. Again friction over so trivial a matter as the erection of a stone pillar embittered the relations between the three capitals, while a sort of religious upheaval, stirred into being by a Buddhist fanatic anxious to bring about a religious revolution, added to the political troubles of the day.

Hence while there was peace for the moment in Gurkha, dark clouds were beginning to form over the valley. With their powers of defence weakened by their incessant internal squabbles, the days of the three kingdoms of the Mallas were clearly numbered; for Prithwi Narayan, inflated by his success a few years after his accession, when he had annexed three of the Chaubisia states and obtained supreme control of the confederacy, was already casting covetous eyes upon the rich valley of Nepal. And it says much for the powers of resistance of the Newars that they were able to hold out against him and his more warlike Gurkhas for as long as they did. For the first siege of Kirtipur—the opening phase in the Gurkhas' campaign for the conquest of the valley—took place in 1765, and it was not until the summer of 1769 that the downfall of the three kingdoms was finally brought about and the seat of power transferred from Gurkha to Kathmandu.

Prithwi Narayan's reputation had been steadily growing since he came to power, and the murder of a king at Patan resulted in the people of that principality inviting him to accept the throne and restore order in the kingdom, where revolution and anarchy prevailed. Feeling that the time to move had not yet arrived, he refused the offer, but deputed his youngest brother to reign in his stead, the latter being himself deposed after a reign of four years. Shortly after this he tried to seize Nawakot, the key to the valley of Nepal, but the unexpected arrival of troops of the King of Kathmandu frustrated the attempt.

Thwarted thus for the time being in his own neighbourhood, he then directed his attention to more distant regions, and by seizing the territory of a brother-in-law that lay in the hills to the east he managed to turn the flank of Nepal. It is a curious fact, by the way, that, despite the warlike qualities of his Gurkhas, Prithwi Narayan was invariably beaten when it came to open fighting in the field. His success as a leader was indeed due chiefly to his sound judgment and tenacity of purpose, in conjunction with an unrivalled mastery of intrigue. Thus, although he was almost invariably defeated at the outset of every enterprise he undertook, his skill in propaganda and powers of persuasion rarely failed to convert defeat into victory in the end. Nor did any man know better how to take advantage of any opportunity that luck might send his way.

The opening of his campaign against the valley supplies a typical example of his methods. The customary bitter and futile quarrel which was raging at the time between the kings of Bhatgaon and Kathmandu led to the former calling on Prithwi Narayan to come to his aid. The Gurkha leader, seeing here a golden opportunity, was nothing loath, and after securing Nawakot, this time without opposition, besieged Kirtipur in the valley. The King of Patan, to whom Kirtipur belonged, did not raise a finger in support, but Jaya Prakasha, the King of Kathmandu, a first-class fighting man, attacked the Gurkhas and completely defeated them, Prithwi Narayan himself being very nearly killed.

The subsequent insane behaviour however of the conqueror in insulting and imprisoning the nobles of Kirtipur when they had come to express their gratitude to him for his aid, lost him the fruits of his victory, for in revenge they delivered some of the forts on the surrounding hills to Prithwi Narayan, who preferred however in the end to achieve his purpose by other means than further fighting with such a formidable enemy. The policy which he adopted therefore was that of starving the valley into submission by cutting off all its supplies. This he effected by posting troops at all of the seven passes by which tracks entered it, and hanging on the spot everyone, man, woman or child, suspected of bringing in food, salt or cotton.

At the same time he proceeded to undermine Jaya Prakasa's influence by fomenting dissension amongst the nobility and by a rigorous religious propaganda to which two thousand Brahmans of their own accord lent their aid. Then in 1765, thinking that his brutal blockade and religious propaganda had now done their work, he laid siege for the second time to Kirtipur, only to be repulsed again with heavy losses and driven back ignominiously to the hills once more. In this action moreover his brother lost an eye as the result of an arrow wound, a mishap for which he subsequently wreaked his vengeance on the unfortunate inhabitants of Kirtipur in a characteristically barbarous manner.

This was some months later when Prithwi Narayan launched his soldiers for a third and final assault upon the heroic city. By this time the kings of Patan and Bhatgaon, realising the danger which now threatened the whole valley, had agreed to compose their differences and stand together in a united effort to keep the dreaded Gurkhas at bay—herein differing from Jaya Prakasa the half insane chief of Kathmandu, who made no effort at all to relieve Kirtipur though it was only four miles away. Moreover, it was he who was indirectly responsible for the ultimate fall of the city. For, after holding out for six months, the lower part was surrendered to Prithwi Narayan by one of the nobles who had been insulted and humiliated in Kathmandu.

Withdrawing into the upper part of the town which was almost impregnable the gallant inhabitants prepared to make a further stand, but in the end despairing of help from outside, they came to terms with Prithwi Narayan, accepting his word that they should go unharmed, and only learning when too late how little such a promise was worth. For two days after their submission an order came from Nawakot to the effect that the noses and lips of all males, except children at the breast were to be cut off and the name of the town changed from Kirtipur to Naskatipur, or the City of Cut Noses. The chronicle adds that the only people to escape this terrible fate were those who could play on wind instruments! Music hath charms—but not enough, it would seem, to soothe the savage breast of this inhuman ruler.

Prithwi Narayan now turned his attention to Patan, and by threatening the inhabitants with a fate similar to that which had befallen Kirtipur, but with the loss of the right hand as well this time, was on the point of compelling the capitulation of this city also. But an unforeseen event, in the shape of the appearance in Nepal of a small British force, under Captain Kinloch, drew the invading army away and for the moment Patan was saved. The Honourable East India Company's troops had been sent in response to an appeal from Jaya Prakasha, during the last assault on Kirtipur, for British aid to expel the Gurkha invader. Unfortunately, with his progress checked by swollen streams and his ranks decimated by the deadly Terai malaria, Kinloch had encountered insuperable difficulties and had in fact actually begun to retire before even encountering any of his Gurkha opponents. Yet, damaging as this withdrawal was to British prestige, the diversion caused by this small force afforded a welcome respite to beleagured Patan, and indeed postponed its fall for nearly a year.

With the retirement of the British force, Prithwi Narayan was again free to resume his operations in the valley, but for the time being he disregarded Patan, and instead made elaborate preparations to besiege the wealthy city of Kathmandu, where Brahmans in his pay had already been engaged in steady propaganda for some time. The capture of Kathmandu proved an easy task. While the inhabitants, including most of the garrison, were celebrating a religious festival, the Indrajatra, the Gurkhas entered the city unobserved. The king, who was worshipping

Entrance Gateway at Patan.

Temples in Bhatgaon.

in a temple at the time, escaped to Patan, but not before he had laid a mine on the temple steps which cost many Gurkhas their lives.

From Patan, Jaya Prakasha, taking with him Tejnarsing, the ruler of that city, sought refuge in Bhatgaon, after which Patan surrendered without a struggle to the Gurkha prince. Contaminated by the propaganda of the Brahmans and cowed by the fate that had befallen Kirtipur, neither soldiery nor citizens had the heart to offer any resistance, and Prithwi Narayan, after solemnly promising to respect not only the lives but also the property of the nobility, made a formal entry into the town. From what has already been said of Prithwi Narayan's character, it will hardly surprise readers to learn that he ordered the nobles who had assembled to greet him to be at once put to death.

Meanwhile, Bhatgaon still held out. Many small towns and villages to the east had displayed magnificent courage in opposing the Gurkhas, and these last knew to their cost the stubborn resistance they would have to meet from the forces of the three kings of the valley, now united in a last desperate stand. There was, however, to be little or no fighting on this occasion, for Prithwi Narayan once more had recourse to treachery, and when eight months later, about July, 1769, he appeared before the walls of the city, he had no doubt as to the issue, for the seven illegitimate sons of the King of Bhatgaon were now securely in his pay. The traitors, however, were to be dearly punished for their treachery, and, ironically enough, by Prithwi Narayan himself, who after denouncing them—incredible as it may sound!—for their infamous conduct in surrendering the city, order their noses to be cut off and their property to be confiscated.

Yet even Prithwi Narayan, brutal and treacherous as he was, seems to have had his better moments at times. Thus, on one occasion he found his way barred by a handful of men led by one Mohindra Rai, who held out against overwhelming odds with the most dauntless courage, disposing of no fewer than three hundred of the enemy. Valour such as this did not escape the notice of the Gurkha commander, and when, on riding over the field of battle the next morning he saw the body of his courageous adversary, he took his family under his personal protection, and maintained them until his death.

Likewise, after the fall of Bhatgaon, no harm befell its aged ruler, Ranjit Malla. On the contrary, mindful of the kindness and hospitality which he had often received in earlier days at his hands, Prithwi Narayan not only treated him with respect and kindness, but even invited him to remain upon the throne of his little principality. Ranjit Malla had, however, had his fill of the tempestuous and dangerous life that was the lot of a valley ruler, and asked only to be allowed to end his days peacefully in Benares, a request which was immediately granted. The King of Patan, on the other hand, was confined in irons until he died, but clemency was shown again to the mortally wounded Jaya Prakasha, the defeated King of Kathmandu, whose last request, that he should be carried to the temple of Pashupati and be allowed to die in the royal ghat, was granted. And therewith the curtain falls upon the last act of the story of the conquest of the valley.

CHAPTER VI

Turbulent Years

THE Gurkhas being now indisputable masters of Nepal, the Newars were relegated to the position of a subject race and their Hindu nobles lost all power, the Brahmans alone retaining their status. From now on the Gurkhas ruled without question, and their Rajput nobles not only held all the positions of trust and honour in the valley but also owned much of the best land. In their conquest of Nepal the Gurkhas had admittedly been much helped by the disunion and ineptitude of the Indian kings who ruled over the Newars, but their own superior powers, due to the infusion of Indian blood into the brave but unenterprising mountain tribes of the Chaubisi Raj, and to the leadership of the Rajput nobles, would almost certainly have achieved in any case the same result.

Now master of the whole of Nepal, Prithwi Narayan made his headquarters at Kathmandu and set to work to ensure the pacification and unification of his new domains. From the first he showed himself strongly antagonistic to European influence, expelling the Capuchin missionaries who had settled in the valley after being driven from Tibet, and closing his passes to all European merchandise.

He did not, however, live long enough to reap the full benefit of his triumphs, for he died in 1771, and after the short reign of his son, Singha Pratap Sah, during which further country to the south-west was added to the kingdom, the latter's infant son, Rana Bahadur Sah, succeeded to the throne in the year 1775.

The new king's uncle, Bahadur Sah, who acted as regent, immediately embarked upon a further campaign of aggrandisement, this time in a westerly direction. Thanks to the well-trained and skilfully-led troops of the invaders, and not a little also to the policy of intrigue in which Bahadur Sah was a past-master, the chiefs not only of the Chaubisi Raj, but also of the twenty-two kingdoms away to the west, surrendered one by one, and thus the whole of the western country—the prize so long striven for—was at last in the hands of the Gurkhas. Flushed with success, they crossed the western boundary of modern Nepal, the river Kali, and invaded Kumaon, of which they rapidly took possession.

With the submission of the principalities in the west thus successfully brought about, the Gurkhas now turned their attention eastwards, invading Sikkim and even threatening Tibet. Finding an easy prey in the latter country, they crossed the frontier and indulged in acts of aggression, such as the pillaging of sacred temples, which they ultimately had cause to regret. For on the Gurkhas refusing to restore the loot which they had taken from the Grand Lama's palace at a place called Tashi-lumpo, the patience of the Chinese, who had long resented their encroachments, was finally exhausted, and in 1792 the Emperor, as the terrestrial protector and spiritual disciple of the Lamas, dispatched an army of 70,000 men against them.

Though the Chinese suffered considerable losses in the mountain warfare, their overwhelming numbers rendered the Nepalese quite helpless in the plains of Tibet, and after desperate fighting they advanced finally into Nepal as far as Nawakot, only twenty miles from Kathmandu. In the treaty of peace which followed, the regent was compelled to acknowledge the suzerainty of China and to undertake to send a commercial mission every five years to Pekin. At the same time Nepal was obliged to surrender a certain portion of her territory, though on the whole she did not come out of the business so badly as might have been expected. Tibet, which had gained a material victory, really lost far more in proportion, for the Chinese Emperor seized the opportunity to impose his yoke even more firmly on that country than before.

The quinquennial mission to China has long since been a thing of the past. The last one took place in 1908, although it had ceased to have any political importance long before that. Once arrived in Peking, these missions had usually been received courteously enough, but the numerous "incidents" that used to occur on the way thither, especially in Tibet, gave rise to much ill-feeling between the Nepalese Government and the districts concerned, and the whole business was wisely abandoned in the end.

It may be added that at the outset of the hostilities between Nepal and China the Nepalese regent applied to the British for military aid. Lord Cornwallis was unwilling to go to the length of sending troops, but he offered to negotiate between the two countries and a mission under Colonel Kirkpatrick reached Nawakot early in 1792. Colonel Kirkpatrick arrived too late, however, to vary in any way the peace terms that had already been promulgated, and finding the Nepalese unwilling to embark on any closer alliance with the British, or to allow the establishment of a British resident in Kathmandu, which he had also been instructed to arrange for if possible, he left Nepal the same year. Although he was unable to fulfil the purpose of his mission, Kirkpatrick was the first Englishman to enter the country, and his account of the valley during that time, which was published in 1811, forms the basis of practically all that is known about that period of Nepalese history to-day.

The defeat which they had sustained at the hands of the Chinese did nothing to check the military activity of the Nepalese in the west, and in 1794 they annexed the provinces of Garwhal and Kumaon. The Gurkha kingdom therefore now extended from Sikkim to the borders of Kashmir, and what are to-day known as the Simla Hill States were at this time also Nepalese.

In 1795 Rana Bahadur Sah removed his uncle from the regency and assumed the reins of government himself. Dissolute and unprincipled—thanks in no small measure to his uncle, who had purposely kept him in ignorance and profligacy during his minority—during the next five years he was responsible for a policy of absolutism and violence such as had been rarely witnessed even in Nepal. Intolerable as was his general conduct, it was his choice of a Brahman's daughter as his wife—his queen, Tirpura Sundari being childless—that proved his undoing. Such an action not only antagonised the Brahmans but also completely alienated the sympathy of his people, and he was compelled to abdicate in 1800. Accompanied by his legitimate queen, he retired to Benares, while his son by the Brahman lady Girvan Juddha, though declared illegitimate by the Brahmans, was put on the throne. To act as regent, Rana Bahadur had nominated one of his concubines, while Damodar Panre, the conqueror of Kumaon and a prudent and able man, assumed the duties of Prime Minister, thereby paving the way for the other notable Prime Ministers whose energy and capability have contributed so much to the prosperity of Nepal.

At this juncture British politics again came into the affairs of Nepal, for fearing that the presence of the deposed Nepalese king in their territory might induce the British to intervene and reinstate him, the regent hastily made a commercial treaty with the East India Company, and agreed to accept a permanent British resident at Kathmandu.

Captain Knox, who was appointed to this delicate post, reached the capital in 1802. Finding the policy of the Government anything but conciliatory, and that their aversion to his presence in the country became more and more marked as time went on, Knox withdrew from Nepal in March, 1803, while in January of the following year the alliance with the Durbar was formerly dissolved.

The conduct of Rana Bahadur in Benares had in the meantime become so scandalous that his queen, Tripura Sundari, tired of her husband's fresh infidelities, and anxious to resume her place as queen regnant, prevailed on Damodar Panre to allow her to return to Nepal. The concubine regent thereupon sought sanctuary in a temple, the Raja of Palpa, who in the king's absence had been scheming for the throne himself, was expelled, and Damodar Panre was entrusted with the conduct of affairs.

Accordingly the way soon became open for the restoration of Rana Bahadur himself, and when he returned he was accompanied by a companion in exile, a Rajput noble from Gurkha, by name Bhim Sen, who subsequently attained one of the greatest names in Nepalese history and who can indisputably be called the first of the series of distinguished statesmen to whom the present prosperity of Nepal is due.

The sudden appearance in Nepal of this man however was to cost the gallant Damodar Panre his life. For family feuds have always been rife in Nepal, and with the arrival of Bhim Sen Thapa upon the scene, the famous quarrel between the Panres and the Thapas—for there had been rivalry between the two families for many generations—now came to a head in a sufficiently decisive manner. For the first action of Bhim Sen on his assuming supreme authority was to put Damodar Panre and all his sons to death.

A man of great capacity and determination, Bhim Sen held the office of Prime Minister for thirty-three years. Although there came times when he in his turn was seriously threatened and his office imperilled by the old antagonism between the Thapas and the Panres, which had cost Damodar Panre his life, he encountered, on the whole, little opposition throughout his career until he reached its tragic end. His power was indeed for the most part absolute; he was in fact Nepal. Further, it was on the foundation that Bhim Sen laid that those other great Nepalese rulers, Jung Bahadur and Chandra Shumshere, built up the prosperity of the country.

After the ruthless manner of the premiers of those days, Bhim Sen, while his hands were still stained with the blood of Damodar Panre, proceeded to the murder of the King of Palpa, who, as previously mentioned, during the absence of Rana Bahadur in Benares, had been conspiring for the throne, and, these preliminaries disposed of, then devoted his energies to the extension of his conquests to the west. Palpa was annexed, the independence of the last of the Chaubisi States vanished, and by August, 1804, the whole of Nepal came under the sway of the Gurkha dynasty at Kathmandu. By the inclusion of these states the warlike population, on which the Gurkha king could draw, was now vastly increased, and generally speaking, the western tribes were admitted to the same social privileges as the Gurkhas; the eastern tribes, on the other hand, being of a lower social and religious development, were not granted them till later, though their value as a recruiting ground for the Nepalese army was in the meantime thoroughly appreciated.

Flushed by his successes, Bhim Sen, through the agency of his father, General Amar Sing Thapa, now tried to extend his conquests still further westward, and invaded Kangra. Amar Sing's efforts to annex Kangra however were doomed to failure, for here he found himself confronted by a redoubtable adversary in the shape of the lion of the Punjab, Ranjit Singh. The famous Sikh leader, engaged at the time in the conquest of the Punjab and Kashmir, had thrown a strong force in the direction of the latter country, and the rivals met in the Kangra valley. Amar Sing's triumphant progress was now arrested; in the battle that followed he had no choice but to retreat; and, instead of the Gurkhas, the Sikhs became dominant in the Kangra valley.

Meanwhile, his return to power in his own country had done nothing to improve the conduct of the king, Rana Bahadur. There were the same excesses, the same outrages, to which was now added a systematic persecution of the Brahmans, whose personal and temple property he confiscated to replenish his own chest. Came the inevitable sequel. Rana Bahadur, at the instigation of the Brahmans, was killed in a dispute with his illegitimate half-brother, who in turn fell by the sword of a nephew of Bhim Sen. The infant son of Rana Bahadur's Brahman wife remained on the throne, while his first wife, Tripura Sundari, was appointed co-regent, a position which she held for the next twenty-eight years. All this happened in the year 1807.

Bhim Sen now began to search for a further outlet for his warlike energy. True, he had conquered Nepal and the hill valleys eastwards and westwards at the foot of the great Himalayan wall on the north, but his way was now blocked in every direction save one. The Sikhs had checked his advance to the west; the Chinese had put an end to any ideas of further encroachments in the north-east; the country east of Sikkim afforded little scope for profitable enterprise; to the north the Himalayas constituted an impassable barrier; only the south remained.

To encroach upon British territory, however, was a perilous undertaking, in view of the possibility of reprisals which might bring his country under British ascendancy—a contingency of which the Nepalese lived in perpetual dread. At the same time Bhim Sen had always regarded the East India Company as his foe rather than his friend; but, in judging it by its somewhat timid and vacillating attitude towards Nepal during the previous thirty or forty years, he made the mistake of underestimating its power at this time. At any rate he decided to see how far he could go, and from 1804 to 1812 the Gurkhas pushed steadily southwards into British territory, until by the end of that time no fewer than two hundred villages in the fertile Terai and Tirhut had been annexed.

A commission, on which both sides were represented, was finally appointed to inquire into the matter, and, the result of the investigation being entirely favourable to the British, a detachment of regulars were instructed to occupy the debatable ground. On these being withdrawn during the rainy season, however, and their places taken by native police, the Nepalese troops raided the territory and put to death many of the latter. War was now inevitable, even though a last chance of settlement was granted to the Nepalese Government, and it was formally declared on 1st November, 1814.

The story of the early part of this war makes pitiful reading. The strategy of Lord Hastings, the Governor General, who himself planned the campaign, was faulty; the generals, with few exceptions, were old and inefficient, constantly breaking down in health or nerves; while the troops, handicapped by the presence of a large number of undisciplined volunteers, were at first quite incapable of making headway against the brave and well-trained mountaineers. Thus in the first season's fighting, three out of the four main columns suffered reverses inflicted by smaller numbers, and only in Kumaon to the west, where a small detachment was operating independently, did the British meet with any success.

To General Ochterlony fell the honour of restoring the prestige of British arms. Assuming command in 1815 of the detachments operating in Kumaon, the new leader conducted operations with skill and perseverance. Leadership and discipline now produced their inevitable effect, and in May, 1815, General Amar Sing Thapa was obliged to capitulate with all the honours of war. Under the terms of the agreement reached between the two generals, the Gurkhas were compelled to evacuate the whole of their territory from the Sutlej to the Kali river, comprising their conquests of the last thirty years, and corresponding roughly to the present districts of Kumaon, Garwhal and Simla. As a sequel to these peace negotiations it is important to note that the Gurkha soldiers who formed the remnants of Amar Sing's forces enlisted in the British army, being the first Gurkha soldiers to serve under the British flag.

Throughout the campaign the Nepalese fought with the greatest gallantry, while they further showed their confidence in their opponents' sense of fair play and sportsmanship by sending, whenever possible, their wounded into English camp hospitals for treatment. Peace was, however, after all, not to be so easily restored. News that the Indian Government was expecting trouble from other quarters—in particular from the Sikhs and the Marathas—encouraged the Nepalese to procrastinate, and eventually to refuse to ratify the terms arrived at. This led to the resumption of hostilities in February, 1816, and Ochterlony, the successful general of the previous campaign, was again given command.

This time he advanced upon Kathmandu by the direct route

HITAURA VILLAGE, NEAR CHURIA PASS.

BHIM SEN TEMPLE AT PATAN.

through the Terai, and marching straight upon his objective, came into contact with the enemey in the neighbourhood of the Churia ridge, thirty miles from the British frontier and on the high road to Kathmandu. Unwilling to cause unnecessary loss of life by a frontal attack, he succeeded in outflanking the Gurkhas, thanks largely to the discovery (by Lieutenant Pickersgill), of a little-known torrent-bed which lay to the west of the Churia Pass road. Forced to abandon their position here, the Gurkhas put up a last gallant but hopeless resistance at Makwanpur, after which, determined at all costs to prevent British troops entering the valley of Nepal, the Darbar sent an envoy to the British headquarters to sue for peace within a march or two from the capital.

The resulting treaty, which was signed at Segowli on the 4th March, 1816, has been maintained to the letter to this very day. By it Nepal was confined to the country between the Kali and the Mechi, thereby giving up all claim to Garwhal, Kumaon and the other hill states on the west, and to Sikkim on the east. To the south, Nepal was compelled to cede the Terai, subject to the annual payment by the company of compensation to certain landowners with whom it had no quarrel, the eastern Terai being also annexed by the British, and the western Terai being handed over to the kingdom of Oudh. A large part of the Terai was, however, restored the same year in lieu of the annual payment, as Lord Hastings was now anxious to establish the best possible relations with Nepal.

An important clause in the treaty, and one which deserves more than a passing reference, was that by which the Nepal Government agreed to receive a British representative at Kathmandu. Nepal being, as I have already said elsewhere, an independent state, the British minister, as the resident is called to-day, occupies an entirely different position from that of a resident in a native state in India. He acts merely as the official intermediary between the two governments, and his duties are confined to reporting events in Nepal as far as they concern Indian interests, to representing to the Nepalese authorities any grievances brought forward by Indian subjects, and to issuing passports. The British representative in Kathmandu, therefore, may be said to combine the duties of a consul with the position of a minister, for he represents the King-Emperor on all ceremonial occasions in Kathmandu.[1]

Immediately after the war, the king, Girvan Juddha Vikram Sahi, died of small-pox, at the age of eighteen, and the succession of another minor, in the shape of his two-year-old son, Rajendra Vikram Sahi, served further to consolidate the powers of the joint regency of Bhim Sen Thapa and the Queen Tripura Sundari, which lasted, in fact, until the latter's death sixteen years later. Although no events of any importance occurred to disturb the peace of the country for several years after the Treaty of 1816, the policy of the Durbar towards the British continued unfriendly, at any rate, for a time. The campaign had certainly taught Bhim Sen to respect his powerful neighbour, but it had not taught him as yet to trust him, and so for some time the Nepalese adopted a policy of pin-pricks that made life anything but a bed of roses for Captain Gardner, the British Resident.

Thus the delimitation of the frontier remained a matter of constant friction between the authorities of both countries, dacoity seemed to be encouraged rather than suppressed, obstacles were thrown in the way of trade, while friendly overtures were made to any likely enemy of the company. The ultimate pleasant relations that have continued unbroken between the two countries for nearly a hundred years had not yet been established.

With the death of the Queen Mother, Tripura Sundari, in 1832, the power which Bhim Sen enjoyed for so many years began to wane, for the young king, now of age, began forthwith to assert his own authority. In 1833, at the annual Panjni, the ceremony at which every state official is either confirmed in his appointment or dismissed, Bhim Sen was not re-elected. It is true that he was restored a few years later, but the mere

[1] The title having been changed so frequently in recent years, the British Representative at Kathmandu is variably referred to as Minister, Resident, Envoy and British Representative in the text.

fact that the king had been able on this occasion to assert his authority against the formerly all-powerful minister showed that his power had been badly shaken. And, oddly enough, it was again the old feud between the Thapas and the Panres that brought about his final downfall.

For the Panres, now led by Ranjang, the son of Damodar Panre, his former victim, had never ceased to intrigue against him, and the net drew tighter and tighter round him. They had much to revenge, and finally achieved their purpose. The death of the elder queen's youngest son gave them their final trump card, for they immediately spread the rumour that the child had been poisoned at Bhim Sen's instigation, and that he had even attempted to poison the queen herself. In the result, Bhim Sen and his nephew Matbar Sing, the late head of the Government in Gurkha, were put in irons and imprisoned, all their property was confiscated and every indignity heaped on them, while Ranjang became Prime Minister.

Through the influence of the younger queen,[1] both prisoners were subsequently released, but although his long services and his recent misfortunes secured for him much sympathy, Bhim Sen decided to retire from public life, though he did not end his days in the peace which he deserved.

Utter confusion now reigned in Kathmandu, a confusion which the dissension between the two queens, each supporting a rival faction, only served to increase. Prime Minister succeeded Prime Minister in rapid succession until, in 1839, the command of the Panre forces was again attained by Ranjang, who determined this time to make quite certain of his old opponent. All the old accusations were accordingly revived, and Bhim Sen was again thrown into prison practically without a trial. As he did not dare actually to assassinate him, Ran Jang attained the same result in another way by the orders which he gave for his treatment in prison. And so, after holding out for nine days, Bhim Sen gave up the struggle and committed

[1] The younger queen and the author of the Kot Massacre was Maharani Lakshmi Devi.

suicide with the khukri which his tormentors had thoughtfully allowed him to retain.

"And thus has perished," wrote Brian Hodgson, Resident at the time, to the Governor-General of India, on the following day, "the great and able statesman, who, for more than thirty years had ruled this kingdom with more than regal sway. He was, indeed, a man born to exercise dominion over his fellows, nor am I aware of any native statesman of recent times, except Ranjit Singh, who is, all things considered, worthy to be compared with the late General Bhim Sen, of Nepal."

CHAPTER VII

Jung Bahadur and his Days

WITH the removal of Bhim Sen, the last obstacle in the path of the senior queen and the Panre party was removed, and by 1839 she had practically ousted the weak and incapable king from any participation in public affairs, and had taken the reins of government into her own hands. The policy of this tempestuous and irresponsible woman was marked by a strong anti-British feeling, and only the arbitrary means which she employed in making preparations for war (which had the effect of arousing public opinion against it) and the skilful handling of the situation by Hodgson, the Resident, prevented a conflict with the British in 1839. Egged on by the war party, however, so far from abandoning her hostile policy against her powerful neighbour in the south, she actually ordered an invasion of British territory the following year, when nearly a hundred villages in the district of Ramnagar were occupied.

On Hodgson demanding the immediate withdrawal, compensation and a full apology, the Queen incited the troops in Kathmandu to mutiny, by spreading the false rumour that their pay was to be reduced under orders from the Indian Government, whereupon a large body of them marched upon the Residency. The personal popularity of Hodgson saved the situation and incidentally his life. The coup failed, and when an official ultimatum was forwarded from Calcutta for the withdrawal of the Gurkhas from Ramnagar, not only was it immediately complied with, but the Durbar agreed to dismiss the Panre Government and to appoint in its place a type of Coalition Government with strict orders to do all that was possible to renew the friendship between India and Nepal.

The death of the Queen herself, in 1841, from malaria contracted in the Terai, removed the last great danger to peace between the two countries. There was an immediate reaction from her hostile policy. No longer under her influence, her weak husband now gravitated to the peace party, and even went so far as to offer the services of the Nepalese army for use by the Company in Burma or in Afghanistan, where a British force had just been annihilated on its retreat from Kabul.

But though the death of the senior Rani had certainly paved the way for more friendly relations between the East India Company and Nepal, chaos still continued to reign in Kathmandu. In fact, the feud between the Panres and the Thapas kept the country in a ferment for over twelve years. Each party in turn clutched at supremacy, only to suffer in a few months the fate that it had meted out to its rivals in its days of power.

Thus, at this particular time, with the succession of the junior Queen to the position of chief wife, it was the turn of the Thapas, whose cause she had from the first supported, to come into their own. To further consolidate their position, the Queen recalled Matbar Sing, nephew of Bhim Sen, from Simla, whither he had been exiled at the time of his uncle's downfall, and installed him as Prime Minister. And bitterly he must afterwards have regretted leaving the peace and security of British protection for the storm and stress of political life in Kathmandu. For inevitably the pendulum swung once again. The tables were turned on the Panre party, and Matbar Sing's vengeance on his uncle's accusers was swift and effective.

His own career was, however, destined to be a short one, for the Queen, disappointed in his persistent refusal to waive the rights of the heir apparent in favour of her own child, plotted with the King to bring about his downfall, and, in May, 1845, only two years after his appointment to the Premiership, he was sent for to the palace and murdered. To complete the story of what must be regarded as one of the most shameful episodes in a black period of Nepalese history, the man chosen by the Queen as the instrument for the murder was none other than Jung Bahadur, Matbar Sing's own nephew, and the man who put into his hand the loaded rifle with which the murder was committed was the King.

The situation in Kathmandu was now more hopelessly confused than ever. Although the courage and ability of Jung Bahadur gave him exceptional claims for the post of Premiership, yet, in view of the great power wielded by Gagan Sing, the Queen's lover, and incidentally, the last person whom the jealous King wished to appoint as Prime Minister, he only consented to act in that capacity for a time. He was, however, as a reward for his services, given the command of three regiments, and made military member of the Council, though Gagan Sing, by being given the command of seven, still remained the most powerful man in Nepal.

The increasing intimacy between the Queen and Gagan Sing, however, in time aroused the jealousy of the King to fever pitch, and in September, 1846, he had him murdered in cold blood while he was at his prayers. The fury of the Queen now knew no bounds and there ensued, an outburst of bloodshed and carnage surpassing in ferocity anything seen even in Nepal for many years. Assembling all the chief civil and military officers of the State in the Kot or Royal Court of Assembly, she proceeded to accuse her entire Council of the murder, and in the massacre which followed, according to the official records, fifty-five of the nobility and high officials, to say nothing of over five hundred humbler folk, lost their lives.

It must be admitted Jung Bahadur certainly figured prominently in the Massacre of the Kot, for as soon as he had heard what was happening, accompanied by his three regiments and a host of adherents, fully armed, he proceeded to the Kot, which he surrounded with his troops. He thus completely dominated the assembly, and, as will be seen, was before long to find himself in the thick of the fray. That he was personally responsible for the bloodshed on this occasion is, however, probably untrue. It was, in the first place, certainly not premeditated, and was, in the beginning, more of a confused mêlée than a massacre. Even the chroniclers are uncertain as to who actually fired the first shots. But once blood was shed, the rest was inevitable.

Everyone distrusted his neighbour, and all who had arms drew them in self-defence. In the promiscuous fighting that followed, a party of Jung Bahadur's supporters, armed with double-barrelled guns, forced their way into the building, and rallying round him and his brothers, commenced firing on all who seemed opposed to them. Those who took refuge in the Kot were, therefore, cut or shot down by Jung Bahadur's followers, while those who came out into the quadrangle were at once slaughtered by the men of his regiments who surrounded it on all sides.

While the massacre lasted, the Queen stood at the open window of an upper story urging on the soldiers with cries of "kill and destroy my enemies." Indeed, had it not been for Jung Bahadur's restraining influence, she would have put the heir apparent to death on the spot. Thus, the chief responsibility for the "Massacre of the Kot" may well be assigned to this blood-thirsty woman,—a fact which is further borne out by Jung Bahadur's own statement to the Resident, given two days later, in which he maintained that the massacre "originated entirely in the violent and outrageous conduct of the Queen, who, holding supreme power at the time, ought to be held responsible for it" (Oldfield).

While the slaughter was at its height, the Queen conferred the office of Prime Minister and Commander-in-Chief upon Jung Bahadur, who thus attained supreme power in circumstances which may well be described as unique. Born in 1817, Jung Bahadur was the second son of Bal Nar Sing Kunwar, who, as a reward for his action in slaying the murderer of Rana Bahadur Sah, had been made hereditary Kazi, and who continued to hold various important posts until the fall of Bhim Sen. He appears upon the scene somewhat suddenly, for during his youth his father was commanding the north-western district and he was thus continually away from Kathmandu. Rumours of his escapades and independent character

—his father was apparently quite unable to control him—reached the capital however from time to time.

From these it transpired that, while he was impatient of the authority of his superiors in the Nepalese army, he was extremely popular with the rank and file, that he was an expert gambler, and that he was, above everything, a past master in all forms of sport. Some idea of his courage and adventurous spirit can be gleaned from the fact that when he and his father lost their posts at the time of Bhim Sen's fall in 1837, he conceived the idea of catching elephants single-handed in the Terai in order to pay off his gambling debts! And so it is hardly surprising to learn that, tiring of his military duties, and seeing for the moment no scope whatever for a man of his energy in Nepal, he deserted before long from the army and, escaping across the frontier into the territory of the old Sikh King, Ranjit Singh, made his way to Lahore.

He appears to have made no great impression on Ranjit Singh during his stay in India, and finding himself after a time in financial difficulties, with a characteristic disregard for consequences, he calmly returned to Nepal. There, curiously enough, instead of punishment for his seemingly grave offence, he received promotion and was given the rank of Kazi—having won the special admiration of the King it is said through his courage in dealing with a wild elephant—though for some years the part which he played in public affairs was small. He was, however, only biding his time. While in exile in India he had not failed to follow the course of events in Nepal, and fully conscious of his own capacities—even if he hardly realised then the importance of the part that he was destined to play—he knew that his opportunity would come in due course. For with a weak and vacillating king, with several different parties all struggling for power, with a government seething with discord and intrigue, a man of such exceptional intelligence and character as Jung Bahadur was bound to come to the front in time, as he did in due course, to the great advantage of his country.

Of the many stories—perhaps legends is the better word—told about Jung Bahadur, some of the most oft-repeated concern his relations with Surendra Vikram, the heir to the throne. This youth, thoroughly decadent and brought up in an atmosphere of murder and intrigue, hated him with an almost maniacal intensity and plotted again and again to have him assassinated. Oddly enough, however, nothing which Surendra Vikram might do or say provoked Jung Bahadur's resentment in the slightest degree—so sacred in his eyes was the divine right of kings—and even the young miscreant's attempts to murder him did not prevent him risking much later to protect his life and secure his succession. Thus we are told how, on one occasion, when Surendra had ordered Jung Bahadur to be thrown down a well the latter defeated his amiable designs by having the well filled up beforehand with bales of cotton, how another time he pretended to be drowned but clung to the sides of the well and was later hauled up again by his friends, and how, on yet another occasion, when crossing a narrow bridge on horseback and ordered by the Prince to return he wheeled round on two narrow planks and got safely back again. I cannot say to what extent credence may be placed in these stories, but they go to suggest at any rate that Jung Bahadur was a man who took a lot of killing!

Still another story is one which tells of his dealing with an elephant that went "must." After killing his mahout, the beast broke loose and became the terror of the neighbourhood. No one coming forward to undertake its recapture, Jung Bahadur volunteered for the job, and taking up a strategic position above a track it was known to frequent dropped on its neck as it passed below him. Then in the struggle that ensued he succeeded in blinding its eyes with a pagri (turban) and eventually tired it out sufficiently to enable another mahout to shackle its feet and secure it again. No wonder, in the light of such exploits as these, and having in view further his achievements in other and more important ways, that Jung Bahadur has become the national hero *par excellence* of the Nepalese.

Such then was the man to whose courage and determination is due not only much of the prosperity and contentment of present-day Nepal, but also—what is hardly less important—the fact that Great Britain has gained in that country a loyal and valuable ally. And even if his rise to power was achieved and maintained by methods that might not commend themselves in all cases to arm-chair moralists, it must be remembered that he was merely acting up to the principles of his day and putting into practice with exemplary efficiency the gospel of the strong man. Certainly he was not one to flinch when the interests of the state commanded. It was by the King's order that he killed his uncle Matbar Singh; it was to save the King's honour that he arranged the murder of the Queen's paramour, Gagan Sing; it was in the interests of the rightful heir that he faced the wrath of the Queen Regent. When in their turn the King and the heir apparent made various attempts to hill him, he bore them no resentment. They were merely exercising their royal prerogative!

To return to the course of events after the Kot Massacre and Jung Bahadur's appointment as Prime Minister. That the latter acted quickly and resolutely it is hardly necessary to say, beginning with the banishment of the whole Panre clan and the confiscation of their property. At the same time all others whose loyalty was in any way doubtful were turned out of office and their places filled by the new Premier's adherents. In the result, order was soon completely restored in Kathmandu. The Queen, who remained nominally Regent, was, however, still a disturbing element, and the inevitable conflict between her and Jung Bahadur was not long in breaking out.

With the object of getting herself confirmed in the Regency and securing the enthronement of her own son, she repeatedly demanded the death of the two princes, the sons of the elder ranee, and on the Premier's courteous but persistent evasion of her request, she hatched a plot to assassinate him. Jung Bahadur was, however, by this time more than a match for this blood-thirsty virago. From his spies he received a timely warning of her plans, and after successfully rounding up the conspirators, rode to the palace at the head of his loyal troops and demanded her immediate banishment to Benares. And so on the 23rd November, 1846, the Queen, accompanied by her two sons and the King, left for Benares, the rightful heir apparent, Surendra, being appointed Regent in his father's absence.

A Village Scene. Nepal Valley.

CHAPTER VIII

Eventful Times

JUNG BAHADUR now assumed the full administration of Nepal, and the lal mohr (red seal), or King's decree, appointing him Prime Minister—a badge of power which all through his career he was most careful to obtain—enabled him to overrule any orders of the banished King and Queen. It was not to be expected, however, that the exiled royal family would allow Jung Bahadur to remain in peace for long. The ex-royal Court at Benares soon became a hot-bed of conspiracy and intrigue, and very soon the King, at the instigation of the Queen, connived at a clumsy conspiracy to murder him. This was once more nipped in the bud, and Jung Bahadur, thinking that the absence of the King would only make for perpetual intrigue, now sent him a message to the effect that the army had demanded his abdication and at the same time invited him to return to Nepal.

This Rajendra proceeded to do, but hardly in the way Jung Bahadur had hoped or expected, for he appeared in the rôle of invader, at the head of an ill-organised force which scattered to the four winds as soon as it came into contact with four of Jung Bahadur's regiments under the command of Sanak Sing. The King was taken prisoner, but though Jung Bahadur treated him outwardly with every consideration, even to the extent of welcoming him with a salute of guns, he decided to put an end for good and all to his ceaseless intriguing, and after compelling him to abdicate in favour of his eldest son, Surendra Vikram, he interned him for the rest of his days in the old palace of Bhatgaon.

With all fear of further internal trouble thus removed Jung Bahadur was at last free to consolidate his position and to exercise for the benefit of his country the unexampled power and authority which he had now attained. His prudent and sagacious policy (he gave his adherents, of course, all the responsible posts, civil and military, in the government), the prestige he obtained by defeating the hated Queen Regent, his reputation for dauntless courage and resolution, and his good fortune generally, all combined to put him on a pinnacle in the eyes of his fellow countrymen, who one and all realised that with such a man at the helm the destiny of the country was at last in safe hands.

Always a firm believer in maintaining friendly relations with his powerful neighbour in the south, in May, 1848, he offered six regiments of Nepalese troops under his personal command to the Indian Government in the event of war breaking out again between the English and the Sikhs. The offer was declined, but in their reply the Indian Government said that, should need arise on some future occasion, they would gladly accept it.

In 1850, considering that his position was secure enough to allow him to leave the country, Jung Bahadur undertook the great journey that it had been his dearest ambition to make from his earliest days. He went to England. He had heard all his life much about the English, but his relations with them up to that time had been purely official, and he wanted to see their country with his own eyes and to decide for himself if they really deserved the enormous power which they exercised throughout the world. Thus, leaving his brother, General Bam Bahadur to act as Prime Minister during his absence, on the 15th January, 1850, accompanied by two other brothers, a staff of twelve members, four cooks and twenty-two domestic servants, he left Kathmandu for Europe, and, after spending some time *en route* via India and Ceylon, arrived at Southampton on the 25th May.

His English visit was little short of a triumph, and incidentally secured for Nepal and the Nepalese such an amount of notice and attention as they had never enjoyed before. The charm and sincerity of the Prime Minister's manner made him at once a popular and striking figure in all circles. Queen Victoria took a special interest in him, making him sit by her side among her children and asking him many questions about the climate and scenery of his native land. He met all the prominent people of the day, from the Queen and Prince Consort downward, and of them it is recorded that the one who impressed him most of all was that fellow warrior-statesman the Duke of Wellington.

Although much of his time was devoted to ordinary sightseeing, it was our military and naval establishments—arsenals, dockyards and so forth—and great industrial undertakings which aroused his liveliest interest. To satisfy himself how coal was hewn, he even went down a mine. Of the endless entertainments and social functions to which he was invited, the Derby seems to have impressed him more than anything else. On the other hand, he considered the opera a rather foolish exhibition, and told his intimates that it compared most unfavourably with an ordinary military brass band!

On the way home he stayed for a short time in Paris, where he was received by Prince Louis Napoleon, then President of the Republic, and afterwards Napoleon III. Here he paid a ceremonial visit to the tomb of Napoleon the Great, visited all the best-known sights of the city, including places like Versailles, Fontainebleau and Compiègne, and attended a big parade of troops.

He returned to Kathmandu on the 29th January, 1851, having been away almost exactly a year. Although he made a triumphant entry into the city, being welcomed with genuine joy by the populace, his unprecedented action in crossing the "Black Water," thereby setting at defiance the religious scruples of his own country, had brought upon him no little odium in certain circles. Wherefore it is hardly surprising to learn that ten days after his return a conspiracy to assassinate him was discovered which had been conceived and organised by no less a person than his own brother, Badri Narsingh. This conspiracy was, however, frustrated by his elder brother, General Bam Bahadur, and the four leaders—Badri Singh, a cousin of Jung's called

Jai Bahadur, and two nobles—were arrested, and brought to trial. Jung Bahadur, however, refused to sanction the punishments—either death or having their eyes put out with hot irons—that the court had decreed, but instead took the somewhat unusual step of asking the Indian Government to take charge of them, and they were in the result confined in Allahabad for the remainder of their days.

In May, 1854, the ill feeling that had long existed between Nepal and her northern neighbour came to a head, and Jung Bahadur, exasperated by the constant ill-treatment of Nepalese residents in Lhasa, combined with the Tibetan authorities' persistent refusal to pay any attention to representations on the subject, declared war on Tibet. Severe fighting and unparalleled hardships, endured by the combatants of both sides on the high mountain plateau of Tibet, the scene of action, characterised this campaign which lasted two years. The passes of Kuti and Kyirong were the first objectives of the Nepalese, but the strict orders issued by Lhasa to the King of Sikkim to close all passes between his country and Nepal, prevented Jung Bahadur from sending another force through Sikkim as he had intended.

At the outset, all went well for the Nepalese, and on receiving the news that Kuti, Kyirong and Jhunga had been occupied by his troops, Jung Bahadur himself proceeded to the front to take command, and secured the positions thus gained. He returned to Kathmandu for the autumn, but in November he received news that Kuti had been recaptured with heavy loss to the Gurkhas, and that Jhunga, though still holding out, was exceedingly hard pressed.

Five regiments eventually succeeded in cutting their way through to Jhunga, and Kuti was also ultimately recaptured, whereupon, not long after, the Tibetans, recognising that the game was lost, began to make overtures for peace and a treaty was signed in Kathmandu on the 24th March, 1856. The terms included the surrender of the territory occupied by the Nepalese as the result of the campaign, the payment of an annual indemnity by the Tibetans of ten thousand rupees, freedom of trade to Nepalese subjects in Tibet, the abolition of customs duties on all goods entering Tibet, and finally the appointment of a Nepalese representative who would reside permanently in Lhasa and protect the interests of Nepalese subjects in that city.

On 1st August, 1856, Jung Bahadur, to the surprise of all parties, suddenly resigned the premiership in favour of his younger brother, Bam Bahadur, giving as his reason for so doing that he was weary of the hard work and responsibility that his office entailed. His action took all parties—even his own brothers—by surprise. As to what exactly took place between Jung's resignation and Bam Bahadur's death the following year authorities are inclined to differ. Thus, Percival Landon says in his book "Nepal" (1927) that a deputation headed by Raj Guru actually offered Jung the Crown, and on his refusing it, proposed that he should be given the title and revenues of the Maharaja of Kashi and Lamjung, whereas Hamilton, who was actually in Nepal at the time, states that these honours were conferred on him by the King.

Further, he is said to have been given the powers of life and death, of making war and peace, of full control over all the state departments, and finally to have had the succession to the Prime Ministership of the country with the title of Maharaja conferred upon his family in perpetuity. Yet, although evidence as to the exact honours and powers conferred on him at this juncture appears to be somewhat vague and conflicting, there is no doubt as to the general principle governing the law of succession in the case of the Premiership in Nepal. It is that of succession by the eldest fit agnate, common in Mohammedan countries, under which, after the brothers and male cousins of one generation have filled the office, it descends to the eldest born male of the next generation, which in due course hands it down to the third, fourth and succeeding generations in the same way.

Whatever Jung's exact position may have been after his resignation he did not occupy it long, for Bam Bahadur died in

May, 1857, whereupon he at once reassumed the headship of the Government, this time with enlarged powers, including even authority to declare war.

Immediately after this the Indian Mutiny broke out, when the good results of Jung Bahadur's visit to England were manifested by his immediately offering to send troops to the Company's aid. The offer was at first declined, but when after the recapture of Delhi, Lord Canning invited the Maharaja to send a contingent to the aid of Lucknow, three thousand troops were at once despatched. Moving by forced marches down the valley of the Tirsul Ganga river the Nepalese occupied two towns strongly held by the rebels, and then swept on through Oudh as far as Chanda and Sohanpur, thereby preventing any chance of a flank attack on the British troops as they were operating towards Lucknow.

Later, Jung Bahadur took the field in person at the head of eight thousand men, and success after success attended the Nepalese arms. Acting with his accustomed vigour and rapidity, he captured Gorakhpur in January, 1858, as the result of which the morale and military strength of the rebels throughout the north of the kingdom of Oudh were completely broken. Two months later again the Nepalese were in the forefront of the battle line at Lucknow, where, after displaying much gallantry in such operations as the capture of Chattar Munzil, the Moti Mahal and the Kaisar Bagh, they played a prominent part in the final battle at the Musa Bagh, which decided the issue and secured the relief of the city.

Even now Jung Bahadur's task had not been fully accomplished, for as the Mutiny drew to its close, thousands of refugee rebels, well armed and in many cases retaining the discipline and organisation of their original units, swarmed across the frontier into Nepal. When, by November, their number had reached 23,000, of whom 11,000 were under arms, Jung Bahadur, thinking that the time had come for prompt and energetic measures, again took the field himself with a mixed force of infantry and artillery, and the rebels were disarmed and dispersed.

In recognition of the loyal assistance and magnificent services rendered by the Gurkhas during this all-important period of the Mutiny, the British Government restored to Nepal a large part of the former Gurkha possessions in the Terai which had been ceded to the British in 1816. During the Mutiny, Jung Bahadur authorised the raising of more Gurkha battalions for the Indian army. And from this time forward the Nepalese Government has not only recognised the existence of the Gurkha regiments in the Indian army, but has actively assisted in their recruitment—a change indeed from the attitude which had been adopted by the authorities in the case of the three battalions raised in 1815, whose service had been *sub rosa*, and laid the families of the men open to persecution.

With the quelling of the Mutiny and the restoration of peace in the Peninsula, the stormier and more eventful part of Jung Bahadur's life may be said to have ended. Now firmly established on his throne, with his constitution working smoothly and his foreign policy on a satisfactory footing, he could henceforth devote himself to internal reforms. Further, he could do so now without fear of interruption by the political disturbances that had hitherto been so prominent a feature in Nepalese politics, for at last peace reigned in the country. Accordingly he gave his attention to such matters as improving communications, establishing a postal system, modifying the somewhat barbarous existing penal code and so on, with the result that great advances were made in civilising the country and the material conditions of the people was vastly improved.

He had indeed brought his ship safely into calmer waters. Although the centralisation of government at Kathmandu made his duties almost more arduous than formerly, office routine now largely took the place of the excitements of his earlier years, and even if up to the last he made a point of personally superintending any special work that had to be done, he was now able to indulge more freely in personal pursuits, and especially in his life's great passion—big-game shooting. His innate reserve and love of seclusion he maintained to the day of his death, while his irritability, which is almost proverbial to this day, increased with advancing years. He received honour after honour during the latter part of his life. About a year after the Mutiny he was nominated a Knight Grand Cross of the Order of the Bath by Queen Victoria, while, in 1872, he received from the Emperor of China the highest honour which that potentate could bestow.

It is pleasant to be able to add, too, that the remainder of his career was entirely tranquil and untroubled. Indeed, almost the last outstanding event of his life was connected with big-game hunting, in which it is said he found his only real happiness in his declining years. For when the Prince of Wales—afterwards the King Emperor Edward VII—visited India in 1876, Jung Bahadur organised in his honour one of the famous big-game shoots in the Terai, when a prodigious number of tigers, leopards, bears and other smaller game were bagged, and a "kheddah"—or the ringing in and capture of wild elephants—was also organised for the royal visitor's entertainment.

Sir Jung Bahadur died the following year. The exact cause of his death has never been quite definitely established, some saying it was due to fever and others to injuries received from a wounded tiger. Nothing at any rate could be done to save him, and he was carried to the banks of the Baghmati at Pathar-ghatta where he passed away peacefully one night in March, 1877. And thus rather suddenly and unexpectedly was ended the career of not only one of the greatest of Nepal's sons, but one of the greatest leaders that have come out of the whole of modern Asia.

CHAPTER IX

Nepal in Modern Days

In accordance with the laws of succession, made in 1856, Badri Narsingh, Jung Bahadur's eldest surviving brother, should by right have succeeded him as Prime Minister. Jung Bahadur had, however, excluded him from the succession because of his attempt to assassinate him, and the Premiership therefore fell to the next below him, Rana Udip Singh. A genial, easy-going man, but with nothing of his brother's personality and very lacking in initiative, the new Prime Minister encountered many difficulties from the opposition of Jung Bahadur's sons. Particularly hostile was the eldest, Jagat Jung, who before long, openly protested—though he had no legal ground for doing so—against Rana Udip's succession.

The latter was, however, fortunate in having as his Commander-in-Chief, Dhir Shumshere, the most capable of Jung Bahadur's brothers, who throughout gave him the most loyal assistance and for a time at any rate kept the trouble at bay, though the ranks of the malcontents were later swelled by the addition of a palace party headed by one of the King's daughters-in-law and by a party of Thapas, headed by the heirs of Matbar Singh. The old business of intrigues, plotting and assassination was once again resumed in Kathmandu, and this time in circumstances even more complicated and involved than usual. In 1881, the King, Surendra Vikram, died, after a reign which had lasted for thirty-four years, during which, however, his power had been purely nominal, and his grandson, Prithwi Bir Vikram Sah, who reigned until 1911, succeeded to the throne.

The following year (1882) a conspiracy by the Thapas to wipe out not only Rana Udip's entire family, but also the King, and the other brothers and sons of Jung Bahadur, was discovered by Jagat Jang who, however, determined to let it run its course so that the way might be cleared for himself while he took shelter in India. But the plot failed, and though he himself escaped punishment by remaining in India, a number of his brothers were removed from the roll of succession, and no fewer than twenty-one of the leading councillors of state were put to death.

The death of the Commander-in-Chief soon after this served in no degree to help matters, for with the removal of his strong hand, the easy-going Rana Udip allowed his nephew (Jagat Jung) to return from exile, and to be reinstated in the roll of succession, and a fierce struggle for power now ensued between him and the sons of the late Commander-in-Chief, Dhir Shumshere, resulting in a victory for the latter. For they, like their father, were nothing if not resolute, and seeing Jagat Jung's influence over the Prime Minister to be steadily increasing, they decided that there was only one thing to be done.

Accordingly, on the night of 22nd November, 1885, they went to the palace of Maharaja Rana Udip and put him to death. Jagat Jang and his son Judha Pratap Jang suffered the same fate, after which, taking with them the infant King and the Queen-Mother, the brothers hurried to the big parade-ground known as the Thuni Khel. Here, in the presence of the assembled troops, the eldest of them, Bir Shumshere proclaimed himself Prime Minister of Nepal, a position which he continued to occupy for the following sixteen years to the great advantage of his country. For if he had obtained power by methods sufficiently ruthless it might be said that these methods were justified, not only by the circumstances of the case, but also by the excellent use which he subsequently made of the position thus secured.

In the course of his rule, Bir Shumshere did much indeed to improve material conditions in Nepal in many ways. Educational, hospital, sanitary and other social services all received his special attention while—perhaps most important of all—he provided a good supply of drinking water to the valley towns. But like so many of his predecessors, Bir Shumshere was not to escape the unwelcome attentions of political opponents, and within sixteen months of his assumption of power, he discovered a conspiracy directed against himself and the young King. The prime mover this time turned out to be his own brother, Khadga Shumshere, the Commander-in-Chief and heir to the Premiership. The plot was discovered, but the ensuing punishment was surprisingly lenient, for Khadga was merely sent to a hill district near Palpa where he was interned. Two years later he was actually appointed Governor of Palpa. The Maharaja (the title of the Prime Minister in Nepal) took the opportunity however to have a royal decree issued detailing the order of succession to the Prime Ministership, in which Khadga Shumshere was excluded, and also, it is important to note, the sons and grandsons of Jung Bahadur.

Maharaja Bir Shumshere visited India three times, and a little misunderstanding which arose on one of these occasions from the procedure of the Indian Government in regarding the visit in the light of a "complimentary mission to Lord Curzon," rather than that of the Royal Ambassador of the King of Nepal, will no doubt be remembered by some. Bir Shumshere died in peace in 1901 and his brother Khadga having been, as previously stated, excluded from the roll of succession, he was succeeded by the next brother, Deva Shumshere, then Commander-in-Chief.

Though of a kindly disposition and genuinely solicitous for the welfare of his people, Deva Shumshere was not fitted for the high position he was now called upon to occupy. As Commander-in-Chief, and working under the eye of Maharaja Bir Shumshere, he had carried out his duties satisfactorily enough, introducing important improvements in the arsenal, and doing much to alleviate conditions on the main route from India, including the laying on of pure water for the use of travellers in the Terai. He further, by freeing some of his own slaves, took the first step in the abolition of slavery in Nepal, thereby preparing the way for general emancipation afterwards brought about by his more famous brother, Chandra Shumshere.

The strength of mind, sense of dignity and capacity for hard work that the office of Prime Minister demanded were, however, too palpably lacking in Deva Shumshere's equipment, and three months after he had assumed office his brothers compelled him to sign his abdication in the presence of the King, who immediately issued a royal decree in favour of the next brother, Chandra Shumshere, a man of a very different character.

Thanks in no small measure to the foundation laid by his uncle, Jung Bahadur, Nepal was already well started on the way to civilisation when Maharaja Chandra Shumshere assumed supreme control in the year 1901. And to show how absolute is the power of the Prime Minister in the ministerial regime under which Nepal has prospered, and which suits it so admirably, it may be worth while giving a brief quotation from the proclamation announcing his appointment. Thus "he is given full authority in respect of passing sentence of death, deprivation of caste, imprisonment for life, confiscation of property, banishment or deportation, conferring or deprivation of honours, control of the Treasury, together with plenary powers in all affairs of the State." Another edict of the King enjoined the entire nation to give complete support to the new minister, failure to do this being regarded as an act of disloyalty, the penalities for which included deprivation of caste, confiscation of property, deportation, imprisonment for life, and even death.

Contrary to the usual procedure following *coups d'états* in Nepal there was on this occasion no sweeping change in the leading Government officials. Having held the post of Commander-in-Chief—which, as will have been already observed, involves in Nepal much more administrative work than the title ordinarily implies—for three months Chandra Shumshere had formed evidently a sufficiently favourable opinion of the existing occupants of the various offices and few changes therefore were found necessary, and he was able to address himself without delay to the work of internal re-organisation which occupied most of his attention during the early months of his career. And happily, too, he was able to do this without any untoward incidents or interruptions. The whole nation

[Photo by Herzog and Higgins.

HIS HIGHNESS SIR CHANDRA SHUMSHERE AND HIS SONS.

welcomed indeed the accession of a far-sighted and determined ruler, whose position had been acquired not at the cost of other men's lives, but because his high character, ability and sterling qualities had shown him to be the best man.

Extremely well-read himself, Chandra Shumshere always took the greatest interest in education. Sent in 1883 to Calcutta University where he matriculated, he quickly developed academic ambitions, but the sudden illness of his father which recalled him to Nepal, compelled him to abandon these. The value of a really first-class education had, however, firmly impressed itself on him, and to this fact is due not only the remarkable education that all his sons and grandsons have received, but the great advance made generally in the matter of public education in Nepal. To-day the scope is even more widely extended, for the College at Kathmandu is now affiliated to the University of Patna, and many Nepalese youths are granted facilities to graduate there, or to attend medical and technical schools in Calcutta and elsewhere.

Likewise in other important matters, where also the foundations had been already laid by his father, Dhir Shumshere, Chandra Shumshere lost no time in introducing many much-needed reforms, not the least notable of which was the abolition of slavery. Slavery had existed in the country for ages, although in a comparatively mild form, not unlike that which prevailed in the southern states of America before the civil war, but the new Prime Minister speedily made known his desire to abolish entirely an institution which constituted a blot on the fair name of Nepal. At the same time, his task was not an easy one, for the uprooting of a custom not only firmly established in the social life of the country, but even sanctioned by religion, called for unusual discretion and tact. Chandra Shumshere, however, proved equal to the occasion, and a decree promulgating the abolition of slavery throughout the country was passed in the winter of 1924.

Four years before this another ancient and evil custom formerly commonly practised in Nepal had also been abolished by the Prime Minister. This was the custom, known as *sati*, of burning a widow alive upon her husband's funeral pile. By insisting on the consent of the highest authority before the suicide could be carried out, and other measures, both Jung Bahadur and Bir Shumshere had already done much to modify this practice, but it was left to Chandra Shumshere to dispose of it finally in June, 1920.

And these were only two of many beneficial reforms which stand to his credit. Thus from the outset he took a firm stand against any form of corruption in the public services, and in the result affected notable improvements in this respect, while the administration of justice was humanised and purified under his direction and the whole judicial system greatly improved. To deal at length with all of Chandra's many reforms would indeed take up too much space, but the briefest record of his achievements in this respect would be incomplete which failed to make mention of the great work which he accomplished in the re-organisation of the army, which was always his first and greatest interest of all. From top to bottom he overhauled and reformed the whole military system of the country in the most efficient and thorough manner, introducing examinations for officers, promotion by merit instead of by favour, payment by cash instead of in grants of land, improved administrative methods, etc. etc.—a gigantic work which alone would have constituted an enduring proof of his amazing energy and capacity.

It was, however, in the wider field of foreign relations that the diplomatic insight and political sagacity of Chandra Shumshere were perhaps best displayed—a notable instance being afforded by the part which he played in arranging terms of peace during the trouble between India and Tibet in 1904. And in his dealing with ourselves he showed always no less tact and judgment, having made it his aim from the outset to continue the attitude of friendship and co-operation inaugurated by his famous uncle, Jung Bahadur.

Hence on the outbreak of the Great War in 1914 he proved himself at once a friend in need, just as in 1857, in the time of the Mutiny, his uncle had done the same. And considering the limited resources at his disposal, the assistance that the Maharaja rendered on this occasion was indeed remarkable, and not less so the readiness with which it was forthcoming. Thus, when on 3rd August, 1914, Sir Chandra Shumshere called on the British Envoy to inform him of his readiness to place the whole military resources of Nepal at the disposal of the British Government, should they be needed, the offer was gratefully accepted, the first request being for a loan of Nepalese troops for general service in India. And so Nepalese troops, to the number of 10,000 left Kathmandu early in 1915, with General Sir Baber Shumshere, G.B.E., the second son of the Maharaja, as Inspector-General of the Contingent. Four regiments under the command of Commanding-General Sir Padma Shumshere, the eldest son of the late Prime Minister, proceeded straight to the North-West Frontier, while two others under the command of General Tej Shumshere were sent to Dehra Dun. And in February, 1916, a second contingent, officered and equipped in the same manner as the previous one, was despatched to India.

It needs only to add that the Nepalese troops won universal praise for their admirable discipline and bearing, several regiments taking part in the Waziristan campaign in 1917, in which they distinguished themselves by their bravery and steadiness under fire. Besides the invaluable assistance given by the dispatch of these contingents, the Maharaja further instituted measures in Nepal to maintain the strength of the Gurkha regiments in the Indian army, and to provide additional battalions. In the result, no fewer than 200,000 Gurkhas joined our service, and suffered casualities totalling 20,000, or rather more than the strength of the entire Gurkha brigade before the war. Not content with giving so lavishly of his country's manhood, Sir Chandra made further contributions in the shape of machine guns, generous monetary donations, army blankets, railway sleepers and produce of the country such as cardamons and tea.

Like his uncle, Sir Chandra, recognising that the only way

to acquire a thorough knowledge of western civilisation was by personal observation of it, paid a visit to England in the summer of 1908, and during the three months of his stay had hardly less success than his famous predecessor. The King and Queen showed him much attention and in all other directions he was most cordially recived so that he was left in no sort of doubt as to the high esteem in which he was held by the British people.

That His Highness Maharaja Sir Chandra Shumshere Jang Bahadur Rana was one of the most notable men of his time may certainly be said. Although it is perhaps too early yet to appreciate to the full all that he did for his country, there can be no sort of question as to the outstanding character of his services and of his reign as a whole. As recruiting officer for Gurkhas, for a period which extended over five years, the writer was brought into fairly frequent contact with Sir Chandra. Nor will he ever forget the graceful grey-bearded figure, strong and wiry despite his sixty years, dressed plainly yet with distinction, and wearing a gold embroidered scarlet peaked cap. Still less will he forget the cordial handshake, the courteous, genial smile and conversation and the strong impression which he invariably left on one as a man of quite exceptional dignity and distinction, who at the same time with all his charm of manner, was the possessor of a very strong and determined character.

Sir Chandra died on the 25th November, 1929, after a reign of twenty-eight years, in his sixty-seventh year, and in strict accordance with the law of the country was succeeded by his brother, Bhim Shumshere. Having had no fewer than twenty-eight years' experience as Commander-in-Chief and Chief Officer of the State Administration under his distinguished brother, Sir Bhim came to his exalted office equipped in a remarkable degree. Being, however, already advanced in years, he was not destined to remain in it long. He died only three years later, but brief though his reign was, he won in that short time the universal esteem of his people, for whom he laboured with unceasing care.

Sir Bhim Shumshere's successor, His Highness Sir Joodha Shumshere, has travelled a great deal and accompanied his brother, Maharaja Sir Chandra on all his important visits to Calcutta and elsewhere, including that to Europe in 1908. Having been Commander-in-Chief during the three years of Sir Bhim Shumshere's rule he has had much administrative experience, while as holder during the Great War of the important position of "Jangi Lat," or Senior Commanding General—the officer responsible for the training and supervision of the whole military forces of the country—he played an all-important part in organising Nepal's magnificent achievement on that occasion.

From a high authority well qualified to speak on the subject I have received the following notes respecting the status and functions of the Prime Minister and the daily routine of the present distinguished occupant of the office which I am sure will be read with interest:

"The position of His Highness The Maharaja Prime Minister of Nepal is somewhat different from that of similar ministers in other countries, inasmuch as he is the *de facto* ruler of the country. Being thus the supreme head of civil and military affairs, he is the centre of the mechanism governing the country, and has to be in personal touch with so many things every day of his life that he can safely be said to be the busiest person in Nepal.

"The present Prime Minister, His Highness Maharaja Joodha Shumshere Jung Bahadur Rana, though over sixty years of age, enjoys most robust health, and leads an amazingly active life whether at home in the capital or when touring the provinces. Rising early in the morning he, as an orthodox Hindu, devotes some time to Puja, after which he begins the day's hard work by reading the daily papers. By the time he has finished this several secretaries get ready the notes they have prepared for presentation to him when he comes out dressed for the morning's audience.

"This morning salaam has become an institution in the country, having probably been imported from the custom of the Moslem Emperors of India, with which it has many points in common, and provides an opportunity for those who cannot do so through the ordinary channels to approach His Highness. Petitions, complaints and appeals, even against the decisions of the various heads of departments, and many things more, are presented to him by the parties concerned in person. The usefulness of this custom in redressing many real grievances is so much in evidence as to preclude any possibility of dispensing with it, even bearing in mind the tremendous advances that have been made in the country's administration.

"The morning's audience over, His Highness will, if the day be fine, go riding or take a walk, and then will sit for two hours or so with his secretaries before the mid-day meal. An hour or so of rest precedes the heavier work of the day, which begins generally at about 3 p.m. About thirty-six main offices have their turn fixed by routine, and these offices cover the whole of the administrative machinery—home (including civil and military) and foreign. His Highness receives directly reports from the various provinces, and also suggestions and criticisms of Government work, which are then discussed. Some of these are forwarded to the departments concerned, and some are dealt with by His Highness's personal correspondence office.

"These matters keep His Highness engaged up to 5 p.m. and sometimes to 6 o'clock or even later, after which he usually takes a drive or has an elephant ride for about half an hour. On his return, the evening Puja follows, and he then spends a couple of hours with the members of his family. His Highness does most of his thinking in the quiet hours after dinner, and it is his special habit to make notes of any instructions which have to be given the following day to heads of departments. The careful thought which he thus gives to affairs of state is reflected in the far-sighted and statesmanlike policy of the Nepal Government both in the zones of home and foreign affairs.

"One whole day of the week and one half-day His Highness sets aside for attending to his personal affairs, and for some well-earned rest."

[*Photo by Herzog and Higgins.*

COMMANDING GENERAL SIR BABER SHUMSHERE JUNG BAHADUR RANA, G.B.E., K.C.S.I., K.C.I.E.

His Highness's eldest son, Commanding-General Sir Bahadur Shumshere, G.B.E., is, as has been mentioned elsewhere, the very keen and capable Chairman of the important Development Board, created as the direct result of the earthquake to develop to the full the resources of the country, while he will also be remembered as the first Nepalese minister to represent his country in London.

Other outstanding figures in the public life of Nepal to-day are Commanding-General Sir Baber Shumshere, G.B.E., K.C.S.I., K.C.I.E., the second son of the late Sir Chandra, who was attached to army headquarters as Inspector-General of the Nepalese Contingent during the Great War, and received high honours for his notable services in this capacity, Commanding-General Sir Padma Shumshere, G.B.E., K.C.S.I., K.C.I.E., son of the late Maharaja Sir Bhim Shumshere (brother of the present Maharaja) who commanded the Nepalese troops stationed at Abbottabad on the North-West Frontier and is now Commander-in-Chief, and General Sir Mohan Shumshere, G.B.E., K.C.S.I., K.C.I.E., eldest son of the late Sir Chandra, who holds the important office of Jangi Lat, or Senior Commanding General.

Another prominent personality at Kathmandu is Commanding-General Sir Kaiser Shumshere, K.B.E., the third son of the late Maharaja Chandra who is Director-General of Foreign Affairs. A man of many hobbies and especially interested in literature and art, General Kaiser is perhaps also the greatest sportsman in a country of sportsmen, with more tigers, rhinos and big game generally to his credit than anyone else in Nepal.

As regards the system of government in Nepal, His Majesty the Maharajdhiraj, as the king[1] is called, is the sovereign, but His Highness the Maharaja, which is the title of the Prime Minister, is the virtual ruler of the country, and is supreme in all matters affecting the government, whether political, administrative, executive or military. In all important matters, however, he is advised by councils composed of Bharadars, or Nobles,

[1] The present king, who succeeded to the throne in 1911, is H.M. The Mahahrajelhiraja Tribubhana Bir Vikram Shaha.

and by certain state officials, according as the nature and gravity of the matter under consideration may require. It may be interesting to add that, in colloquial parlance, the Prime Minister and the King are known as Tin Sarkar and Panch Sarkar respectively. These somewhat curious appellations are due to the number of Sris (an honorific prefix much used by Hindus) to which each is entitled, the Maharaja bearing three (Tin), as originally granted to Jung Bahadur and his successors in commemoration of his services in the Tibetan War and in the Mutiny, and the King five (Panch).

For purposes of administration the country is divided into circles, each under an official who is the local representative of the Government in all matters, both civil and military, and whose position is not unlike that of a district commissioner in India under the old regime, when civil and military duties were combined under one official. The laws, based on the Hindu Shastras, but modified to suit the spirit and customs of the times, do not really differ greatly from the code in force in British India, and punishments usually take the form of imprisonment or fines. Cow-killing and murder were formerly punished with death, but in 1931 Sir Bhim Shumshere abolished capital punishment except in cases of high treason and certain breaches of military law, as a tentative measure for five years, thereby removing the anomaly of discrimination in favour of women and Brahmans, who had always been exempt from it.

The bulk of the revenue of Nepal, apart from that derived from the Government of India as the result of the various treaties, comes from land dues, which are collected by village officials known as Mukhiyas (headmen) and paid into the nearest district headquarters. Other sources of revenue are customs duties, fines levied in the courts of justice, the sale of timber (which, as I have noted elsewhere, is perhaps the country's greatest asset), and also of hides and skins. There is no direct taxation in Nepal, practically the whole revenue of the country—amounting it is believed to about one and a half crores of rupees yearly—being raised in the manner stated.

Landlocked as Nepal is, its only neighbours—apart from Great Britain—are China and Tibet. Except in the matter of trade, there is really little intercourse between Nepal and the last-named country, though under the Treaty of 1856 Nepal receives an annual tribute of Rs. 10,000 and there is always a Nepalese representative in residence at Lhasa whose duties are to safeguard the interests of his countrymen. As regards relations between Nepal and the British Government. Enjoying as she does complete political independence, the position of Nepal is perhaps best described as an ally with whom we are on particularly friendly terms. Further, relations between the two countries are regulated by the Treaty of Friendship concluded in 1923. This Treaty was signed on the part of the British Government by Lieut.-Colonel W. F. T. O'Connor,[1] C.I.E., C.V.O., British Envoy at the Court of Nepal, and by His Highness Maharaja Sir Chandra Shumshere on the part of the Nepal Government on December 21st of that year, and its most important clauses accord to Nepal permission to import arms, ammunition and other stores from and through British India.

[1] Now Sir Frederick O'Connor, K.C.S.I., C.I.E., C.V.O.

CHAPTER X

The Gurkha* as he is

THE origin of the Gurkhas is even to-day not definitely known, but his linguistic researches have led my friend, Dr. R. L. Turner, M.C., to think that the Mongolians, whose advance down the southern slopes of the Himalayas appears to have taken place at a comparatively late period, may possibly have overlaid an earlier population, though he confesses his inability to say with any certainty what it was. That the present population of Nepal has been brought into the country as the result of various migrations can be seen from the diversity of the languages which are spoken there, numbering at least twenty, in a population of under six millions. Further, so distinctive are the dialects into which some of these again are broken up that within the confines of a single valley the inhabitants of one village may speak a language quite unintelligible to those living in another village only two miles away.

For present purposes it will be sufficient to state that these multifarious languages belong in the main to three distinct families—(*a*) Munda, a division of Austro-Asiatic, the language that recent researches show to have been spoken probably by the earlier inhabitants of Northern India; (*b*) Tibeto-Burman, the language largely spoken throughout Tibet and Burma and related to Chinese; (*c*) Indo-Aryan, which is descended from the ancient Sanskrit and to which most of the languages spoken in Northern and Central India belong, such as Bengali, Marathi and Urdu. It is a dialect of this last big family, the Indo-Aryan, variously called Khaskura, Parbatya, Gorkhali and Nepali, that is now the language of government and administration, and as such the lingua franca of Nepal.

* Although amongst Nepalese the word Nepal is actually only applied to the Nepal Valley, the word Pahar (hills) being used for the country as a whole, the words Nepalese and Gurkha have identically the same meaning and are used quite indiscriminately throughout the text and index of this book.

Nepali is, according to Dr. Turner, more closely related to Kumaoni than to any other Indo-Aryan dialect, and "must have been brought, eventually, into the valley of Nepal by those movements of conquest and infiltration from west to east which culminated in the conquest of Kathmandu by the house of Gurkha."[1] With the exception of certain tribes, nearly all Gurkhas are bilingual, speaking both their tribal languages which belong to the Tibeto-Burman group, and the lingua franca of the country, Nepali, though their proficiency in the latter varies greatly. Certain tribes for instance, like the Gurungs, who inhabit the more inaccessible parts of the country, have a very imperfect knowledge of it.

In consequence of the uncertainty of their origin and the futility of appealing to Nepalese history for light on the subject, the whole question of the ethnology of the Nepalese people is a difficult one. Of the large number of tribes however into which the Gurkhas are grouped, the chief are the Thakur, Chetri or Khas, Newars, Gurung, Magar, Rai, Limbu, Sunwar and Tamang, to which should be added also the Brahmans, though these can hardly be described perhaps as Gurkhas proper. They occupy, however, the same high social standing that they do in India, and it is from their ranks that the official priesthood of the country is exclusively drawn.

Of the other tribes I have mentioned, the pure-blooded Thakur occupies the highest social standing—the Brahman excepted—of all Gurkhas. They claim royal descent, and the head of their best clan—the Sahi or Sah—is the King of Nepal himself. Very intelligent, smart in appearance, and endowed with the highest military qualities, the Thakur is the beau-ideal of the Gurkha soldier. While, owing to their Rajput ancestry, in appearance Thakurs resemble Chetris in certain cases, the majority are hardly distinguishable from the Mongolian-looking Magars or Gurungs. I have already spoken of the Khas or Chetris in my reference to the Moslem invasions during the

[1] Dr. R. L. Turner, in *The Gurkhas* (W. Brook Northey and C. J. Morris, London, 1928), Ch. IV, p. 70.

twelfth century. Owing to the strain of Indian blood that runs in their veins, they differ greatly in appearance from the purely Mongolian tribes, being generally taller, and less thick-set, and without the strongly Mongolian cast of countenance that the others possess, while their customs approximate more to the practice of orthodox Hinduism than those of any other tribe. Rather more intelligent than Magars or Gurungs, they too make excellent soldiers, a large proportion of officers in the Nepalese army being Chetris.

The remaining tribes I have named are clearly of Mongolian descent, the Magars and Gurungs, from whom eight out of the ten Gurkha regiments are composed, coming roughly from the country that lies to the west of the Nepal valley, and the Rais, Limbus, Sunwars and Tamangs who are residents of eastern Nepal. Magars and Gurungs are also to be found in eastern Nepal, but they are usually of inferior quality and are not normally enlisted for the Indian army.

As regards the Newars, they comprise the bulk of the population of the Nepal valley, and to them frequent reference has been made elsewhere. Perhaps owing to the geographical position of their valley which prevented them wandering far afield, they possess more marked racial characteristics than any other tribe. With a literature of their own, they are far more civilised than the others, while the trade of the country is largely in their hands. To their skill as artisans and craftsmen I have given much space elsewhere.

Although, as has been noted, a certain amount of doubt may still exist as to the precise origin of the Gurkhas, yet from the physical features that the bulk of the population display, it is clear that as a whole they can be classed as belonging to Mongolian or Mongoloid stock.

I have used the words "bulk of the population" advisedly, for although the Aryans, to whom I have already referred as having entered Nepal at the time of the Mohammedan invasions, were undoubtedly far less in number than the Mongolian element, yet they were bound to affect the physical type to a certain extent.

Gurkha Rifleman (Magar) in Uniform.

]Photo by Major R. A. Briggs.

Gurkha Rifleman (Gurung) in Mufti.

Thus, amongst certain classes such as the Chetris, men and women may be often seen whose features really differ but little from those of the natives of the Indian plains. None the less, speaking generally, the Gurkhas as a race are decidedly Mongolian in appearance, possessing the high cheek-bones and almond-shaped eyes peculiar to that race.

In stature they are decidedly on the short side, for the average height of a full-grown man is a mere five foot three inches. To be tall in Nepal brings, indeed, no special admiration, as it usually does in other parts of the world. On the contrary, in a community where all are of short stature, a tall man is apt to be regarded as rather in the nature of a freak. There is certainly one regiment in the Nepalese army, the rifle regiment, in which the men are all six feet and more. But they are quite exceptional —for it may be added that they are usually of correspondingly fine physique in other respects also, resembling in this our own household troops—and do not alter the fact that the Gurkha is generally a small man.

As regards colouring, it may surprise some European readers with fixed ideas as to dark-skinned Orientals, to learn that among the Gurkhas fair complexions are always much preferred to dark, and further, that a well-bred Gurkha is almost invariably fair-skinned. But throughout all classes it may be said that a dark complexion is the exception rather than the rule among the Gurkhas, and when it does occur the owner will not be allowed to forget the little trick that nature has played on him, for amongst his friends and in the bosom of his family he will invariably be known by some such nick-name as "Blackie" or "the Dark one."

Though I am, I fear, ignorant of the precise nature of the factors that affect the pigmentation of the human skin, it seems not unreasonable to ascribe the fair complexion of the Gurkha chiefly to the equable climate and—certainly as regards eastern Nepal—comparative absence of sun in the hill country in which he lives.

There are curious cases however of dark men coming from

exceptionally high-lying districts, and in my own regiment a Gurkha officer who was almost black being known, as might be expected, throughout the regiment as the "Black Subadar," furnished a typical example of this fact.

Long residence in the plains, on the other hand, seems to have the effect of darkening the Gurkhas' complexions to a great extent, though they themselves will often attribute the circumstance rather to the bad quality of the water which they have had to drink.

Illness is another factor often responsible, in their opinion, for the same result, and I myself was informed on one occasion on my return to the regiment after a bout of some kind of fever that I had become "very black indeed"!

As is usual in the case of Mongolian races, the Nepalese have very little hair on face and body, and until they approach middle age usually but a few sparse hairs on the upper lip. Thus they are generally spared the burden of the early morning shave, though the alternative method which they adopt, when necessary, of pulling out each hair separately with a small pair of pincers can also be a laborious and not unpainful process!

In their general physical characteristics and appearance the Gurkhas have often been likened, and with considerable truth, to the Japanese—meaning, however, not so much the more highly educated, alert and sophisticated specimens of the latter that one encounters abroad as the heavier and less cultivated peasant types that make up the mass of the population at home, whose affinity with the average Gurkha is indeed often surprisingly close. Certain it is that in the Boxer campaign of 1890, men of the 4th Gurkhas who formed part of the British contingent from India, used often to express surprise that they were unable to converse with the Japanese troops when they met them, so closely did they appear to resemble their own people. This likeness may be said to apply also to a great extent to Gurkhas and Chinese, though as the result of being able to observe Chinese at close quarters when I travelled on the same river steamer with six hundred of them in Mesopotamia during the Great War, I am inclined to say that the affinity between the Gurkhas and Japanese—affinity in the matter of physique I mean—is the closer of the two.

Generally speaking, the Gurkha is sturdy and thick-set, his nether limbs are exceptionally well-formed and admirably adapted to bear him over the rough and pathless country of his mountain home.

It is his Mongolian strain that makes the Gurkha the cheerful soul he is. For he differs from his Indian brother as much in character as he does in appearance. He possesses in particular that most precious of all characteristics, a sense of humour, to an extent that is rarely found in the more solemn and austere man of Aryan descent, while his frank, open character permits an intimacy in his intercourse with Europeans that is seldom achieved by other native races in the East.

His ability to fraternise with the British soldier, especially with those of Highland regiments, between whom and himself there seems always to be a special sort of freemasonry, is proverbial. Few things are more amusing, indeed, than to see a diminutive Gurkha and a tall British soldier engaged in an animated conversation, the flow of which is not hampered in the least apparently by the fact that their knowledge of each other's language is practically nil. In the art of making himself understood in a foreign country, Thomas Atkins must surely stand supreme.

The camaraderie between the British soldier and the Gurkha dates back many years. Describing the Battle of Bhartpur, Captain T. Smith, in 1852, wrote, "it was an interesting and amusing sight to witness the extreme good fellowship and kindly feeling with which the Europeans and the Gurkhas mutually regarded each other. A six-foot-two Grenadier of the 59th would offer a cheroot to the 'little Gurkha' as he styled him; the latter would take it from him with a grin, and when his tall and patronising comrade stooped down with a lighted cigar in his mouth, the little mountaineer never hesitated a minute in puffing away at it with the one just received, and they are consequently patted on the back and called 'prime chaps.'"

Gurkhas are extremely independent, possess the utmost confidence in themselves, and in their own country are apt to be suspicious of foreigners and somewhat self-assertive. The thought of such a thing as cringing in connection with a Gurkha is inconceivable. Thus, in the eyes of people who do not know him and his ways, and who are accustomed to the—generally speaking—more docile and subservient men of the plains, he seems on occasion rather too independent, while his ignorance of the traveller's language (few Nepalese know any Hindustani and the peasantry none at all) which makes him seemingly unable to understand what is required of him, gives at times the impression that he is somewhat surly and aloof. Ability to speak his language is consequently a prime asset in gaining the confidence of the Gurkha. Even after many years' service he often remains entirely uninterested in people, European or otherwise, with whom he is not directly concerned, or who cannot speak or understand his language.

On the other hand, though shy and somewhat reserved at first, he attaches himself closely to those under whom he takes service, and once his confidence is gained, he reveals little by little, his true character and proves himself the most staunch and faithful of friends.

The devotion and loyalty of the Gurkhas to their British officers are too well known to need enlarging on. One little illustration may suffice. "Are you ever homesick?" I once asked a young Gurkha from a remote village in Nepal after he had been a year in his regiment. "I was terribly so at first," he replied, "but I am no longer. The regiment has become a second home."

Imbued as they are with the warlike qualities of their ancestors and with the traditions they have inherited of their military achievements as conquerors of the Nepal valley, it is but natural that the Gurkhas should cherish the military spirit to a high degree, and this from their earliest years. There is indeed nothing which the youngsters enjoy so much as forming themselves into small squads and "playing at soldiers"; and the results are quickly seen as they grow up. Their active physique, their keen sight and hearing, and the fact that they have from their earliest childhood been instructed in all forms of sport, all combine to make Gurkhas almost unrivalled in jungle country and eminently capable as riflemen on the mountain side.

Further, the fact that their country is to all intents and purposes run on military lines, gives the wearer of a military uniform exceptional prestige. Few travellers can fail to be impressed indeed by the tremendous respect inspired as they pass through the country by the uniform of the often quite youthful escort who accompanies them. In the matter of commandeering supplies, arranging for accommodation and so forth, his word is law, and no one would ever dream of questioning it. And somewhat Prussian though this system sounds, it is what the people have been accustomed to for centuries, and they certainly do not appear to resent it.

Yet despite the militarism that prevails, remains the paradoxical fact, to which reference has already been made, that at heart the Gurkha is not really warlike. He asks for nothing better than to be left alone and, hardworking peasant that he is, to be allowed to till his fields and mind his herds and flocks in peace.

And rather fortunate it is perhaps that this is the case. For the khukri, the short heavy knife with its broad curved blade, which is carried by all males, would be a dangerous weapon in the hands of a quarrelsome or unruly people, and might easily give rise to trouble. As it is, the scenes of violence and the inter-family or tribal feuds that are only too familiar in certain parts of India and elswhere, can be said to be virtually unknown in Nepal, with the result that it is as a general utility instrument rather than as a lethal weapon that the khukri is generally employed.

Beyond the very rare occasions on which it figures in some personal quarrel, the decapitation of buffaloes' heads during the Dasehra festival constitutes perhaps the most awe-inspiring use to which the khukri is put in the ordinary way in these days. A hundred years ago, however, it was often devoted to much more sinister uses. It was by means of the khukri, for instance, that an injured husband did justice on an erring spouse by slicing off her nose, while at the same time dealing still more forcefully with her betrayer.

Surgeon Oldfield relates[1] for instance how one Kahsing, havildar (sergeant) of the Residency guard, showed him one day the khukri with which he had cut down the man who had violated his wife's honour. "He was at the time using it to cut and pare some radishes, which he was eating with great gusto," continues laconically the writer.

"And what did you do to the woman?" he asked him.

"Oh, I cut off her nose and turned her out of doors, but I gave her five rupees to prevent her from starving," replied the gallant havildar, proud in the fact that though he might be stern he was generous and not unmerciful at heart. And in connection with this custom of former times, it can be added that the seducer could always save his life by passing under the uplifted leg of the outraged husband—an ignominy, however, to which death was nearly always preferred.

Many fantastic statements have been made as to the manner of using the khukri in war time. A popular one is that it is thrown, some people going so far as to suggest that it is, in fact, a sort of boomerang fulfilling much the same function as the weapon of the Australian aborigines. In point of fact it is never in any circumstances employed in this fashion, being for one thing far too valuable for the owner to let it out of his hand.

It hardly needs saying that the Gurkha is nothing if not a sportsman, as is indeed only natural. Living in a country which abounds in game, and where the game laws are the reverse of strict, opportunities for indulging in his favourite hobby are well nigh unlimited.

The methods which he employs when out shooting can hardly

[1] *Sketches from Nepal*, Vol. I, Ch. XIX, p. 245.

be said to resemble those of English sportsmen, but they are none the less effective on this account. It is not without reason that the Gurkha calls his ammunition "khazana" or "treasure," for his aim is always to get the utmost possible value for the cartridges which he expends. Thus it is very rare to find a Gurkha who will even attempt to shoot a bird "on the wing." The risk of losing a cartridge would be far too great. So what he does is usually to stalk his prey until it is within a few yards of the muzzle of his gun and then to fire, with the result that not infrequently the victim is practically blown to bits!

In other cases, inspired by the same irrepressible desire to get the maximum value for his "treasure," he will not only hold his fire until he can make an absolute certainty of his prey, but even then reserve it still further until he has manoeuvred himself into such a position as to get actually three or four birds in one line!

There are few families in Nepal of which at least one member does not possess a weapon of some sort or description. Most of the men who enlist in the Gurkha regiments of the Indian army purchase guns in India before their retirement to take with them to their villages, and though neither guns nor ammunition are easily procurable in Nepal itself, muzzle-loading weapons of a somewhat primitive design can be obtained.

For those in turn who have neither the means nor the opportunity to possess themselves of firearms there is always the pellet-bow. A familiar sight in India in any place where Gurkhas are stationed or domiciled is a solitary Gurkha, bow in hand, walking slowly along the side of some hedge or stream, gazing anxiously upwards in the hope that some unsuspecting bird may offer him a target on which to try his skill.

The method which he used for fishing are also no less unorthodox at times. When following a path by the side of a stream in Nepal the traveller will often catch sight of a gentleman bending down and carefully placing something in the water. Let him not be too shocked when he discovers that it is a disciple of Izaak Walton who is laying a charge of gunpowder in place of the more familiar forms of bait. After all, why waste time with a line that is going—and that, too, only if you are lucky!—to bring you but one fish, when a single charge of gunpowder—incidentally, illegal in Nepal—may be trusted without fail to bring you a bag of half a dozen! It may seem unsporting according to our western notions, but it is extremely logical none the less.

Though I may seem to have spoken somewhat lightly of the Gurkha as sportsman, his achievements in this respect are in fact by no means to be underrated. Primitive and unorthodox though his implements and methods may be, the fact none the less remains that the Gurkha is a most plucky and enterprising sportsman, for whom no labour is too irksome, and no danger too great when the opportunity of securing a good trophy, small or great, comes his way. To which it may be added that the love of sport is universal in Nepal, and is indulged in by all classes, from the lowest to the highest, with equal enthusiasm.

On the other hand, mere games such as football, tennis, cricket, and so on, play but a small part in the lives of the Nepalese. It is true that those who take service in India, especially those who enlist in the army, take readily enough to football and hockey, in which they often do remarkably well, as they do also in basket ball, which has acquired such popularity in recent years. As a consequence, ball games are by no means unknown in Kathmandu, where the number of those who have learnt to play them, either from service in Gurkha battalions or in the Nepalese contingent who served in India during the Great War, is probably fairly large. In the villages and country districts generally, however, they are not played at all.

CHAPTER XI

Customs and Characteristics

THE upper classes in Nepal have a very distinctive national dress, for their double-breasted garment known as a *chaubandi*, which fits tightly over the waist, and is fastened at the waist and inside and outside at the shoulder, is worn only by the Nepalese. Padded with cotton wool, and made as a rule of a double layer of thin cloth with a polished surface, it is as comfortable as it is picturesque.

The trousers are loose and of the same material as the coat, while a long, thin, white cloth is wound round the waist sash-fashion. The cap, high on one side and low on the other, is also peculiar to the country. The stout, simply-designed Nepali shoe is, however—certainly in the Nepal valley—gradually being discarded in favour of European shoes, while nowadays a tweed coat of European pattern is often worn over the chaubandi.

The full dress of a Nepalese general, which is the dress His Highness the Marahaja wears on state occasions, does not differ very greatly from that of a general in the British army, being also of scarlet cloth, and differing only in such minor details as the epaulettes, badges of rank and so on, and the same uniform is likewise worn by most of the members of the ruling family who are generals *ex officio*.

The magnificent head-dress worn by the King, the Prime Minister, and indeed, by all members of the royal and prime ministerial families on similar occasions, deserves, however, special mention, for it is as unique as it is beautiful. That of the Prime Minister, for instance, is composed of a cap of closely sewn pearls ornamented in front with three circular plaques composed of large diamonds, with a row of heart-shaped diamonds carried round from the front to back of the head-dress, and a profusion of enormous emeralds, and here and there cut rubies; while that of the King, it is hardly necessary to say, is equally gorgeous on much the same lines, save that he has five plaques in front instead of three. Nor is this all, for each of these splendid coronets is further adorned with a wonderful bird of paradise plume—rising from the head like a fountain of brown, white and orange as someone once put it—set in a head-piece mounted in pearls and gold—similar plumes, though of varying sizes, being worn by all members of the royal and ruling families, with an effect which, it is easy to believe, is striking indeed on great occasions.

The country people wear what may perhaps best be described as a thin kilt, for they wind a thin piece of cloth round and round the waist, without folding it, which comes down to just above the knees. They also wear the distinctive chaubandi, but in this case it only reaches as far down as the waist, and is of a rough country homespun. Over this again they wear a thin cotton waistcoat of European design, which is usually black in colour, and as often as not with Indian four-anna pieces doing duty for buttons. The inevitable khukri is tucked into the top of the "kilt."

Some of the tribes that live in the higher regions wear in addition a thick, course sheet made of nettle fibre over the top part of the body, which, knotted about the centre of the chest in such a manner as to leave the arms bare, forms a bag in the small of the man's back in which he can carry provisions or anything he likes.

Besides being distinctive, this dress suits the Gurkha remarkably well, showing off, as it does, his admirable lower limbs to the greatest advantage, for although usually sturdy and thick-set, he is perhaps less well developed above the waist than below.

It must be admitted, however, that picturesque though his national dress may be, it is often far from clean. For cleanliness is a virtue not held of much account by the inhabitants of these far-away Himalayan villages, so that while the average Gurkha recruit on first joining may be very honest and absolutely

Lalsing (Gurung) and His Wife.

Men of the Magar and Gurung Tribes.

GURKHA WOMEN (MAGAR TRIBE).

truthful, he will also almost certainly be rather dirty where his person is concerned.

The women in turn wear a bodice and a skirt formed of a cloth wound many times round the waist, while, somewhat after the manner of Italian peasant women, they wear a shawl or veil, usually of some bright-coloured material over the head.

But the most important feature of the Gurkha woman's costume is her jewellery, for, besides its ornamental purpose, this can be considered in the light of a bank, since it is the custom to preserve the family savings in this form. Large gold ear-rings, bracelets, anklets, and various types of necklaces, amongst which a heavy ornament composed of alternate reels of gilt and coloured thread is distinctive, constitute usually the principal items, nose-rings being also affected by many, though not universally worn.

The practical purpose served by the women's jewellery in the domestic life of the Gurkha hill tribes may be better understood when it is added that in cases of marital infidelity in a Gurkha regiment (which are generally tried by a court of Gurkha officers) the guilty wife is frequently ordered to return all her jewellery to the injured husband, representing as it does the savings of the family rather than her own personal possessions.

In Nepal itself, cases of infidelity are dealt with through the medium of the law-courts should the parties reside in the Nepal valley or in the vicinity of a town where law-courts exist, but in the villages the case is tried by a court of arbitration consisting, as a rule, of eight or ten village notables. In nearly every case the husband is awarded his original marriage expenses, an award that meets with universal approval, being adjudged as ample compensation for the loss of a faithless spouse.

The Gurkha is extremely amenable to discipline and is ordinarily very well-behaved. But, of course, like everyone else, he has his little failings, one of the commonest of which, in earlier days especially, was a tendency to drink. "Drunkenness and dirtiness are more frequent than in the plains," wrote many years ago that very eminent authority, the late Brian

Hodgson; and it would certainly be going too far to say that the former failing is nowadays unknown. But it is very far from being a national vice, and the average Gurkha is no more of a sinner in this respect than the members of many other nations which might be named!

It may be added, moreover, that matters have greatly improved in this respect in recent times, thanks to the good judgment with which the late Sir Chandra Shumshere tackled the question of the manufacture and sale of liquor in Nepal. While too wise to adopt so drastic a measure as prohibition, he took steps to insure that only the best and most wholesome spirits were manufactured, largely reduced the number of liquor shops, and prohibited the sale of liquor altogether at any of the fairs and festivals held at the various holy places in the country. Simple measures it might be thought, but they achieved their purpose most effectually, so that to-day in the valley of Nepal it is quite exceptional to see an obviously drunken or disorderly person.

The favourite drink in the Gurkhas' own homes is a kind of beer made from fermented rice, or Indian corn, which they brew themselves. This, however, is not so easy to obtain in cantonments, where special permission to make it is required, and so there they fall back on commissariat rum as sold in the regimental canteens. Not all, however, take this by any means, and to recruits it is actually forbidden in most regiments, with the excellent result that not a few never acquire the habit of drinking at all, and remain abstainers to the end of their days.

But, speaking generally, of course, the Gurkha is as fond of his liquor as most other men, and ready to enjoy it in any form. With Tommy Atkins in the latter's canteen he will quaff a glass of English beer with the greatest relish, while the pipe-major of a Gurkha regiment is never likely to refuse the whisky offered him by the mess president on a "guest night," when—after the manner of Highland regiments—the regimental pipers play round the mess table.

If, however, the Nepalese can be acquitted of any undue tendency to drink, the same can hardly be said of their passion for gambling, to which they are certainly inordinately addicted. In general, gambling in public is strictly prohibited in Nepal, except on certain very special occasions such as that of the Diwali festival. But as we all know, it is one thing to make laws of this kind and quite another to secure their enforcement, and the Nepalese in point of fact gamble at all times and in all places whenever they can possibly manage to do so.

Here, as in the case of drink, Sir Chandra Shumshere was fully alive to the evil, and, as one means of checking it, introduced legislation prohibiting the giving of credit to the loser and compelling the payment of all debts of this kind in cash on the spot, whereby a certain amount of good was certainly affected, though naturally hardly making much difference in the case of such orgies as those of the Diwali festival when all restraint is thrown to the winds.

The street scenes in Kathmandu and the other towns of the valley on the occasion of this particular festival must indeed be seen to be believed. Upon the beat of a drum—the signal that the gambling may begin—every other occupation is immediately abandoned by one and all and the whole population gives itself up forthwith to its one all-absorbing passion, for which, as it is hardly necessary to add, opportunities in plenty are provided. For not only are there innumerable booths in every street with their enticing "tables", but practically every house and shop in addition has its own gambling party all feverishly engaged in some form of play.

Cards, dice and a form of "Tommy dod" are all favoured. With cards, a kind of three-card trick is generally the game. The packs employed are almost invariably well-thumbed, and more often than not somewhat damaged, so that it is by no means unusual for certain cards to be easily identified by all the players immediately they have left the dealer's hand—a circumstance which, however, appears to add to rather than detract from the general hilarity of the proceedings.

Cowrie shells provide, however, the commonest form of gambling in Nepal, some sixteen or so of equal size being taken in the hand, well shaken and thrown down on a board, while the players bet as to whether the majority fall face up or face down.

Thus, drifting from one booth to another, joining any crowd that has gathered where stakes run high, or the betting is particularly keen, at times playing himself, at other times watching others play, does our Nepalese spend the Diwali in his own country. And by the time it is over, even such an inveterate a gambler as he is should assuredly have had his fill, for the festival—or at any rate this part of it—lasts at least five days.

Many and extraordinary too, not to say incredible, are the stakes for which they play, as authentic records attest. Thus men have been known to stake their wives and children on a throw of the dice, while one man is even said to have cut off his left hand and put it down under a cloth as his stake. It is recorded further that on winning the game, he insisted on his opponent cutting off his hand, or else restoring all the money which he had previously won.

Being as it is a Hindu festival held in honour of Lakshmi, the goddess of good fortune, the Diwali is similarly observed in India wherever Hindus are to be found, and like scenes are to be witnessed all over the land. Yet, perhaps because it is the only time when public gambling is permitted here by the authorities, nowhere else can be matched the scenes of almost delirious excitement evoked by the Diwali in Nepal.

As regards the food of the Gurkhas, their staple diet is decidedly monotonous from a European point of view, for it is—when they can obtain it—nothing but rice. Rice is, however, usually procurable only in the valleys and low-lying districts, so that dwellers in the higher regions have to content themselves with what their less fertile soil can offer them, namely buck-wheat, millet and Indian corn. From these they make a rough kind of bread, and also a species of porridge.

There is, fortunately for them, nothing in the laws of their caste forbidding them to eat meat, with the exception of cows and female goats, while with a few minor exceptions, they are also partial to most kinds of game. The usual dish for all big ceremonial occasions is buffalo and this last all Gurkhas, except Brahmans, Thakurs, Chetris and Magars, will eat without any hesitation in their homes. Yet in any case, meat in whatever form, is only an adjunct to the Gurkha's meal, and, as often as not, forms no part of it.

To make the cooked rice more palatable, when meat is not available, he will add the dal—the split pulse or lentils known to every Indian—or any kind of vegetable, though failing such he will eat the plain boiled rice without any additions at all. It is the rice, however, that seems to give him his stamina, and he relies on it implicitly to carry him through any particularly severe undertaking demanding all his physical strength.

With the spreading of Hinduism in Nepal and the gradual extinction of Buddhism, to which I have made reference elsewhere, it is not surprising that the rites and ceremonies practised in the matter of births, marriages, deaths and so on, tend to approximate more and more closely to those observed in India by orthodox Hindus. Further, as this Hindu influence has extended, so have the customs of the various races in the country tended to become more and more standardised, so that the day is not far distant probably when such small differences as still obtain in the matter of their various ceremonies will have disappeared altogether.

It may be said indeed that the standard for religious and ceremonial ritual throughout the country is now set by the three tribes who possess the highest social standing of all the Gurkhas, and who are at the same time the most orthodox Hindus in Nepal—namely the Brahmans, the Chetris and the Thakurs. One of the largest of the Mongolian military tribes, the Magars have adopted this form of ritual in its entirety for all their ceremonies, and the remaining tribes practice it to a large extent. Thus, in a country where, apart from its rulers, and from the dwellers in the actual Nepal valley, the inhabitants cannot, as a whole, be considered very strict followers of any religion so far as their ceremonial observances are concerned, the influence of Hinduism is steadily extending.

Although Brahmans and Chetris marry at an early age compared with Europeans, the system of child-marriages as practised in India, where the contracting parties are literally children, cannot be said to obtain in Nepal, for in cases where such marriages do take place, the children remain with their respective parents until both are fully grown up. In any case, public opinion in Nepal against child marriages in any form is growing rapidly, as it is in many eastern countries; and although betrothals take place before puberty is attained, the age at which most Nepalese are married nowadays—say, between seventeen and twenty-one—can hardly be considered in any way abnormal.

Except in some parts of eastern Nepal where, amongst the poorer people it is not uncommon for the parents to know nothing about the marriage of their daughter until she returns from the ceremony a married woman, marriages are arranged by the parents. I will not attempt to describe in detail a Gurkha marriage, especially as I have already stated that in essentials it conforms to the ordinary Hindu ceremonial, but it may be of interest to note that the presentation of curds figures prominently in this, as in many of the Gurkhas' ceremonies.

Thus, in the preliminary negotiations for a betrothal, the father of the bridegroom often brings with him a bowl of curds when he visits his son's prospective father-in-law, while at one point in the actual wedding ceremony the mother of the bride feeds the couple with milk and curds. What may be the origin of the employment of curds so frequently in this curious way I do not know, beyond the fact that they are supposed to have an auspicious significance—a circumstance which would naturally appeal to the superstitious Gurkha.

That feasting, singing and dancing play an important part in all Gurkha ceremonials it is hardly necessary to add, so that even funerals are made the occasion of gargantuan feats entailing the consumption of enormous quantities of liquor.

Though polygamy is not illegal in Nepal, in actual practice

Women Weaving. Palpa District.

Gurkhas—certainly those of the Mongolian hill tribes—rarely have more than two wives, this being the usual number, and in such cases, when the man has for any reason to leave home, the senior wife is as a rule left behind to look after the house and cattle, while the younger one accompanies her husband. Should the latter, for instance, enlist in the army, it is she who will be the one to go with him. The younger wife's position is, however, apt to be somewhat insecure, owing to the fact that the proper marriage ceremony is not performed in her case, thus making it possible for the husband to get rid of her should he feel so inclined.

This state of affairs occasionally gives rise to amusing situations, as in the case of one which I recall. While a young Gurkha was at the front during the war, his wife went off with another man. On the husband's return he invoked the law against his erring spouse and took the case before his company commander. The latter noticed, however, that, while curiously indifferent about his wife, he seemed none the less to have something on his mind, and wondered what it was. The explanation came at the end of the proceedings when, on being assured that his partner would be restored to him, he blurted out, "Oh, I am not worrying about my wife at all, but the other man has gone off with my umbrella!"

Again, discrepancy in years may give rise to humorous incidents in cases where the wives number more than one. Thus, when on one occasion shortly after the Great War I complimented the Subadar Major of the Recruiting Depot—a portly, grey-haired veteran recalled to service though well "over-age"—on what I imagined to be his two charming daughters, he replied, to my slight embarrassment, that the ladies in question were his wives! "The elder one has come down from the hills to spend a short holiday in Gorakhpur, but," he informed me, "my daughters were also very attractive at that age. Now, of course, they have themselves been married many years!"

It may be noted by the way that there is no ceremony, whether that of marriage, burial, naming of children or what not that can be performed without the family priest's approval of the date, which he determines by consulting the horoscope of the party concerned, this being a matter to which the greatest importance is always attached.

Among the many other queer customs of the Nepalese, one of the most curious is that of singing for a bride. It is in eastern Nepal that this practice prevails. Open singing competitions are held at which either the girl or the boy commences by singing a couplet to which the other must reply. The couplets must be composed on the spur of the moment, and each succeeding one should improve on its predecessor in humour and repartee. The contest proceeds until one or other is unable, for lack of further ideas, to continue, so that in order to win a bride the man must produce a couplet of such dazzling brilliance that even the usually nimble-witted Gurkha maiden is at a loss to reply.

The birth of a child of either sex is made the occasion of much rejoicing for eleven days, but a boy, especially in the case of the first born, is always hailed with greater delight than a girl. The reason for this is somewhat unexpected, the explanation being that only a son can properly carry out the funeral rites of the parents.

In this connection it may be noted as somewhat surprising that the Nepalese have no one exclusive method of disposing of their dead, but practise both cremation and burial, the place they select for the purpose being, in the case of most of the tribes, on the banks of a river. As opposed to the European custom of black, they wear white for mourning, the head, eyebrows and moustache being shaved, while for about a fortnight they are forbidden to eat anything but rice, and that only once a day.

I have said little or nothing so far as to caste among the Nepalese, but the subject is by no means to be overlooked, even though it does not play quite such an important part among them as it does in the case of the Indians. For though, as I have already had occasion to point out, those that belong to the Mongolian military tribes are not very rigid in such matters, it is very different in the case of the upper classes, whose lives are completely ordered by it, as one speedily discovers. Instances arising from it are indeed constantly cropping up, presenting as often as not problems that are most difficult even for the Brahmans and others who are considered experts on the subject to solve.

If, for instance, a man of the high Chetri caste has, quite inadvertently even, eaten cooked rice with a man of a lower caste, he at once loses his own caste, and can only gain readmission after performing a special ceremony which entails the presence of a Brahman. Again, should a Chetri marry a woman of a menial caste, he at once becomes himself a complete outcast, no one being allowed to enter his house or even touch his drinking water. In this case, however, reinstatement is impossible. His original caste is irretrievably lost, and nothing can give it back to him. Which being so, it is not difficult to understand how carefully a Nepalese must regulate his conduct throughout the whole course of his existence if he is not to suffer the direst consequences. It is indeed hardly too much to say that he never performs a single action of any consequence without first considering whether his caste will be in any way affected thereby.

As strict Hindus, the ruling family and aristocracy of Nepal are rigid in complying with all the customs and observances of their faith, while their etiquette in general is also very strict, with the result that they come much less into contact with Europeans than the corresponding classes—Princes, Rajahs, and so on—of British India. Considerations of etiquette may have something to do also with the fact that they go in so much less for games—polo, cricket, tennis, etc.—than the Indian nobles, although this is not due to any lack of sportsmanship on their part, since they excel in big-game shooting, for which, as I have made plain elsewhere, their country affords such abundant opportunities. Otherwise the upper classes of Nepal may be described as very amiable and attractive people, while from their homes one derives very often an impression of wealth and culture which would certainly come as a surprise to the ordinary European visitor. Thus General Sir Kaiser Shumshere, the third son of the late Sir Chandra Shumshere, is the possessor of a magnificent library and of gardens which have not inaptly been compared with those of Hampton Court.

Although trade, as also arts and crafts, such as they are, is almost entirely in the hands of the Newars, pasturage and cultivation form the chief occupations of the Nepalese. During the summer season those who possess cattle and sheep send them up into the higher elevations, often only just below the snow line, for grazing. Here the shepherds erect rough shelters of hurdles and leaves, and here they pass their days until the monsoon is over, when they return to their villages, often far away. Of industry in the country, little can be said, for beyond homespun cloths, paper made from the bark of trees, brass, copper, iron and wooden utensils for personal use, but little else is manufactured.

CHAPTER XII

Sports and Diversions

THE Nepalese are fortunate in having in their own country what may truly be described as a sportsman's paradise. For as a haunt of big game, the Terai, composed as it is for the most part of swampy tracts and overrun with tall grass and rank vegetation, is probably unequalled in the world. This is the abode of such animals as sambhar, buffalo, chital, hog-deer and swamp-deer, while among the larger animals, elephants, rhinoceros and tigers are found in larger numbers, it is said, than anywhere else in the world.

Herds of elephants roam in its dense jungles, emerging in the rainy season to do considerable damage to the crops. The rhinoceros in turn, which is practically extinct in India, save in Assam and northern Bengal, lives chiefly in the large tracts of level country covered with dense, high grass jungle that lie in the Chitawan district, and although many are shot annually, no appreciable diminution of their number has apparently been effected, nor has it become any less of a terror to the villagers in the rainy season, when it wanders forth seeking how much of their rice crops it may devour.

Thus it will be seen what opportunities are available to devotees of sport among the ruling classes of Nepal, and the enormous "bags" of tigers, rhinoceros, bears, leopards, etc. which fall to the guns of the Prime Minister's relatives and other members of the aristocracy who organise shooting expeditions during the cold weather in different parts of the Terai, will be readily understood.

On special occasions, such as the visit of some foreign royalty or other exceptionally eminent personage, shooting expeditions are indeed organised by the Prime Minister on a truly prodigious scale, necessitating weeks and even months of careful preparation, and entailing a correspondingly large expense. Two such expeditions which will long be remembered were the one organised by Sir Chandra Shumshere at Kasra in honour of His Majesty the King in 1911, and that organised, again by Sir Chandra, for the Prince of Wales during his visit to India during the winter of 1921.

On special occasions such as these, an area which may measure some thirty or forty miles in length and ten in depth is selected in a favoured district—often that of Chitawan—in the Terai, and into this chosen area are driven rhinoceros, elephants, tigers, wild boars, bears, leopards and other smaller game by an army of beaters who have been employed for weeks or months beforehand in combing the warm, damp jungles of lower Nepal. Ultimately a vast number of animals are concentrated within this area and allowed to grow accustomed to their new surroundings.

As to the actual manner of hunting there are two different methods practised. In the one case "kills" are tied up, and on news being received of the presence of tigers or some of the other beasts that have been beaten in, the game is either stalked or ridden down in the open.

The other system—and this is the method with which the Nepal Terai is chiefly identified—is that of encircling the tigers or other game by an enormous ring of elephants. In this case, the tigers discovered and reported from the various "kills" are surrounded by the elephants and kept penned in in this way until dawn and the arrival of the guns. The ring is then gradually contracted until the tiger is eventually completely shut in by a living wall of elephants—there may be as many as two hundred and fifty—through which escape is practically impossible.

Next, in order to get the tiger out of the particular patch of jungle in which it is hidden, about a dozen elephants, specially trained for the purpose, are formed into line and marched direct upon the beast's lair. This constitutes, naturally, one of the

[Photo by Sir F. O'Connor.

MOVING UP INTO POSITION AT A TIGER SHOOT.

[Photo by Sir F. O'Connor.

A FINE TROPHY.

most exciting moments of the proceedings, and though the tiger will contrive on occasion to evade the search in the most astonishing manner, it is, of course, almost invariably dug out eventually and compelled to break loose and runs the gauntlet of the waiting rifles in its dash for liberty. His chances, however, are small, as may be imagined, and even a moment's halt or hesitation will almost certainly prove fatal to him.

On the other hand there are occasionally times when he does manage to escape. Thus he may charge the ring of elephants, and by so creating a momentary panic amongst them succeed in breaking through and getting away. I recall this happening, indeed, actually twice in the course of a shoot given by Sir Frederick O'Connor, British minister in Nepal at the time. The undergrowth was, however, very thick, and the grass particularly high on that occasion, thus making visibility difficult. Also, in a private shoot of this kind such as the British minister is accustomed to give from time to time during the cold weather, the number of elephants employed is much smaller than on the occasions of the big government shoots for royalties, etc., so that the ring is less compact and much more easily broken through.

Sometimes again a tiger will spring upon an elephant's head and manage to effect its purpose in that way. It may be noted, however, that an elephant, though in such a case as this it will naturally not escape a severe mauling, is as a rule quite capable of dealing with a tiger, and curiously enough, much smaller animals such as leopards, or even jungle cats, will often cause more alarm to elephants then the larger kinds of game.

The royal game *par excellence* in Nepal is, however, the rhinoceros, for permission to shoot which the direct permission of the State must be obtained. The killing of a rhinoceros in Nepal is, moreover, a more important event than that of any other animal, for amongst the superstitious shikaris (hunters) of the jungle there are many half-magic uses to which the carcase of a rhino may be put. Magic properties are, for instance, credited to a rhino's horn, from the scrapings of which an aphrodisiac is composed, and there are other occult purposes for which it may be used, making it a most coveted object to secure.

Again a little blood from a rhinoceros smeared on the head of a dying man is supposed to ensure him a happy reincarnation; and these are only a few examples of the part magic plays where a dead rhinoceros is concerned. The Duke of Windsor, then Prince of Wales, accounted, I may add, for one rhinoceros at the big shoot organised in his honour in December, 1921.

There were no fewer than four hundred and twenty-eight elephants collected on this occasion, while the total bag consisted of eight rhinoceroses, eighteen tigers, two leopards and two bears. Yet even this pales into significance when compared with the royal shoot at Kasra ten years before. On that occasion the number of elephants—including a certain number borrowed from India—amounted to over six hundred, while the total bag was thirty-seven tigers, eighteen rhinoceroses and four bears, out of which twenty-one tigers, ten rhinoceroses and two bears fell to King George's own gun.

If elephants are not unduly frightened by tigers, they generally go in deadly fear of rhinoceroses, and almost invariably bolt when they hear the latter's peculiar grunt, resembling that of a bear, as they approach.

While on the subject of elephants in Nepal, mention must not be omitted of the great elephant-catching operations known as the kheddah. For many years the Nepalese employed the methods that obtained in northern India, whereby a herd of wild elephants was run down with others especially trained, and the particular elephants required were separately secured and tamed.

This method proving costly, however, and often entailing damage to the animals so secured, the Nepalese decided to introduce the kheddah system that has for many years now been in vogue in southern India. Under this system the wild elephants are rounded up by specially trained elephant-catchers, and finally induced to enter an enormous stockade composed of immense tree trunks where they are—by no means unprotesting, of course

—one by one tethered to trees and so made ready to begin the long period of training that awaits them.

Jung Bahadur, the famous Prime Minister to whom I have referred elsewhere, used to capture elephants himself single-handed. Mounted on a specially selected tame elephant, he would, on coming upon a herd of wild ones, lassoo one of them, after which, by fastening one end of the long rope to a large tame elephant which went in front, leading the way, and the other to his own which followed behind ready to administer a prod or push with his tusks should the captive jib or protest too violently, he would return in triumph to his camp.

Jung Bahadur was indefatigable in pursuit of any game. Thus, if he heard of a large elephant that he was particularly anxious either to catch, he would be off at daybreak and follow the track over the worst ground, often on foot, all day and all night perhaps without any food but a little fruit. His courage too knew no limits.

On one occasion when he was present at a duel between elephants—he delighted in witnessing such fights—one of the mahouts was thrown off. The elephant, however, was not riderless for long, for the Prime Minister without hesitation took the mahout's place.

Tiger and rhinoceros shooting was Jung Bahadur's favourite sport, and anything less than a deer he used to refuse to classify as game at all. Small game such as snipe, partridges, parrots or pigeons he considered quite unworthy of a sportsman's attention, nor could he ever understand why some birds were dignified with the name of "game" and others not.

The sagacity of elephants is well-known, but it is not until one has had first-hand experience of them in such places as the jungles of the Nepal Terai that one can appreciate it to the full. The wonderful skill which they exhibit in removing all obstacles from their path, and the cleverness with which they pick their way up and down the steepest banks, often overgrown with jungle, must be seen to be believed.

When shooting from an elephant's back, the sportsman is

usually seated in a howdah, in which he is not only comfortably accommodated, but also effectually secured against any risk of falling off. Riding on a pad which is merely a large, stuffed bag strapped to the elephant's back may, however, entail—certainly in the case of the uninitiated—considerable risk of this when the going is rough. But to the old hand one way is just as acceptable as the other. I have myself traversed part of the journey from Raxaul to Kathmandu on both howdah and pad elephants with equal comfort and security.

I had, however, an amusing experience on a pad elephant in the Terai on one occasion. This was when returning from a shooting expedition near Tribeni, that charming spot on the Rapti river and close to the British India frontier, where the British Envoy often has a camp, and the cause of the contretemps was my own elephant, a huge beast rejoicing in the name of Krishnamurti.

Krishnamurti had been displaying the sagacity peculiar to her kind during several miles of the homeward journey when she, or at any rate, her front legs, suddenly disappeared into a nullah, or deep drain, completely hidden in the long grass, that lay right across our path. The suddenness of the shock unseated me from my pad, and I was thrown heavily forward on to the mahout's back, pinioning him face downwards, with the whole weight of my body lying on top of him.

To prevent myself from slipping head foremost off his back down into the nullah I clung desperately to Krishnamurti's huge ears—an edifying snapshot for a photographer had there been one there! Fortunately, however, Krishnamurti did not roll over, but with the assistance of her trunk, and the skilful manipulation of her ungainly limbs, succeeded in completely regaining her balance and successfully surmounting the further side of the nullah. The effect of this last manœuvre was to propel me into a sitting position and on to her back once more, though I was now wedged in between the mahout, now released from my unwelcome presence on his back, and the front of the pad.

[Photo by Sir F. O'Connor.

RETURNING TO CAMP.

This little episode had been enacted in a clearing of the jungle, and after elephant, mahout and myself had, so to speak, straightened ourselves out again, I observed that several other elephants with members of our party had made their appearance and had been interested spectators of the little side-show which I had unintentionally provided. On the nearest elephant to me was my Gurkha orderly Lalsing (who had, fortunately as it happened, my rifle) and a couple of Brahman soldiers belonging to the Envoy's Escort in Kathmandu, most of whom are, through their long experience, an invaluable asset to any shooting expedition.

Lalsing, true to his Mongolian bonhomie, made no effort to conceal his merriment, while even the more sedate Brahmans held discreet hands to their faces to avoid giving full play to their emotions. The day had not been distinguished by any superabundance of sport, and I had, in their estimation, contrived to enliven it by this gratuitous entertainment to no small degree. I could neither speak nor understand the dialect of my mahout on this occasion, and so was spared his version of the little incident, in which, however, I do not doubt that he alluded to Krishnamurti's, and possibly even my ancestors, in no very decorous or endearing terms!

If I have dwelt at some length on the subject of sport in these pages it is because it has always played so prominent a part in the national life of the country and had so large a share in the development of the character of the people.

It is indeed fortunate that the Nepalese have such abundant facilities in their own country for indulging in their favourite hobby, for the amusements open to dwellers in cities are, of necessity, lacking in the little mountain villages in which they live. Thus it falls to the lot of the people themselves to make their village life cheerful or the reverse, and fortunately, the cheery, buoyant nature of the Gurkha enables him to rise to the occasion and to dispense with the ordinary distractions of the outer world.

Dancing and singing play a very important part in the

Gurkha's life. The soldier sings in camp and in the barracks, while the peasant sings as he works in the fields. During important festivals such as the Holi and the Dasehra, they will sing incessantly throughout the duration of the festival, which in the case of the Dasehra, at any rate, means ten days.

To European ears, their songs, by virtue of their constant repetition of the same short refrain, are frankly somewhat monotonous as a rule, although some of them, especially the harvesting songs of the Limbu and Rai tribes in eastern Nepal, have a definitely tuneful and fascinating lilt about them. In any case, whatever the quality of the actual songs, a Gurkha sing-song is a pleasant and exhilarating function to attend, at any rate, for a short time.

There is nothing ominous or mysterious in the distant throbbing of Gurkha drums. It does not, as in some countries, portend warning of coming danger, or some general summons to arms. On the contrary, should you make for the source of the sound you would merely find a group seated on the ground—if at night round the cheerful blaze of a camp fire—singing innumerable choruses to the accompaniment of one or more oval drums and the clapping of their own hands, which beat out the time as they sing, while in the centre one of their number slowly gyrates, his feet beating time to the throb of the drum.

It is only on very rare occasions that the women dance, although in certain parts of the country there is no objection to their joining in the singing. Indeed, at times of festival and on other special occasions, men often dance dressed in women's clothes, and so graceful are their movements that with their smooth Mongolian faces, and bedecked with the jewellery beloved of the Gurkha maidens, they are not easily distinguishable from the genuine article. As regards Nepalese folk songs, a large number are connected, like those of most other lands, with prominent physical features of the country—mountains, rivers and so on. Thus the Kali Ganga (river), the Devi Ghat (ford) and similar well-known landmarks, form frequently the themes of some of the best known examples, a great many others being woven not unnaturally, round Kathmandu and other places in the Nepal valley. "As I gazed up at the monument, my hat fell off"—runs a popular couplet, referring to Bhim Sen's monument on the Kathmandu parade-ground. Although exceedingly primitive for the most part, many of the folk songs surprise one by the thoughts and feelings expressed.

In the heavens above are more than nine lakhs of stars.
I cannot count them.
Thus the words of my heart surge up into my mouth.
But I cannot utter them,

—is a typical example of the more sentimental kind, while of the humorous variety—for the Gurkha cannot remain sentimental for long—the following may serve as an example:—

After seventeen years of married life a son was born to me
But unfortunately he was eaten by the cat.
I searched for him all over the house
And finally found his head in the pantry.

Although I fear a sophisticated European audience might consider this last silly rather than funny, it is none the less sufficient to send the more simple-minded Mongolians into convulsions of laughter—so little does it take to amuse them. There are various kinds of songs for special occasions and ceremonies. Thus, in central and western Nepal, the Ramayana, Chalitra and Mahabharata, which are the Hindu classics and mythological songs known throughout India, are considered appropriate for certain ceremonial occasions. Amongst songs unconnected with questions of ceremonial, the Sorati, best described as a kind of Hans Andersen fairy-tale put to music, and the Juwari Kheliako, a song in which a boy and girl take part in question and answer form, are perhaps the most popular and widely sung. The tunes of the old-established songs do not change, but the composition of new songs and tunes is in the hands of professional female singers known as Gainis who wander from village to village, exploiting their talents in the musical line. In the case of central Nepal, the music for the songs is invariably written in the pentatonic or black-note scale; this is, however, not the case in eastern Nepal, where, as I have already said, the music is more melodious and the effect not unlike European songs.

Apart from those of the simplest form, such as roughly-fashioned shepherds' flutes and the drums for accompanying the songs, musical instruments are rarely seen in Nepal. The few that there are are played exclusively by the professional musicians of the country, known as Damais, who, in addition to being hereditary musicians, are also the tailors of the country. Lovers of the art will, I fear, be distressed to learn that the caste of musician is one of the very lowest in Nepal, although it may be noted that the mere fact of performing on an instrument would not seem to be considered in any way derogatory, since the musicians of a Gurkha regimental band in India will often be men of good caste. The bands of the Nepalese regiments cannot be said to compare very favourably with the average regimental band in the Indian army, although the band of the rifle regiment can give a pretty good account of itself.

My reference, a few paragraphs back, to women joining in at sing-songs and the like calls to mind that the Gurkha woman enjoys, in general, a greater measure of freedom than is allowed to her sister in the Indian plains. Unhampered by any trammels of caste, she takes an interest in life and what is going on about her in a manner that approximates more to that of a European woman, herein being akin amongst eastern women, to the vivacious, cheroot-smoking Burmese. Bright and intelligent as a rule, she has the same gift of humour and repartee as her male counterpart; like him, too, she is a great smoker and shares his predilection for rice, beer and any other kind of intoxicating liquor that may be obtainable. In consequence of this exceptional freedom which she enjoys, the married life of the Gurkha woman has little of Oriental submissiveness about it, but may be said to run more on European than on eastern lines, with the wife enjoying life as well as the husband, but faithfully doing her duty by him and their children, looking after his uniform if he be a soldier, knitting gay stockings and mufflers for him to smarten his appearance, and so on.

For the Gurkha, it may be said, takes a great pride in his personal appearance, and delights to affect bright colours, besides adorning his cap and person with flowers, of which he is passionately fond. He might, in fact, be described as rather vain.

In the matter of the Gurkhas' looks it is difficult for the European to speak to much purpose until he has had sufficient experience to enable him to discriminate between individuals, since, naturally, with their Mongolian type of features, they all look much alike at first. In time, however, one learns to be more discriminating, and then has no difficulty in perceiving that they differ from one another just as much as Europeans, that some are good-looking, some plain and so on, although it must be admitted that not many foreign observers seem disposed to admit as much.

"Little, ill-made and abominably ugly," is how Laurence Oliphant described a regiment which he saw at a review in Kathmandu about the middle of the last century. Oliphant was, however, perhaps more prejudiced than most foreigners against the Mongolian type, for, after seeing a party of Bhotiyas and Tibetans in a temple in the same city, he delivered himself as follows: "Had I been asked to determine the origin of this race, I should have pronounced it to be a mixture of Naples *lazzaroni* with the scum of an Irish regiment"! Similarly, words like "debased" and "squalid" figure in an entirely unmerited denunciation of Nepalese women.[1]

Yet, biased and inaccurate in his fulminations though Oliphant might be, he is only one of many foreigners who have been unwilling to concede even a modicum of good looks to the Nepalese, though it should be understood, of course, that reference is made in this connection only to the Mongolian

[1] *Journey to Katmandu*, Chs. VII and XIII.

hill tribes and lower classes as a whole. The higher castes and the upper and ruling classes, possessing as they do the blood of ancient Rajput stock in their veins, belong naturally to a different category.

And so, too, as regards the women. Like the men, they too disclose individual differences in plenty when one gets to know them, though almost all of course are of the Mongolian type and hardly beautiful, for the most part, in European eyes. Many, however, are not uncomely, and not a few, especially in eastern Nepal, and particularly in Darjeeling, might with justice be called distinctly pretty.

CHAPTER XIII

The High Road to Kathmandu

About a mile to the north of the little railway station of Raxaul, in the Province of Bihar, in northern India, stands a trimly-built bungalow, surrounded by a pleasant garden. Many such are to be seen throughout the length and breadth of the great Indian peninsula, but none possessing the same interest for the writer as this little red-brick building that lies secluded amongst the trees, on the outskirts of the straggling bazaar. For, situated on the border line between Nepal and British India, this bungalow is the Residency rest-house, and on the other side of the little bridge that spans the Raxaul river the high road, flanked by dusty mango and pipal trees, runs northward through flat, paddy fields, to Kathmandu.

So, as one looks northwards from the verandah of the rest-house across the plains to where, a hundred miles distant, like a white lace border, the eternal snows overhang a rampart of dark, forbidding mountains, one knows that before one lies Nepal. Some two miles away, a landmark in the foreground, stands a high and imposing white house with projecting eaves—its unfamilar architecture peculiarly Nepalese—the residence of some important Nepalese official.

A stranger who sets out for the first time upon the journey to Kathmandu never fails to experience a curious sense of adventure—the feeling of entering into the unknown. As I have said elsewhere, the laws regulating the entry of foreigners into Nepal are absolute, and admit of the fewest possible exceptions, so that even to-day the number of Europeans who know the old arduous track that led up to the valley of Kathmandu from the plains of India is very small. The distance from Raxaul to Kathmandu—along what may be called the beaten track of Nepal—is seventy-five miles. The journey to-day, however, presents no great difficulties or hardships. A part of it which traverses the Terai is now performed by rail, for, in 1927, the late Sir Chandra Shumshere, as part of the progressive policy that characterised his able rule, promoted the construction of a light railway that runs from Raxaul to Amlekhganj. Hence, part of the journey, which formerly occupied a whole day, is now accomplished in a few hours.

From Amlekhganj as far as Bhimphedi, the little town that stands at the foot of the Sisagarhi Pass, the road is good, and the appearance of an occasional motor car arouses only mild interest to-day among the Mongol inhabitants. It was very different some twenty-five years ago—to be precise, in 1910—when I made my first trip to Kathmandu to take up the appointment of training officer to the Nepal escort. Not without reason, indeed, did Mr. Percy Brown, Principal of the Government School of Art, Calcutta, then write (in his charming book, *Picturesque Nepal*) "at least sixty miles of this journey can be described as a materialised nightmare."

Yet, arduous as the journey undoubtedly was in those days, I never regretted the repeated occasions on which I made it. The spirit of adventure, the delight of penetrating the unknown country that was the home of the attractive people with whom one's lot as a soldier had been cast, more than outweighed any discomforts and fatigue experienced on the road, while the beauty of the scenery encountered alone made the journey worth while.

In those days a palanquin, borne by relays of not always willing bearers or "kahars," took the place of a railway carriage or motor car. These bearers, not hillmen, but natives of the adjacent Province of Bihar, shuffled through the long hours of the night—one used to leave Raxaul at dusk—with a steady, grunting chorus, broken only by occasional louder supplications to their gods. This, combined with the hum of insects and the soft patter of the men's feet, had a certain soporific effect as one lay at full-length in the dooly, inducing, in fact, a kind of delightful coma. But that this peace of mind and rest of body should continue unbroken throughout the night was, of course, hardly to be expected. Mishaps of one sort or another were, indeed, of constant occurrence, one of the commonest arising from the breaking of a worn-out palanquin pole, to be replaced, without undue hurry, from a neighbouring clump of bamboo, of which in the forest there is no lack. Alarums and excursions of other kinds were also to be looked for at any time—as when, during a halt, a bearer would run off into the forest, his crime in deserting being, at any rate in part, atoned for by his courage in facing the dread Terai jungle alone at night.

Of the twenty-seven miles that comprised the first stage of the journey, ending at Churia—where the night was spent at the little rest-house picturesquely perched scarce fifty feet above the Churia river—twelve miles ran through virgin forest. It is this strip of forest that has given the Nepalese Terai the unenviable reputation of being the unhealthiest region in Asia. One tribe, indeed, the Tharus, are immune from the deadly Awal, or malarial fever, which prevails here between the months of April and October, but otherwise its victims are innumerable. Indeed, after sunset it is only at the risk of his life that anyone lingers in this impenetrable jungle, where overhanging trees shut out the sky and a warm oppressive stillness prevails. By day, the Terai is comparatively safe, but should any traveller be compelled to make the journey to Kathmandu during the malaria season, he would certainly be wise to avoid spending a night in this deadly tract, and preferably make for some place like Sisagarhi, high up in the foothills. Even the little rest-house at Churia is said to lie high enough to ensure immunity.

Formerly, to the fear of disease and attacks from wild animals —for the traffic had not then driven the game into the denser parts of the forest—was added, as a further hardship for the humbler wayfarers in this region, a lack of drinking water, which added immeasurably to the discomforts of the journey. In more recent times a lady of the royal family of Nepal, grieved at the suffering which she witnessed when on a journey by this route, provided the well-made and ornamental drinking fountains which are now to be found every few miles throughout the forest—the water being conveyed by pipes from the mountains to spouts fashioned, it is said, to resemble the hands of the donor, and falling in a continuous stream into tanks, a boon to man and beast that only those who know the Terai can properly appreciate.

I have referred already to the little rest-house at Churia. Behind it lies the ridge bearing the same name which played so important a part in the Nepal war of 1814, which I have described elsewhere.

And thus it comes about that not a little historical interest attaches to the thick woods and stony river beds of the country round about here.

The vastly improved condition of the road enables the traveller in these days to step from the railway train at Amlekhganj into a waiting motor car, which conveys him comfortably and rapidly to Bhimphedi. He is, therefore, spared the extremely tiring part of the journey, familiar to those of us who used to make it in days gone by, with whom it abides as an indelibly unpleasant memory.

I refer, particularly, to the seven miles approach to Churia, and the first seven miles of the march on the following day, where the track lay along the stony bed of a river. At this stage progress became extremely slow and somewhat painful, especially when darkness set in. Coolies, palanquin bearers and traveller—the last usually on foot, to avoid the jolting of the dooly—stumbled and scrambled over huge boulders and trunks of trees, and as if this were not enough, every now and then foaming torrents would almost sweep some members of the toiling caravan off their feet.

As I bowled along the new road in a motor on my last visit to Kathmandu a few years ago, I could not help thinking of those earlier days—the slow groping along the river bed in the dark, and the subsequent delight at seeing the lights of the Churia rest-house at the end. Almost entirely cut off from the modern world as it is still to-day, the march of progress has yet effected some improvement even in remote Nepal.

So on through fine wooded scenery, to the sound of the music of the Rapti river as it ripples below over its rocky bed; on through the lovely valley that broadens out and loses itself in the plain of Bhimphedi, till the picturesque little town, Bhimphedi itself, comes into view. There was always much bustle and animation here, for this was where the road ended, and for the remainder of the journey everything had to be carried by hand.

To-day, not only a new cart-road but also a rope-way has facilitated transport, so that so far as the high road to Kathmandu is concerned, far less is now conveyed by human labour. Yet, when necessary, there would seem to be nothing too heavy or too large for the sturdy little hill-men to carry, as visitors to this Himalayan fastness cannot have failed to observe. Some of the loads in former days were, indeed, of incredible weight and size. Yet, cruel as such burdens seemed, the bearers never appeared dissatisfied with their lot. Accustomed to this kind of work from their earliest days, they accepted it as a matter of course; nor were they badly paid for their services.

Many of the older buildings in Bhimphedi remind the traveller of the India he has now left behind. They exhibit characteristics peculiar to Newar architecture—about which I shall have a little to say later on—though the introduction of cheap, modern tin roofing is tending to destroy the essentially Nepalese charm which they formerly possessed.

On leaving Bhimphedi, one is faced with an ascent of over 2,000 feet, and although it has been improved out of all recognition in the last few years, the path, as it used to be, must have been the worst approach to any civilised capital in the world. It was, in reality, hardly more than a torrent bed, boulder-strewn and with a gradient varying between twenty-five and thirty-five degrees. It was while climbing this path on one occasion that I saw an example of what I have previously alluded to, namely, the fact that nothing is too heavy or unwieldy for the Nepalese to transport by human labour. On that occasion it was nothing less than the parts of a heavy traction-engine which were being slowly carried up this track, which one found difficult enough to climb unhampered by even the lightest load. A hundred coolies had been engaged for the purpose, and, urged on by their leader, who led them in the singing of a chant not unlike the hauling songs common to Russia and other countries, they moved the bulky mass of metal forward, step by step. In this way, advancing, perhaps not more than a hundred yards or so in a day, they would eventually reach Kathmandu.

So, too, have I seen motor cars—not on wheels—making a precarious descent of the massive steps of stone that constitute the track from the top of the Chandragiri Pass down into the valley, the crux of the whole route, and once I saw a grand piano being negotiated over a broad, swift-running stream—at the imminent risk, apparently, of being precipitated into the torrent at any moment. And these examples are but a few of many which could be cited illustrating what miracles unaided human labour can achieve in the way of transport.

Actually, the heaviest single objects that have been carried over the mountain passes of Sisagarhi and Chandragiri are the statues of the Prime Ministers on the Maidan, as Mr. Percival Landon has recorded, each being said to weigh about four tons.

Besides a small bazaar, there is an old fort at Sisagarhi, relic of distant times, when it formed part of a chain of defences that bade defiance to intruders from the Indian plains, while there is also a garrison of two hundred troops. On the path stands a sentry with fixed bayonet, clad in the picturesque blue uniform and quaint head-dress with silver rim, too soon, I fear, to be replaced by the prosaic khaki. We are 6,000 feet above the plains here; the air is cool and the hum of the mosquito is never heard. From the ramparts on a clear day we can trace the course of much of the road we have traversed. Beyond the endless ridges, shimmering in the evening haze, can be

On the Road to Kathmandu.

THE ROAD NEAR CHITLONG.

seen the plains of India as they stretch away to the furthest horizon. Whatever the trials of the road in bygone days, the traveller found solace and reward in the beautiful view from Sisagarhi.

From Sisagarhi there is a climb of a few hundred feet to the top of the Chisapani Pass, from where the first glimpse of the snows is obtained. From here the path falls steeply to the Panoni river through country of great beauty at all seasons of the year, whether the sides of the road are gay with bushes of pink mimosa, or resplendent in their spring clothing of rhododendron and wild apple blossom.

Perched on some smooth patch of grass above the path, at intervals of a few miles, are rough shelters where some enterprising and commercially-minded Nepalese dispense light refreshments to thirsty and footsore wayfarers. The diet offered is unpretentious; highly sweetened and strong-flavoured tea being the most popular, if not the only, item on the bill of fare. Leaving their loads in serried line propped up against the banks of the track, the sturdy coolies squat round the open-air kitchen, sipping their hot tea and puffing at their cigarettes with an air of supreme contentment. At that moment they are at peace with themselves and all the world.

A soldier on leave from a Gurkha regiment in India, who is "trekking" to his home, some three marches beyond Kathmandu away to the west, joins the group. He is sturdily built and smart in his well-fitting black coat and shorts. The coloured tops of his stockings are of a brightness that even the most daringly-garbed devotee of plus-fours in Europe would tremble to affect. Here, however, they do not seem exaggerated or out of place; the little soldier with his cap set at a jaunty angle, and his treasured khukri slung bandolier-wise by a red cloth, presents a debonair and pleasing appearance. To the coolies, he is essentially a "man of the world"; and his stories of life in his cantonment and the big teeming cites of India—possibly somewhat highly coloured—are listened to with silent respect. The comely damsel of the inn, who ministers to his wants, glances at him with approval not unmixed with admiration. "There is something about a soldier," as a popular ditty has it, and the sentiment holds equally good on the road to Kathmandu as nearer home.

You will notice that the heavy copper coins which most customers of the tea-shop proffer in payment for their refreshments are of crude appearance and design, and also that the soldier pays with Indian money which is accepted without any difficulty. There is no paper money in Nepal. Copper, silver and gold coins provide the currency, though the gold coins are little used except for the purposes of ceremonial gifts. There are, however, several silver coins of varying value in circulation, of which a rupee (which stands at a discount of 25 per cent. compared with the Indian rupee) and a half-rupee piece, known as a mohur, are the most commonly used, the others, owing to their smallness of size, being inconvenient for handling. The copper pice, on the other hand, which our friends of the tea-shop are using, are in universal use throughout Nepal, though British Indian rupees are freely circulated also in the Terai, where, for convenience, the collection of Government revenues is made in that currency.

Sometimes entertainment is provided on these occasions by strolling minstrels from Tibet, who foresee a chance of reaping a harvest of small coin from the open-hearted patrons of the booth. An old man draped in a garment that leaves his left arm and elbow bare, produces strange, untuneful sounds from an instrument of three strings shaped like some prehistoric mandoline. Two young Tibetan women dance. Flat-faced, with cheek bones of a pronounced red hue, their heads encircled by a disc set with coloured stones and with their hair hanging in two heavy plaits over their shoulders, they revolve with quaint, rhythmic step. They roll their eyes, and flap and shake their large sleeves; and, as if the noises wrung from the old man's instrument were not enough, they add to them by chanting with shrill voices. The audience looks on with good-natured amusement; taking neither the performers nor their efforts very seriously. Some of them probably do not even understand what the "Bhotes" say.[1]

To extract a smile from a Nepalese is no difficult matter for he has a keen sense of humour and is easily amused. So, after exchanging a few sallies, which, though far from brilliant, are sufficient to cause much laughter, and after bestowing largesse upon the Tibetan maidens, who are as the daughters of the horse-leech in their demands, we take once more to the road.

On both sides of the river the hills rise bare and steep; the path runs sometimes beside, at others within, the bed of the river, till it brings the wayfarer by numberless fords—for the stream winds constantly—to the village of Markhu, that lies at the extremity of the gorge. The high water and a strong current make this river road impassable in any time of the year except the dry season, so a *détour* has to be made over the mountain side, where a road rambles, in places somewhat recklessly, over the cliffs.

The noise of jingling bells, faint at first, then growing louder and louder, which is a familiar sound on Nepalese high roads, denotes the approach of the runner carrying mails. The almost total absence of roads as we know them throughout the country renders the conveyance of mails in Nepal no easy problem, but, although in the country districts post offices are few and far between and post infrequent, letters do seem eventually to arrive at their destination, however distant or inaccessible it may be. The stamps are, however, only valid for the national service, letters addressed to India or beyond having to be franked by Indian stamps.

From Markhu the road runs over a range of hills, low, bare and undulating, till it enters the smiling valley of Chitlong, sometimes called Little Nepal. This is the last place of cultivated land before we ascend the Chandragiri Pass, beyond which lies our goal.

[1] Although the term "Bhotiya" refers primarily to inhabitants of Bhot or Tibet, there are also Bhotiyas of Sikkim and Bhutan, while the Murmis, Lamas and Tamangs of Nepal are often called by the same name.

A steep, but not unduly difficult, climb through groves of rhododendrons takes one to the summit of Chandragiri, and it is from here that we get our first view of the far-famed valley of Nepal. Spread out like some dream picture, 2,000 feet directly below, it surpasses in beauty even that other fair valley, Kashmir, in comparison with which it is so little known.

The panorama, which includes practically the whole part of Nepal accessible to Europeans, is indeed magnificent and worth coming any distance to see. Dotted here and there among the Newar cultivation, brown patches show where the three cities of the valley lie.

Far away at the eastern end of the valley, nestling in a fold of the hills is Bhatgaon. A tall, white tower, that rises from a mass of red-brown roofs more towards the centre of the picture, distinguishes the capital, Kathmandu. A little to the south-east lies Patan, the largest city in Nepal, which in the valley's stormy history has suffered most of all. On a hill, richly wooded and to the west of Kathmandu, a white dome, with gilt spire shimmering in the sunlight, indicates the temple dedicated to the "self-existent one"—the famous Swayambhunath.

Everywhere, extending well up the bases of the hills that surround the valley, are cultivated fields. Divided into squares by crops of varying colour, they look, from where we stand, like some chequer board of brown and russet green. We see the sacred rivers of Nepal, the Baghmati and Bishnumati, winding their way through the valley like threads of silver, till, growing fainter and fainter, they lose themselves in the folds of the distant hills.

In the background, above mountains, some thickly wooded, others gaunt and bare, stretches the main snowy range of the Himalayas, standing guardian over all. Beautiful as it is at all times of the year, this view is perhaps at its finest immediately after the monsoon. Then come days half-cloud, half-sunshine, when at times banks of clouds hide snows and distant mountains, and veils of mist blot out cities and temples that lie below. Never, however, is the colouring more beautiful, nor are the

Ascending the Chandragiri Pass.

varied effects of light and shade more striking, than at this time of the year. On days such as these the picture is ever changing. At one moment, when a stronger breeze has lifted the misty curtain, a tract of sunlit country discloses itself in dazzling brightness, bringing into relief some city or temple; at another, huge quick-moving shadows cast the green and gold of the rice fields into gloom.

For reasons that I have never been able to discover, really good amateur photographs of the snows from the Chandragiri Pass have seldom been obtained. Few of the small band of foreigners privileged to enter the country come unequipped with the requisites for taking pictures, but with few exceptions they meet their Waterloo, photographically speaking, on gaining the summit of the Chandragiri. It may be due to atmospheric conditions or to the difficulty of choosing the right moment. Whatever the reason, successful results would appear to be the exception rather than the rule.

It so happened that I found myself once on Chandragiri when conditions were very nearly perfect from a photographic point of view. But alas for the vanity of human wishes! My roseate expectations came to naught—for reasons which I will explain. Put briefly, the charms of a Bhotiya maiden were, I fear, the principal cause. Accompanied by the cheerful, pleasant retinue with which the traveller is wont to travel in Nepal—usually a Nepali policeman, a sepoy or two from the envoy's escort, a Nepali syce (groom) and possibly some kind of orderly—I was slowly ascending the steep path that leads from Chitlong to the top of the Chandragiri Pass.

Prominent amongst my small following on this occasion was one Lalsing Gurung, my batman from my regiment. Lalsing was in every way a typical Gurkha. About five foot three inches tall, in appearance he was decidedly Mongolian, with the high cheek-bones, almond-shaped eyes, and the fair yellowish-brown skin common to well-bred specimens of his race. Simple in character, fearless and extremely straightforward, in common with all his compatriots he was a stranger to the flattery so much practised in the east. With anyone whom he disliked, Lalsing was sometimes outspoken to the point of rudeness, but to those who had won his confidence he was a loyal and devoted friend.

To return, however, to the path up Chandragiri. As we were resting for a moment in one of the glades through which the track passes, there came into the open, stepping blithely, and followed closely by two girl companions, a young Bhotiya woman of decidedly attractive appearance, and adorned with the coloured necklaces and many bangles popular with girls of her tribe. The impression she created in our small assembly, now augmented by other wayfarers, was favourable in the extreme. When, therefore, it was suggested that the lady was in every way worthy of being photographed I readily acquiesced. The fact that I had exhausted all but two of my supply of plates for the day was the only matter that caused me a moment's concern. Previous experience having led me, however, to be utterly sceptical as to the likelihood of getting a really good view from the summit, I decided to expend one plate on the object of our admiration.

After a little persuasive oratory in which everyone present, including spectators, took a hand, the lady consented to face the ordeal of the camera, and the preliminary operations, the camera being of the stand variety, were taken in hand. Certain minor difficulties, however, had to be overcome during the process of posing. So anxious, for example, were my retinue to avoid any possibility of being left out of the picture, that at one moment they completely obscured the principal figure herself. There was some slight objection also in certain quarters to the pose adopted by Lalsing. It was held—not perhaps unreasonably—that his exceedingly slender acquaintance with the girl hardly warranted his placing his hand caressingly on her shoulder, a gesture accompanied also by a slight inclination of his head. Eventually, however, these details were satisfactorily arranged, the task was accomplished and the party resumed the ascent of the hill.

On reaching the summit I saw the whole of the range revealed for once in a way in absolutely perfect conditions—presenting a scene of grand, impressive beauty, such as no words of mine can possibly describe. It was the opportunity of a lifetime. But how was I to take advantage of it? Where half a dozen plates seemed barely sufficient, I was the possessor, at such a moment, of one only. Rarely have I expended such care in the taking of a photograph. Rarely, perhaps never, could I hope to have such a subject again. I little knew, however, what the fates had in store for me. Developing the plates the same evening in the Residency, I observed, not without some consternation, that curious, and as it seemed, superfluous objects were coming out on the plate devoted to the view of the valley. The disclosure that the other plate in the holder remained supremely indifferent to any immersion in the developing solution—however lengthy—provided the clue to the mystery. I had forgotten to change the plate after the first exposure, and intruding upon a landscape (where the snows were clearly traceable) and half obliterating villages and temples, were figures of abnormal proportions. Amongst these, I could recognise Lalsing Gurung, and the innocent cause of all the trouble—the Bhotiya girl.

The descent from the top of Chandragiri to Thankot, the village lying at its foot on the Nepal valley side, is in these days quickly accomplished. Before the road which has thus facilitated travel was constructed at this point some ten years ago, this final stage—the last eight miles from Thankot to the capital being always quickly covered by carriage or car—was, as I have already stated, the crucial part of the whole journey. The track was composed of enormous stone boulders, rudely shaped into a semblance of steps, while the gradient was in places as much as forty-five degrees. The rough going, however, was in no small degree compensated for by the beauty of the route.

Almost every foot of the way as far as Thankot, heavy foliage of varying shades of green formed a graceful canopy, through which, as in a natural frame, distant views of the valley, with its towns and villages, its winding rivers and its carefully tilled fields could be obtained. For the inhabitants of the valley, the journey by this rough and primitive highway possessed no terrors at all. Women and girls climbed up the massive steps of stone with agility; sturdy coolies, heavily laden, paused to look at the perspiring stranger with curious gaze; now and then one even met a sick man, carried on the back—or more luxuriously in a basket slung behind the shoulders—of a friend.

Though bullocks and goats floundered somewhat precariously between the rocks and boulders, even they never seemed to come to any harm. More anxious was I for my plains-bred pony that I took with me on my first visit to Kathmandu—for on this occasion I was to stay in the valley six months. Accustomed, however, to the hills from my having served in a Himalayan station, he jumped cleverly and courageously from boulder to boulder. But I was thankful for his sake at least when this part of the journey was at an end.

Kathmandu Street Scene. (Figure of Kal Bhairab in Foreground.)

CHAPTER XIV

The Capital of Nepal

[*Note.*—Since the following chapters were written grievous changes have been wrought in many of the places and buildings described by the disastrous earthquake of 1933. I have considered it best, however, to leave them as they stood, relegating particulars of the devastation caused and other details to a later page. (See end of Ch. XVII.)]

It is perhaps the entire absence of everything Indian that strikes the foreigner more than anything else on his first entering the city of Kathmandu. Barely a hundred miles from the frontier, not only in the appearance of the people, but in the architecture of its pagoda-like buildings, the capital of Nepal bears no similarity whatever to a city of the plains. The buildings suggest countries like Burma, Japan or China, for the most characteristic types of the architecture of the Newars, as the supposed original inhabitants of the valley are called, are in the so-called pagoda style. Yet, curiously enough, according to Professor Sylvain Levi, the eminent French Sanskrit scholar, the Newars had not been influenced by architects from the countries I have mentioned; on the contrary, in company with other critics, he is inclined to believe that China, at any rate, obtained the idea of the multi-roofed pagoda from Nepal. The actual origin of this pagoda form of building Professor Levi has traced to the early wooden architecture of India, known to have existed in that country even before the time of the ancient monuments in stone.

Kirkpatrick, one of the earliest European historians of Nepal, in his description of the valley about the year 1811, wrote "there are nearly as many temples as houses, and as many idols as inhabitants, there not being a fountain, a river or a hill within its limits that is not consecrated to one or other of the Hindu or Buddhist deities."[1] One can hardly find fault with this description even to-day, for in every town—be it Patan, Bhatgaon or Kathmandu—temples of every conceivable style and age confront one at every turn.

Kathmandu itself is a picturesque town, with a vitality and an atmosphere of its own, which the other two cities of the valley hardly possess. It is further, a city of contrasts; of narrow congested streets, carved old archways, red-smeared idols and images of burnished brass on the one hand; on the other, of roads well kept and spacious, flanked by high walls behind which are modern palaces, the last word in luxury and style. A cheerful Mongol crowd throngs the streets from morning till night. All types of the Gurkha race are to be seen, though Newars are most conspicuous, most of the trade of the city being in their hands.

It is amusing to observe the people as one walks slowly through, although it is the foreigner himself who is, of course, the object of wonder to the natives. A group of thick-set Bhotiyas from the Tibetan borderland are sitting closely-packed before a refreshment booth; they look up as one passes with wide-staring eyes, a lot of sturdy, jolly-looking schoolboys. Pretty Newar women in bright-coloured dresses, with marigolds in their smooth black hair, pass by carrying brass trays with offerings. Unfettered by any "purdah" regulations, they chatter gaily amongst themselves. There is nothing of gloom in their daily pilgrimage to the temple, nothing in their religious observance that can be said to be forbidding.

Bargaining with the Newar owner of a shop displaying the wares of Nepal—cotton cloths printed in the gayest colours, shining brass utensils, "hurricane" lamps, cigarettes and so on—stands a soldier, on leave from some British India Gurkha regiment. He is by profession a man of war, and his khukri hangs, suspended by its red sash, in a business-like manner at his side. Despite his martial air, however, nothing is further from his mind at this moment than thoughts of war. The

[1] *An Account of the Kingdom of Neprul,* Ch. VI, p. 150.

Street Scene in Kathmandu.

A Jemadar—Purano Gorakh Regiment, Nepalese Army.

transaction upon which he is engaged is one indeed to exclude all other thoughts, for our friend is selecting what is perhaps the most prized of all the Gurkha's few possessions—an umbrella, imported from the Indian plains.

In the matter of money the Gurkha has an outlook that might be described as Anglo-Saxon. He regards it as something that should be spent. In this he differs greatly from the Indian of the plains, who loves to hoard his "pice" as carefully as a Frenchman does his "sous."

A considerable police force, conspicuous in blue cotton uniforms and scarlet pagris, maintain law and order in Kathmandu. Outside the valley, police functions are largely undertaken by the soldiers of the various provincial garrisons, whose duties in fact consist of little else. Parties of prisoners, recognisable by the light steel wire fastened to each leg, can often be seen working in the streets of Kathmandu. No one is in charge of them, and, their task accomplished, they return to prison of their own accord. They are not paid for their labours, but the fact that they are clothed and fed seems to make them contented with their lot, for the idea of trying to escape never seems to occur to them.

Apart from the occasional soldier from a Gurkha regiment to British India, there is plenty to remind one of the military spirit that pervades this little mountain country as we stroll through the streets of Kathmandu. Khaki-clad soldiers belonging to the Nepalese army are much in evidence. To an occasional Nepalese officer, easily recognisable from his red-banded peaked cap, and usually mounted on a sturdy Bhotiya pony, all and sundry will at once give way.

As befits a race in whom, though not at heart warlike, the martial spirit burns keenly, the Nepalese possess, in the Thuni Khel, a natural parade-ground which, with its smooth, green turf, and its large and shady trees forming an ideal saluting-base, has hardly its equal elsewhere.

Including militia, the Nepalese army numbers some forty thousand men. Drawn from the so-called fighting classes of

Nepal—all dwellers in the hill country—the material is excellent, and admirably adapted to the purpose for which the army is primarily intended, namely, the defence of the country. The officering of so large an army is, as can be imagined, a matter that presents considerable difficulty, and the fact that most of the officers are awarded their commissions more on grounds of social position than of military efficiency, constitutes perhaps the chief weakness of the force.

As elsewhere, there are, of course, certain "crack" regiments in the Nepalese army. Thus, corresponding to our Household troops, is a regiment known as the Rifle Regiment. Among a people where a tall man is the exception rather than the rule, the men of the Rifle Regiment are in this respect remarkable, since all are about six foot in height and of a physique to correspond. The Rifle Regiment is certainly the *corps d'élite*, but there are a few other regiments that are distinctive in another way, in virtue of the fact that their members are strictly confined to men of the same tribe.

Regiments of this description are the Kali Bahadur, composed solely of men of the Gurung, and the Purano Gorakh, of men of the Magar tribe. As will be noticed, Nepalese regiments are not numbered, but have, as a rule, picturesque and magniloquent titles, suggesting usually some martial quality such as contempt of danger or valour in war.

If, in matters of drill, tactics and military efficiency in general, Nepalese regiments can hardly be said to rank as high as the finest European troops, this is by no means to say that they would not prove a formidable foe if ever called upon to fight. Of the two Nepalese contingents that served in India during the Great War, and which won golden opinions for their bearing and discipline wherever they were stationed, I have spoken elsewhere.

To have been associated with the Nepalese Contingent, during at any rate a portion of their stay on Indian soil, was a delightful and altogether memorable experience, especially in so far as it afforded opportunity to get to know their officers in the higher command. Undergoing as they did, "in the exigency of the service," a certain amount of discomfort, especially in the matter of quarters, they were brought into the closest contact with the British officers attached as instructors with the happiest results, the best of good fellowship prevailing all round.

The writer will always look back with the greatest pleasure to the days at Kakul when Sir Padma Shumshere, Commander of the Nepalese contingent, and nephew of the late Sir Chandra Shumshere, occupied detached quarters next to him, and only slightly bigger than his own. And amongst his most treasured possessions, too, will always be a badge in silver, bearing "a strange device," the regimental badge of the Pashupati Parshad.

To one side of the parade-ground at Kathmandu is the tall white tower, to which I have already referred when describing the view of the valley from the Chandragiri Pass, and which is a notable landmark from many other parts of the valley as well. Known as Bhim Sen's Folly, and towering above all other buildings—it is 200 feet high—it was built by the Gurkha General Bhim Sen Thapa, Prime Minister of Nepal (1806–1837) during his administration. And the fact that it was built more for the purpose of gaining notoriety than for any other reason is reponsible for its present name.

Popular tradition links the name of Jung Bahadur, the greatest Gurkha hero, with the Dharara, as the monument is also called. He is said to have jumped with two umbrellas as parachutes from the top of the column to the pavement below for a wager, coming through the ordeal unscathed. That, at any rate, is the story to which the loyal Nepali steadfastly clings. The true version of Jung Bahadur's action—for the tradition is based on an actual episode—records that it took place during the construction of the tower, its height at the time being left to the imagination of the listener. Close to the tower is an equestrian statue of Jung Bahadur himself.

In the heart of the city of Kathmandu is the Darbar Square. From here streets radiate in all directions, to pass in their course, sooner or later, other small squares in which the city abounds. Kathmandu is, in fact, built on the general plan common to all large towns in the valley. In every one there is a large Darbar Square—with the royal palace or "Darbar" on one side, and with temples and shrines sacred to the locality on the others—in the centre of the town. And round the Darbar Square are again smaller squares (tols), connected with one another and with the main square by streets or narrow lanes.

A large image of Hanuman, the monkey god, well protected against the elements by a heavy coat and a silk umbrella, guards the main gateway of the old royal palace—the much-revered Hanuman Dhoka.

Of the many important temples situated in the Darbar Square, most of which are dedicated to Mahadeo, the most celebrated is the royal shrine, known as Taleju. An imposing building of five storeys, it is said to have been erected in honour of Taleju or Tulaja Devi, the protectress of the ruling family of Nepal, by a demon from Ceylon. The many pagoda roofs, the profusion of carved wood-work, and the artistic colouring that is so often associated with Nepalese masonry, all combine to give the Darbar Square a picturesque and somewhat Chinese appearance—an appearance that even the modern-looking Darbar Hall, a structure of recent years, and certain prosaic and unsightly electric-light standards have not been able to destroy.

In a little square close by, now used as a fruit market, stands the ancient wooden building from which the city takes its name. It was in 1596 that one Raja Lachiman Sing erected this somewhat ramshackle-looking house as a place of accommodation for fakirs—a function it continues to fulfil at the present day. One of the most characteristic of the old Newar buildings in the city, the Newars still allude to it as Kathmandu, or the wooden temple. According to legend, it was entirely constructed from the wood of one tree, whence came the name Kathmandu—"kath" meaning wood, and "mandu" temple.

The early history of Nepal is so shrouded in doubt and

Approach to Darbar Square. Kathmandu.

uncertainty that it is impossible to fix with any degree of confidence the date of the actual foundation of Kathmandu. Tradition has it that in 250 B.C. the Emperor Asoka, whose dominion at that time comprised the whole of northern India, including Kashmir, and whose capital was at Pataliputra, the modern Patna, came to Nepal. His daughter subsequently settled there and founded Devapatan or Patan.

Thus has tradition assigned a date for the origin of one, at least, of the cities of the valley, and as Patan is but a mile away to the north-east of Kathmandu, everything points to the fact that the latter city was also certainly in existence at, or possibly even before, this time.

Asoka was a zealous Buddhist, and many edicts and inscriptions on rocks and pillars in various parts of India are traceable to this king. One of the most interesting of these is to be found within the boundaries of modern Nepal itself. This is the inscription on a pillar, discovered quite accidentally by the archæologist Dr. Führer in 1895 at Rummindei, the Lumbini Garden, certifying that the pillar marked the actual birthplace of Buddha. "Here the Blessed One was born" runs one sentence in the short inscription which "King Piyadasi, beloved of the gods"—this being the personal formula used generally by Asoka in edicts and inscriptions—has thus handed down.

The Residence of the British Envoy is built on a slight rise a little to the north of the city, and all this quarter which comprises, besides the legation, the residence of the legation surgeon, a post office and the lines of an English escort, is known as the "English Lines."

It is the area round the British Legation that may be described as the residential quarter of Kathmandu. Here are no narrow streets, no pagoda-roofed temples or houses. Instead are well-made roads lit with electricity, and one gets every now and then a glimpse of an imposing modern palace. The glimpse is only a fleeting one, for these palaces, the residences of members and relations of the ruling families, are invariably surrounded by high brick walls.

The palace of the king is one of great magnificence, surrounded by fine grounds and well-laid-out gardens. Another splendid palace is the Singha Darbar, or home of the Prime Minister, the centre, it might be said with reason, of the whole life of Nepal. There is nothing of Nepalese architecture in this imposing building, as it is essentially modern and European in style and possesses a noble frontage, in the centre of which is a handsome entrance, the Corinthian columns of which rise between three archways of graceful form.

CHAPTER XV

Temples and Shrines

THOUGH there is no shred of evidence to support the assertion, Buddha is said to have once visited the Nepal valley, where he found that the fundamental principles of his teaching had already been introduced amongst the Newars. That Buddhism flourished in Nepal some three hundred years before Christ is at any rate always accepted as an historical fact, while there is no doubt further that at one time Buddhism was the predominant religion of Nepal. At the present day, however, the great majority of the people profess the Hindu faith, although they cannot be considered very strict followers of it.

Orthodox Hinduism is, in fact, fast replacing the Buddhist faith of the original inhabitants of the valley, the Newars. Even the tribes who inhabit the northern and north-eastern parts of the country bordering on Tibet, and whose religion, therefore, approximates to the Lamaistic Buddhism of the Tibetans, will to-day call themselves Hindus. The fact that the ruling family are strict Hindus is largely responsible no doubt for the way in which that faith is so steadily gaining ground.

Thus there exists in Nepal at the present time a curious admixture of the two religions, although everything points to the eventual extinction of Buddhism. To which it may be added that even when it holds its own, Buddhism as it exists to-day has been very much modified by the adoption or retention of Hindu doctrines and practices which have naturally been introduced into the country by outside influence.

Temple architecture in Nepal may be broadly classified as belonging to either the "Chaitya" or the "Pagoda" style. Built of solid stone or masonry, and severely simple in outline and design, the former is fundamentally Buddhist in origin, and, in nearly all cases, of early date. There are many temples of this type in different parts of the valley. Such a one is Swayambhunath, whose white dome and shining gilt spire is a landmark for many miles around. As a temple it is considered the finest and most perfect specimen of a Buddhist "chaitya" or mould temple that exists. A stone stairway of some six hundred steps, ever steepening and getting narrower as the summit is approached, leads to the plateau on the top.

At the foot of the hill are three colossal figures of Buddha that seem to stand sentinel over the sacred building. Countless monkeys gambol amid the trees that grow thick on this side of the hill. They appear and disappear as one climbs up the "sacred way," staring at the toiling human with a look that is half pitying and half malicious. At the summit, a colossal copper-gilt and double-headed ornament on a stone pedestal confronts one. Representing the thunderbolt of Indra—the "Bajra"—as this is called, is to be found in some form or other in nearly every Newar temple in Nepal. Around the main dome-shaped structure of the temple is a profusion of small monuments—chaityas statues, Buddhas of colossal size, some black, some white, some red.

There is much of interest and beauty to be seen at Swayambhunath—sacred pillars crowned with images of peacocks or divinities, pillars lotus-carved in gilded bronze, and statues that are masterpieces of Newar sculptural art. In a "holy of holies" to the west of the stupa, Buddhist priests tend and keep alive a sacred flame. Regarded as a symbol of the Supreme Deity, this is supposed to burn for ever and for all time, nor has it, legend goes, since the beginning of time itself, ever once been extinguished. On the four sides of the base of the spire are painted in crimson, white and black, two large eyes—the eyes of Buddha. Try as you will, you cannot evade their grave all-seeing gaze. Swayambhunath is the most revered Buddhist shrine in all Nepal, and yet, situated in its very cloisters stands a purely Hindu temple—a striking example of the curious blending of Hinduism and Buddhism to which I have referred already.

A Corner of Swayambhunath.

SHRINES AT SWAYAMBHUNATH.

The story of how this little Hindu temple has come to be erected within the precincts of a sacred building belonging to a rival religion is sufficiently curious to merit recording here. On the occasion of small-pox epidemics Hindus are in the habit of invoking the aid of the goddess Devi Sitla to help them to free themselves from that dreaded scourge. It so happened that at one time, in days long past, the disease was rampant in the valley. Heedless of age, rank or religious persuasion, it exacted a fearful toll. The Buddhists, however, found themselves in somewhat of a quandary, for though they were no more immune from the disease than their Hindu neighbours, they had no appropriate deity of their own to whom they could apply for aid. So they built a new temple and dedicated it to the Hindu goddess, and, ever since, Hindu and Buddhist worship with equal reverence at this little Hindu shrine.

It needs but a visit to Swayambhunath to see how important is the part that religion plays in the life of the people in the valley of Nepal. At all hours of the day the faithful may be seen moving about amongst the shrines and metal images or doing obeisance before the image of some favourite saint. Intermingled as the two religions are here, perhaps India is somewhat eclipsed by Tibet.

The "Om mani padme hum" is to be seen everywhere laboriously written in Tibetan letters. It is interesting to watch the worshippers and observe how one and all make their devotions in their own particular way. The Tibetans prostrate themselves at full length on the stones, arms outstretched, murmuring some prayer; the Newars content themselves with bringing flowers and other offerings, as would a worshipper of Shiva or Vishnu. Yet there is nothing noisy or strident to disturb the air of sanctity that enshrouds Swayambhunath. The droning of the Tibetans, the slow chanting of hymns, with flute accompaniment, even the unceasing clanging of a temple bell is half-hushed and subdued. Everywhere, whether in art, in colour or in sounds, it is the Orient that seems to speak.

From the platform of the temple a lovely view of the valley

and city of Kathmandu unfolds itself. A monkey sitting on the ground at a little distance has observed us as we look over the low parapet and draws closer to where we stand. Little heeds he that the ground on which he lives is hallowed, and the view of the valley—it is fairly safe to presume—impresses him not at all. It is, however, considered an act of merit to feed these creatures, and of this he seems almost conscious, as he throws occasional furtive glances at us through wide, expectant eyes.

As is so often the case where the temples and other monuments of antiquity in Nepal are concerned, there is no really authentic record telling the age and history of Swayambhunath. Tradition assigns the building of the existing temple to one Gorades, a Nepalese raja, and the date between two and three thousand years ago. It further relates that the hill on which the temple stands was raised by Manjusri after he had converted the lake of Naga Vasa into the valley of Nepal.

The legend tells how a single lotus flower remained floating on the lake. In it was embodied the spirit of Simbu (Swayambhu), and on the spot where this flower finally came to rest the present hill was raised. Fantastic and picturesque though the story may be, it is to some extent based on fact. In early days the valley was known as the Tank of the Serpent, and that the whole of it was at one time filled with water geological evidence exists to prove.

Another temple in the same "chaitya" style of building is that known as Bodhnath. Though somewhat less popular and decorative than Swayambhunath, whose picturesqueness is further enhanced by its commanding position on a hill, Bodhnath has none the less an impressiveness that is quite its own. Standing entirely alone, and in the centre of flat, cultivated fields, it forms a no less conspicuous landmark, while when near at hand, one notices that painted in clear colours high up on each face of the square base of the spire are again great pairs of eyes. Bodhnath is the largest of all the Buddhist temples in Nepal, and its administration is entirely in Buddhist hands. Hindus rarely

The Buddhist Temple of Bodhnath.

THE TEMPLE OF PASHUPATINATH.

visit it, though the Newars, who recognise its sacred associations, make use of it from time to time. The temple is kept in repair at the expense of the Tibetan authorities, for Bodhnath is visited annually by hordes of Bhotiyas and Tibetans.

So it is first and foremost a sanctuary for Tibetans, and the pilgrims encamped in the surrounding fields or in the "vihara" —a kind of hostel built round the temple—have, in nearly all cases, come from Tibet. "The links between Lhasa and these two shrines near Kathmandu are still strong"—records a modern writer, "and for northern Buddhists Bodhnath is the holiest shrine out of India."[1]

A link between Kathmandu and Benares is the sacred wooden temple of Pashupatinath—the most important Hindu shrine in Nepal. Situated on the banks of the Baghmati river, in a picturesque gorge, it resembles in more ways than one the holy city of the Indian plains. Though on a smaller scale, here are the same ghats backed by temples and other buildings, and as the Ganges does at Benares, the sacred waters of the Baghmati lap the feet of pious Hindus brought not only from the valley but also from far and wide to die on its banks.

Here the principal temple is built in the "pagoda" style, and a vast collection of smaller temples, shrines and chapels surrounds it. Two romantic Chinese-looking bridges cross the river; seeming to suggest, with a small pagoda-roofed shrine close by, a picture on a willow-pattern plate. It is perhaps the great natural beauty of Pashupati that has made it the subject of the countless legends which have endeared it so much to the sentimental Nepalese heart. One alleges it was built to commemorate the flight of the god Shiva, who, in the form of a gazelle, took refuge in the sacred wood known as Shlesmantaka, in the remains of which the temple stands.

There is a bright, one might say almost a barbaric, aspect about Pashupatinath. As the sun mounts higher, groups of women and girls dressed in the brightest of colours, and men and boys hardly less gaily attired, come to perform their

[1] Percival Landon, *Nepal*, Vol. I, p. 203.

prayers and ablutions. Priests of various orders, some in the well-known saffron and others in robes that are nearly blood-red, pass constantly amongst the devotees, the temple and its surroundings providing a picturesque setting harmonising with the gaily-coloured throng.

In the courtyards are images and shrines, vermilion-painted; roofs shaped like pyramids cover the temples, their edges often ornamented with a profusion of gold leaf; there are sculptured lions, a vast bell and many other sacred objects, while before the main temple, superbly gilt and made of copper, is a large figure of a kneeling bull. Here all is life and colour. Yet but a few yards lower down a wreath of smoke is rising. It comes from some funeral pyre on a buttress that projects into the Baghmati river—smoke from the fire of the dead.

The part that Pashupati plays in the lives of the people is all-important. It is a name that is constantly before one, for nearly all new projects are dedicated to this god. No act of devotion ranks higher than a pilgrimage to this holiest of Nepal temples; in no other deity is the very spirit of Nepal so deeply enshrined.

Though less holy than Pashupati, the richest from a historical and artistic standpoint of all the Hindu shrines in the valley is that of Changu Narayan, dedicated to Vishnu. This temple is built on a steep spur of the Mahadeo Pokhri, one of the principal hills that enclose the valley to the east, and some eight miles distant from Kathmandu. As an example of a Nepalese pagoda, Changu Narayan can hardly be surpassed, and nowhere else in the valley is the religious architecture of the Newars, with its profusion of colour, carving and embossed metal, more picturesquely displayed.

"Not only is Nepalese art of an intensely religious character, ordained and consecrated to the service of the country's creeds," wrote Percy Brown, "but hand in hand with this, it is also supremely symbolic; there is no unmeaning ornament, almost every element in its composition being emblematic of the creed

In Pashupatinath.

it adorns."[1] In the centre of a small courtyard and amidst a seeming confusion of gods and goddesses, animals and weird monsters sculptured in bronze and stone, small shrines and subsidiary altars, rises the main pagoda, the actual shrine.

Of this, all four sides are most artistically and symbolically adorned. On one, in which is the main entrance, is a mass of hammered brass where reptiles and fishes, angels and devils, flowers and other devices can be seen carved by a skilful hand. Ferocious-looking griffins in brass and mounted on pedestals guard the portals; pillars of stone with lotus capitals, one supporting the disc of Vishnu in brass, the other crowned by a metal conch-shell and rising from the back of a huge tortoise, are on each flank. On another side the doorway is of richly-carved wood, encrusted with plaques of beaten brass; time has mellowed the vivid colouring that once adorned the woodwork, and the strong hues have been toned down till they harmonise completely with the picture as a whole. Here the sentinel griffins have given place to two elephants mounted on pedestals carved from stone.

The struts that support the pagoda eaves are profusely and gracefully carved, for it is perhaps in these ornamental brackets that one of the most striking characteristics of Nepalese architecture is to be found. On the pavement in front are bells of varying sizes suspended from stone supports, dragons of ferocious mien, brass umbrellas, altars, while carefully protected by a screen of ironwork is here an effigy in metal—of the founder himself.

Around the courtyard of the temple is the "Dharmsala," or pilgrim's quarter. With its richly carved windows, wooden arcade, and quaint projecting eave-board, it forms a fitting background for the most beautiful of Nepalese shrines.

I have been unable to give anything but the baldest description of Changu Narayan temple; yet what I have said as to the wealth of art distinguishing this and all the other temples and buildings which I have attempted to describe will perhaps suffice to show

[1] *Picturesque Nepal*, Ch. IX, p. 129.

what an exceptionally artistic people the inhabitants of the valley were. This feeling for art and love of everything that the word implies seem to have been instinctive with the Newars, and fortunately it was fostered and stimulated not only by their religious authorities but also by their rulers to the highest possible degree.

Even if the worker in wood has been the most prolific of all Nepalese craftsmen in his productions, it was as metal-workers in copper and bronze that the Newars supremely excelled. Few monarchs and rulers indeed can boast memorials so pleasing and artistic as those of the Newar kings, whose statues in copper-gilt perched on high stone columns are so frequently seen in the Darbar squares of the cities of Nepal.

Regarded from every point of view, these memorial statues reveal a profound knowledge of the principles of art. The pillar itself is graceful and well proportioned; above the lotus capital, round which a snake—the emblem of eternity—will be seen entwined, is a throne of metal-gilt; on this, seated or kneeling in a dignified pose, frequently with hands clasped, is the monarch gazing complacently down upon the city where he once lived and ruled. Fringed with little metal tongues that tinkle not untunefully, a golden umbrella protects him from the sun, or in other instances a canopy of cobras with expanded hoods forms a background no less striking and picturesque.

Besides human beings, figures of gods, lions, elephants, fishes and peacocks often occupy commanding positions on the carved stone pillars; perhaps the *garuda*, the vehicle of Vishnu, part bird, part beast, part human, is the most often to be seen. I know indeed of few, if any, public monuments so attractive as these of the Nepal valley, in which is displayed to the full the supreme excellence of the metal-workers' art in Nepal.

Often in the forecourts of temples portrait figures in metal are to be seen. Though they generally represent people of less eminence than those whose monuments adorn the public squares, these, too, are often objects of great veneration and respect.

Column in the Village of Temi, near Kathmandu.

A Temple Entrance. Kathmandu.

They are the benefactors, sometimes even the founders, of the temple; and in these also is often to be seen work of great artistic merit.

That the Newar metal-worker could be equally skilful and artistic in his smaller creations is proved by the excellence of that branch of his art for which he is perhaps best known, namely, the temple furniture. Full of grace and beautifully proportioned are the lamps, whether standard or hanging, the incense burners, the rice-bowls and the many other temple accessories that the Newar ritual requires.

Though statuary carved from wood is virtually non-existent there is abundant evidence of the wood-workers' craft in Nepal. It would seem, indeed, as if the architecture of the Nepalese houses, with their roof-struts supporting the overhanging eaves of the pagodas, the elaborate door lintels, the beams above and below the window and so on were expressly designed to enable the wood-carver to show his skill. Picturesque above the average, too, are the houses themselves, quite apart from the often exquisite carving by which they are adorned. The plain red brick of which they are generally built is of a rich cardinal maroon.

Most of them are three storeys high, and the projecting eaves are stayed by numerous props. The lowest storey being, as a rule, open in front, columns support the frieze and cornice, again affording rare opportunities for decorative art. Endless indeed are the opportunities afforded to the Newar wood-carver to display his skill by the variety of his designs and the finish of his workmanship. Windows especially come in for the most ornate treatment. Not only, as in the case, too, of the doors, are their lintels and sills prolonged, as if for the wood-carver's special benefit, but to add to the general decorative richness window openings themselves are often filled by lattice-work. Here the dovetailing together of small bits of wood succeeds in producing a most attractive form of window-screen, and the innumerable patterns and devices employed in these are yet another tribute to the Nepal craftsman's art.

Both for structural and for purely decorative purposes terra-cotta is another material freely used in the valley; and although, according to experts the work in this medium hardly comes up to the high standard of that in wood and metal, one sees many columns and capitals in terra-cotta beautifully executed, while many of the figures in front of the temple entrances are also executed in the same material. It is a matter for regret that the Newars of to-day no longer seem able to construct the beautiful buildings with their wealth of wood-carving such as those which adorn the cities of the valley, having lost apparently not a little of their former skill.

A familiar architectural feature of Nepal, alike in town and country, is provided by the stone spouts for drinking water, formed from the *Makara* or dolphin, from whose large open mouth the water flows. The *Makara* is, however, by no means peculiar to Nepal since it is to be found also in Tibet and southern India, as well as in Java and Bengal.

Percy Brown states that it is in fact "a feature in Asiatic art of all countries and all ages," and that it is one of those strange mythical creatures like the *garuda* (vehicle of Vishnu) or *Kirti Muka* (face of Glory) that are always "displayed in connection with certain architectural features, some of which have a complete history of their own."[1]

Though the *makara* appears in many other forms in Nepalese architecture, it is chiefly associated with water, and there is hardly a well or fountain in the valley where the dragon-like mouth through which the water gushes cannot be seen. There are few prettier sights than the long row of *makaras*—there are twenty-two of them—at Balaji, a delightful spot some two and a half miles distant from Kathmandu, where there is a shrine to Narayan.

Balaji is one of those sheltered nooks, which with their almost ideal surroundings of forest and mountain, are often such attractive features of Nepalese scenery. It lies at the foot of a wooded knoll, which is a spur of the mountain known as

[1] *Picturesque Nepal*, Ch. x, p. 166.

Nagarjun, the game preserve of the royal family. Limpid streams gush forth from the hillside to feed a number of ornamental ponds, where the water is clear as crystal and the home of numbers of large carp. Below the terrace where lie the fishponds, rises, castellated and picturesque, a retaining wall. From out of this project spouts, through which the water falls in rippling cascades into a tank below. Splendid trees cast their shadows over the water, and the grass here is green and velvety as that of a lawn at Oxford or Hampton Court.

In a small tank near the entrance to the garden reclines at full-length on a stone bed the god Narayan carved in stone. A canopy of snaked heads projecting above the water surrounds his head, and his arms and head are pillowed on cushions of stone. Only his features are left uncovered by the gently flowing water, and they appear serene and untroubled, though it is nigh on two hundred years since he first reclined on his watery bed. There is no temple to Narayan himself here, the only thing in this way being a small one, Chinese in appearance, dedicated to Durga.

The Nepalese flock in great numbers to Balaji, especially the women, and everyone as he or she enters does obeisance to the god. It is the pilgrims, too, who feed the fishes, buying rice and grain from sundry enterprising people who supply their needs in this respect. But Balaji is popular with both picnic makers and pilgrims. Dotted about on the grass in the sunlight or beneath the shade of the trees are peasants from the neighbouring villages and the more sophisticated folk from Kathmandu. The children, charming as Mongolian children always are, play about, their shrill voices mingling with the murmuring song of the stream. Some wash their garments below the fearsome-looking *makaras*, others comb their jet-black hair. The picture is one of life and colour; yet the religious atmosphere is not lacking, for above the children's laughter and the music of falling water can be heard, clear and never ceasing, the tinkle of the temple bell.

At a place called Bara Nilkantha at the foot of the northern hills of the valley is another shrine of Narayan. Here also there is a sculptured figure of the god in the middle of a basin of stone very similar to that at Balaji, save that it is four times larger. Though the place is invested with much sanctity, it lacks the outward charm and picturesqueness of Balaji. The surrounding buildings are devoid of architectural interest, and only a few trees overhang the shrine.

Though this is actually the chief shrine of Narayan in the valley, it was found necessary to carve a second figure of the god elsewhere. The reason for this is sufficiently curious to narrate. Narayan is an incarnation of Vishnu, of whom the king of Nepal is considered to be an incarnation, but by an age-long custom the king of Nepal is debarred from visiting the Bara Nilkantha, as the two must never meet. Consequently, the smaller image at Balaji was built in imitation of the larger, in order that the king and members of the royal family could pay their devotions to the shrine. There is no objection to their visiting the smaller reproduction.

The splendid woods that clothe the slopes of Nagarjun behind Belaji are full of game. Below, where the undergrowth is thicker, are innumerable chital, also several kinds of deer; on the higher slopes are the familiar ghoral and other wild goats of the Himalayas that frequent this central zone.

THE DARBAR SQUARE. PATAN.

CHAPTER XVI

Patan

THE three cities of the valley are all so attractive to the eye and full of interest, each having its own special charm, that it is difficult for the stranger to decide which of the three makes most appeal to him. Yet, even if there is not much to choose between them, I venture to think that most will probably give the palm to Patan, the city founded by Asoka over two thousand years ago, which lies a little to the south-east of Kathmandu. The road crosses the Baghmati by a brick bridge and enters the city through a picturesque and massive stone gateway.

There is a special dignity, if somewhat tinged with pathos, attaching to Patan. Once a wealthy and important city, it was the capital of the three principalities into which Nepal was formerly divided, and the residence of one of the Newar kings.

In the year 1768, however, it was practically destroyed by the all-conquering Prithwi Narayan and his Gurkhas. The royal palace was dismantled, the houses of the wealthy were plundered of all their valuables and even the temples were desecrated by sacrilegious hands. Traces of what Patan suffered at that time may even still be seen. Yet, though its importance has now completely dwindled, the city still retains much of its ancient charm. Few people can describe Patan as the late M. Sylvain Levi has done, and though he has been often quoted, yet as I was fortunate enough to meet him in Kathmandu in 1922 when he was studying Sanskrit manuscripts, and to accompany him on some of his rambles, I cannot resist quoting him again.

I may add that it was only a few years ago, during a visit which I paid to his wife and himself in their charming house on the *rive gauche* in Paris, that he told me he still considered Patan the most beautiful place he had ever seen. Writing in his book *Le Nèpal*, in 1905, he said: "Patan is a vision of fairyland, more charming than the too uniform Jeypore. Everywhere temples, pagodas, charityas, all the types of Indian architecture adapted by the most picturesque taste, red bricks, green bricks, gilded bronze, brown wood, sport deliciously in the sunlight."[1]

And again, "The last remains of a dying past still call forth visions of dazzling beauty. Who could describe this jewel, this Darbar square? Under the living brilliance of a sky that still leaves the eye undazzled, the royal palace spreads out its front, enriched by the hands of sculptors and carvers glorying in their work. Upon it the hues of gold and blue light up the darkened timber, and over against it in the centre, like the idle caprice of a great artist, is a work of almost luminous white stone, of pillars crowned by bronze statues, of light-filtering colonnades and of fragile dream temples—guarded all by a company of fantastic beasts, chimeras and griffons."[2]

Such is M. Levi's description of this ancient city. Yet, as I have suggested, there is a certain melancholy air of abandonment and ruin about much of Patan. The Darbar square, however, never fails to leave a deep and lasting impression, for here in this "Street of Palaces," perhaps more than anywhere else in the valley, seems to abide the very essence of the spirit and romance of Nepal.

There are still in evidence at the present day the five stupas that Asoka set up in Patan as a memorial of his pilgrimage to this part of the Himalayas—the most notable memorial in all his mighty empire, so it has been said, that the emperor ever raised. The one in the centre of the town has been rebuilt and thus altered considerably in appearance from the original, but the other four, at the four points of the compass, remain much as they were in those far-distant days when they were first built.

Externally, there is nothing artistic about any of these stupas; they appear merely as hemispherical moulds of plain brick, severe and simple in form, while of anything in the way of ancient inscriptions M. Levi found not a trace. Whatever

[1] *Le Népal*, Vol. II, p. 341-2. [2] *Ibid.*, Vol. I, p. 63.

The Darbar Square. Patan.

A Temple at Patan.

secrets they may contain are most jealously guarded, for throughout the ages these stupas have remained intact, and bid fair to do so to the end of time.

Patan is the scene of the greatest and most important of all the Newar festivals, the Machendrajatra, for amongst other temples in this city is that of Machendranath. Although all classes of Nepalese observe the three well-known and purely Hindu festivals, the Holi, Dasehra and Diwali, yet there are certain festivals in Nepal which find no counterpart in the plains of India, and are peculiar to the Newars. Such festivals, which may therefore be regarded as purely national, are the festivals of Narayan at Balaji and Bara Nilkantha, the Bhairabjatra, in honour of Bhairab, the Gaijatra, the Indrajatra and the Great and Small Machendrajatra, to mention only a few.

With the two religions intermingling with each other as they do in Nepal, it is often difficult to define the exact religious significance of many of the festivals such as I have just named, which take place at intervals throughout the year. Thus in the Indrajatra, which is a so-called Hindu festival, the officiating priests are Buddhists, for they are Banhras—a purely Buddhist sect. On the other hand, Hindus join heartily in the Machendrajatra, which is in character essentially Buddhist, the temple itself having been originally built—in the beginning of the fifteenth century—as a purely Buddhist shrine.

The Machendrajatra is with good reason the most popular of all the festivals, for whatever his religion may be, every Nepalese believes it to be the one that brings the rain, and rain, which is wanted at this time for the sowing of Indian corn, is certainly said always to fall during the Machendrajatra. In fact, of course, as the festival takes place in the early days of June, the phenomenon is really due to the arrival of the south-west monsoon. What St. George is to England, Machendra is to Nepal. Further, like the other deities in that country, he is worshipped by the followers of both creeds. In the festival which bears his name, the god is exhibited to thousands of his followers who flock to Patan from all parts of the valley to do honour to their patron saint. The image that represents him is, however, neither costly nor artistic, for it is merely a block of wood, roughly hewn and painted dark red. There are three distinct phases in the festival.

First, when the god is taken out of the temple at Patan, and, in the presence of a large crowd, undressed and bathed; secondly, when the image is paraded in a processional car through the streets of Patan; and lastly, when the image is disrobed by the officiating priests, and his shirt exhibited for all to see and worship. After this, a smaller car bears the image, now unclothed, amidst much acclamation, to a spot near Patan, where it remains for six months.

The dragging of the car through the streets is the most striking part of the whole ceremonial, and one, too, that might be considered eminently characteristic of Nepal. The car itself is a huge unwieldy object with eyes of startling colour painted on the wheels, and with an upper structure nearly seventy feet high which contains the deity. Neither vehicle nor road being adapted for rapid progress, the procession, even if it be triumphant, is always painfully slow. It takes in fact about four days to traverse the distance—some one and a half miles. Volunteers from the crowd however are never lacking to replace casualties amongst the hundred or so stalwarts who have harnessed themselves to the ropes and from time to time fall exhausted by the way.

So to the accompaniment of strident and barbaric music, creaking, bumping and swaying, the great car with its precious burden passes slowly along the narrow streets. Elephants, gaily caparisoned, with members of the royal house seated in the howdahs of silver and gold, add a touch of Oriental splendour to the scene, while girls bearing garlands of flowers entertain the multitude with oft-repeated refrains. Every wooden balcony is packed with excited spectators, as are also the platforms of the temples and larger buildings that front the street.

Although many centuries have elapsed since the Machendra-jatra first figured thus prominently in the religious life of the valley, its popularity would seem each year to increase rather than to wane.

In writing on Kathmandu and the other cities of the Nepal valley, such repeated reference has been made to the temples, festivals and religious observances as to create the impression that the Nepalese are an intensely religious race. This cannot be said, however, to be entirely the case. The rulers of the country are of course strict followers of the Hindu faith in all its details, and it is really owing to their example that the majority of the people have adopted Hinduism as the fashionable cult. But the constant pilgrimages to the various temples, the vast attendances at the various festivals, the punctilious observance of the ritual and so on, are chiefly confined to the dwellers in the valley itself, and as a race the Nepalese are not very strict followers of any religion, be it Buddhist or Hindu. So far as most are concerned, it is the dancing, music and general hilarity —considered practically indispensable at most of the festivals, Hindu especially—which are the chief attractions.

In the more important Hindu festivals are to be found certain features which are peculiar to Nepal. Thus on the seventh day of the Dasehra festival, the day known as Phulpati, a grand review of the Kathmandu garrison takes place on the fine Thuni Khel parade-ground in the centre of the city. There are few who do not make an effort to be present on this occasion, especially as it is one of the rare opportunities of seeing the king. A feature of the parade is a *feu-de-joie* lasting some twenty minutes, in which the artillery join—a fine test of endurance for one's ears. All round the parade-ground the people stand many deep, dressed in their best clothes, the feminine element adding further touches of colour to the natural brightness of the scene. In the centre of the troops are the combined bands of all the regiments. Some of the tunes they play are not discordant to European ears, but they are unfamiliar, for it is the music of Nepal. Consistent with the military spirit which pervades the country, the ninth day of the Dasehra is devoted to the worship of arms, the principal actor in this ceremony, generally known as the "Blessing of the Colours," being the commander-in-chief. The form the ceremony takes is the sacrificing of innumerable bullocks and goats to the goddess Durga by the usual method of decapitation.

I will forbear to describe this spectacle in detail, less because of its gruesome nature than because this has been so often done. Decapitation of a fully-grown animal with one stroke of the khukri is a feat demanding exceptional strength and skill, and the executioner is invariably acclaimed with tumultous applause. He is further rewarded with the gift of a new white pagri or turban, which the highest in rank present at the ceremony ties round his head. On the other hand, failure to sever the head completely with a single stroke meets with audible disapproval, being considered an omen of ill-luck. Unpleasant also is the form this disapproval takes, for the face of the unskilful performer is smeared with the blood of the victim which has just suffered at his hands. The principal scene of this phase of the Dasehra festival is the courtyard of the Kot, or Darbar council chamber at Kathmandu.

Barbaric as is the ceremony described, this rather ordinary looking courtyard has been the scene of events far grimmer than this. There is no space here to deal at length with the famous "Massacre of the Kot" in 1846. Suffice it to say that within this historic enclosure, chiefly to satisfy political ambitions, many of the highest in the land lost their lives—the prime mover in this "reign of terror" being the then ruling queen.

Though to-day the ceremony involves the slaughter of animals only, the scene in revoltingly wild and savage. Every officer is expected to contribute at least one victim, the senior ones providing two or three, and as there are no fewer than seven regiments in the Kot, the number of animals slaughtered is very large.

By the time the head of the last victim has fallen to the ground the arena has become an absolute shambles. Headless carcases lie about on all sides, and the ground is literally running with blood; the heap of bleeding tokens almost hiding the Brahman priest who officiates at the ceremony, and before whom each head as it falls has been placed. Then follows the blessing of the colours, at which, as I have said, the commander-in-chief assumes the principal rôle. Advancing to them as they stand, all resplendent with garlands of flowers and coloured streamers, and from the commencement of the ceremony grouped in the centre of the court, he blesses each regimental colour in turn. Here, too, must the goddess of war be propitiated—in token of which, his hands that clasp the fabric of the flag leave on each side a clear impression, for they had been dipped in a large basin of vermilion.

Another great Hindu festival celebrated with much enthusiasm by the Nepalese, and one that is much more pleasant to describe, is that known as the Diwali, held in honour of Lakshmi, the goddess of wealth. This festival, which is celebrated by all Hindus, takes place some twenty days after the Dasehra, and lasts for five. It is to commemorate the great victory of Vishnu, the husband of Lakshmi, over the giant Marakasur. The illumination at night by rows of little earthenware lamps placed in the windows of each house making a fairyland of the landscape is traceable also to the same myth. The legend goes that after slaying the hitherto invincible giant, Vishnu entered his city in triumph the following day, and to do him honour the citizens illuminated their houses. Hence the Diwali is known as the "Festival of Illumination" to this day. All this is ordinary Hindu mythology, and in no way especially connected with Nepal. Whatever its religious significance in early days, however, the Diwali has at any rate a special significance of its own for the Nepalese.

Though cards and other games of chance are indulged in all over India during this festival, yet it is the only occasion on which gambling is permitted in Nepal, and for three glorious days and nights the Gurkha is allowed to gamble to his heart's content. Being a born gambler it is hardly necessary to add that he takes full advantage of the opportunity that has—all praise to Lakshmi!—come his way.

CHAPTER XVII

Bhatgaon and Nawakot

PICTURESQUELY situated above the cliff of the Baghmati river and standing out a patch of red and brown amongst the green of the rice-fields, is Bhatgaon, the third and last of the important cities of the valley. It lies in a fold of ground at the foot of Mahadeo Pokhri on the eastern edge of the valley and is distant about eight miles from Kathmandu.

Though this city was also captured by Prithwi Narayan, it escaped much of the plunder and maltreatment meted out to others of the valley. Hence the buildings and ancient monuments are in a better state of preservation, and there is an air of life and prosperity that is lacking in Patan. If the Darbar Square is smaller than that of Patan, in its colouring and in the grouping of its monuments and temples it is hardly less picturesque. But the chief attraction of the Darbar Square at Bhatgaon will always be the celebrated golden door forming the entrance to the palace, and known always as the Golden Gate. Nothing indeed could well exceed this doorway in splendour of ornamentation. "Perhaps the most exquisitely designed and finished piece of gilded metal-work in all Asia," was how Percival Landon described it, and he went on to say that nothing could rival this superb piece of Newar craftsmanship either in Lhasa or in Peking.[1]

If the Golden Gate is the most beautiful of many beautiful things in the city, the temple of the five stages, known as Nyatpola Deval, is easily the most conspicuous building in Bhatgaon. The most monumental example of a Nepalese pagoda to be found in the country, it is said to have its almost exact counterpart in the Pagoda of Horinje, in Japan, constructed at least ten centuries earlier. It was built early in the eighteenth

[1] *Nepal*, Vol. I, Ch. X, p. 217.

IN THE DARBAR SQUARE AT BHATGAON.

TEMPLES IN BHATGAON.

THE TEMPLE OF THE FIVE STAGES. (NYAT POLA)

Street Scene in Bhatgaon.

century by the king, Bhupatindra Malla, and is very striking, if not unique, in design, being built on five terraces or stages one above the other, and connected by a flight of steps, on either side of which are ranged symbolic figures of colossal dimensions carved in stone.

The lowest figures represent two giants, said to be Jaya Malla and Phatta, athletes of Bhatgaon Raha, each of whom is reputed to have had the strength of ten men. Above them are two elephants supposed to be ten times stronger. The third pair are lions supposed to be ten times as strong as the elephants. Again, in their turn, ten times as strong as the lions are the sarduls, or dragons, which make the fourth pair, till one comes to the last, the goddesses Baghini (Tiger) and Singhini (Lion), whose strength is far superior to all. Five roofs, one above the other, and each slightly smaller than that immediately beneath it, compose the upper part of this striking-looking building—one of the most characteristic perhaps in the whole valley of Nepal.

There is an old-world air about Bhatgaon, due perhaps to its comparative isolation and distance from the main roads of the valley, which constitutes its distinctive charm. In the bazaar the shops are well-stocked and numerous, but the streets lack the bustle and activity of Kathmandu. Smaller than either of the other two cities, Bhatgaon is perhaps the most attractive. Like the others, too, it is surrounded by an atmosphere of romance and historical association. Yet Bhatgaon has perhaps, in some ways, an air of the "country-town" about it. Nepalese who have travelled outside the valley say that in its daily life it is more like a town in the outlying parts of Nepal. They see in its peaceful squares something that is a little different from any other town in the valley, much as in Paris a Parisian, provincial-born, will sometimes see in some "place" away from the beaten track of the tourists *un petit coin de province*.

There is nothing that could really be called unhealthy about the climate of the valley at any time of the year. Its elevation being, however, only some four thousand feet, it is apt to be somewhat warm and enervating during the summer and the rains. Though the British Residency is built on slightly elevated ground, and is actually one of the healthiest spots in the valley, Sir Chandra used to relate with a smile that it was originally selected by his predecessors as being the most unhealthy part of Kathmandu.

But a change of air is still very necessary at times, and so on the north-western and eastern hills respectively two hot-weather resorts, known as Kakani and Nagarkot, have been created, where no mosquitos exist, and where a cool wind always blows.

The ascent to Nagarkot from Bhatgaon is a short and easy one. It is a pretty little village, and is the summer residence of various members of the royal family. From here there is a magnificent view of the unexplored country to the east, and the finest view of the snows, it is said, that can be obtained. I have only been to Nagarkot once, and on that occasion, though the day itself was fine, the snows were completely obscured by clouds. Winding away into the distance is a path that one gazes upon with interest, for it is the main track to Tibet.

Kakani, a tiny hamlet, lies on the same range of hills, some distance to the west, the Kakani ridge, with the mountains known as Manichur, Sheopuri and Kaulia, forming the northern boundary of the valley of Nepal. On a flattish crest, and at the spot where the main track to Nawakot begins to trend downhill, stands the summer residence of the Envoy. This is a white bungalow, unpretentious enough in itself, but with a view that must be one of the most magnificent in the world. For on a clear morning the whole range of the Central Himalayan system stands revealed, making a truly grand and impressive picture. Beyond the fertile and well-watered valleys, rugged and lofty mountains, capped with snow, rise to east and west. Amongst the higher peaks can be picked out some bearing well-known names. On the east Everest is clearly visible, while far away to the west, Machha Pucchar, the "Fish-tail" subject of countless Gurkha songs, raises its twin-peaked head. Between these again are other mighty giants of the Himalayas—such as Yassu, Dhaulagiri and Gosainthan.

At the foot of the last-named is a deep and sacred lake, to which devotees from all parts of India make annual pilgrimage, though it entails a toilsome journey of eight days up rocky, perilous tracks. In this lake, whose elevation is said to be 15,000 feet, is a massive boulder, considered by the faithful to represent the god Mahadeo.

The following words were written by Oldfield, but no European's eyes have ever gazed upon the sacred lake of Gosainthan. "The pious worshippers of Shiva, as they stand on the edge of the sacred lake, look on this unhewn rock as a divinely carved representation of Mahadeo, and they can trace out in it the figure of the deity reclining full-length upon a bed of serpents. This rock must have been deposited in its present position when the lake was filled by an ancient glacier, and sunk as it is in the centre of the ice-cold waters it can never have been touched by mortal hands."[1] The scene must be one to stir the emotions; the background of snow-clad mountains, with the pilgrims round the still, transparent pool.

There are other pilgrimages to distant eastern shrines, both arduous and painful, yet few can surpass in toil that made by those who climb the narrow ice-bound path that leads to Gosainthan. From where one stands on the ridge in front of the Kakani bungalow, one can see the Tadi and its tributary the Likhu threading their way through the rice-fields in the fertile valleys below, while away to the south-west the red bricks of some pagoda-shaped buildings in Nawakot stand out clearly in the morning sun.

The number of Europeans who have visited Nawakot is limited to an occasional British Representative or members of his staff who have spent a few days there on fishing bent. Sir Chandra, however, was kind enough to accord me permission to go there on one occasion, as I was anxious to see a place so inseparably connected with the past history of Nepal.

[1] *Sketches from Nepal*, Vol. I, Ch. II, p. 31.

From the rest-house at Kakani the path falls almost precipitously in some places to the south-west. With my companion, Donaldson, of the 2nd Gurkhas, who was training the Nepal Escort that year, we descended for several miles through rough, scrubby country, only relieved by occasional bright-coloured patches of Indian corn. A few miles of this brought us to the Likhu valley that had been so clearly visible to us from the ridge above, and where the maize had given place to rolling fields of corn. Thence through the cornfields, till we reached the Nawakot valley, where we crossed the Tadi river by a fine suspension bridge. Here we were in the region of the rice-fields, and the air had lost its freshness, for we were only two thousand feet above the level of the sea.

For fruit and garden produce Nawakot stands unrivalled in Nepal; guavas, tamarinds, bananas, custard apples—all common to India—grow there in profusion. Its mangoes and oranges are said to be second to none in the world, while its pears, apples, apricots and plums rival those grown in the orchards of Kashmir.

Nawakot to-day is a place of no importance or attractiveness. Once the favourite residence of the Regent Bahadur Shah, and for many years the scene of Prithwi Narayan's court, the little town has lost all the glamour of its byegone days. It is rarely visited nowadays by any member of the ruling house, and then only as a temporary halting place on a journey to some province in the west. To-day it possesses merely a double line of houses, the buildings that we had seen standing out amongst the sal trees, as we looked down from the distant Kakani ridge, being the Darbar and a temple dedicated to Bhairavi, built in the Chinese style of Kathmandu.

The town itself is on a spur that runs south-west from Mount Dhaibung or Jibjibia and is flanked on the west by the Tirsul river, with the Tadi running about a mile below it to the south.

The Tirsul—or Tirsul Gandaki as it is also called—is a beautiful river. A deep arrowy stream, blue in colour, it guides the pilgrims up to Gosainthan, as it does also the traveller and trader to Tibet. Skirting the town on the west, it joins the Tadi river at Devi Ghat. The scenery at Devi Ghat is wild and romantic. Over stony beds and between stupendous boulders, the river roars and foams, and here again the water is absolutely transparent and of the same azure blue. Devi Ghat itself is a very holy spot under the protection of Bhairavi whose temple stands in the little town some eight hundred feet above.

We walked beside the Tirsuli for some three miles up river, to where a picturesque bridge spans the stream. On the further side runs the highroad to Gurkha, the historic capital of Nepal, and cradle of the ruling dynasty, but through what kind of scenery it passes must be left to the imagination, for no European has ever crossed this bridge.

As in the Terai, so in the warm damp valley of Nawakot, malaria rages from March to November. The inhabitants are of a different race from those who live in the town, which stands on a ridge. Only tribes like Tharus and others immune or semi-immune can live with impunity in the disease-infested atmosphere of the valley. In the town are Newars, Chetris, Gurungs, Magars and representatives of all the other Nepalese tribes.

From the high ground behind the little town we looked out upon a scene all the more attractive for its being so little known. To the south-west we could trace the course of the Tirsuli river, flashing here and there in the sunshine, a winding silvery thread. Westwards, across the river we could follow the road to Gurkha as it ascends the pass known as Manibhanjang, till growing fainter and fainter, it disappears behind the hill. Immediately below us lay the little town, its many-storeyed houses bearing witness to an importance that has vanished, with Bhairavi's temple and the Darbar building raising their heads proudly amongst the roofs of red and brown. Below the town again, and stretching eastward far into the Likhu valley, lay the rice-fields in their terraced squares of emerald green. To the south, on the very crest of the ridge, the glint of the sun on its windows revealed the bungalow at Kakani some twelve miles away.

Though it be to-day but a shadow of its former self, yet the name Nawakot is one to conjure up much past history. Above all does it recall memories of Prithwi Narayan Sah. For it was from here that in 1768 he directed his attack upon the valley, Nawakot being in those days always regarded as the key to the valley of Nepal. To-day only the pagoda roofs of the Darbar are there to remind one of the past.

We camped for the night on the little Thuni Khel, or parade-ground above the river. Above its gentle murmuring we could hear from time to time the sound of singing or laughter from some party of Gurkhas who were tramping, doubtless heavily laden, along the road to Kathmandu. And of all the sounds in this country, that is one of the pleasantest, for in the cheerful, uncomplaining spirit of its simple inhabitants, more perhaps than in anything else, is to be found the greatest charm of Nepal.

We would have given much to have been able to take the road as far as Gurkha, or alternatively to have followed the Tirsuli river, as it winds its way through the valley into the unknown west. But neither course being possible, we could philosophically congratulate ourselves on having at least seen Nawakot.

For my part I have been exceptionally lucky for a European in seeing as much of Nepal as I have, and though in some cases I have had little more than glimpses, yet they have been sufficient to afford a very good idea of what the rest of the country is like; and if this little country, tucked away in a far corner of the Himalayas, is attractive to all Europeans, it can be understood how greatly it must appeal to anyone in a Gurkha regiment, with all the associations with its attractive people which that implies.

When we returned from Nawakot we found that the Diwali festival, the "Feast of Lights," was about to begin. And to see the valley during the Diwali is a thing to be remembered.

To appreciate what is to be seen at its best, one should climb a little way up the hill at the back of the Residency at night. It is very peaceful up there. Now and then you catch the ring of a Gurkha's laugh on his way home to a distant village; sometimes the echo of a temple bell comes up from the valley

THE JUNCTION OF THE TADI AND TIRSUL RIVERS AT DEVIGHAT.

[Photo by Major R. A. Briggs.

STREET SCENE AFTER EARTHQUAKE.

[Photo by Major R. A. Briggs.

REPAIRING A TEMPLE.

below; otherwise all is still. But from where one stands the valley seems transformed into a kind of wonderful fairyland with lights in all directions from the big glow below that marks Kathmandu and the other towns to the tiniest glimmerings high up and far away where some peasant has illuminated his humble home. And as you think of where you are—how far from the western world—and of the many things that have happened in the valley below, with its old-world cities, its beautiful rivers, its palaces and its temples, you realise as perhaps never before all the charm and the spell of Nepal.

The earthquake of the 15th January, 1933, which ravaged Bihar and north-east India generally, wrought terrible havoc in the valley of Nepal, with the result that some at least of the former architectural glory of the country has departed. By eliminating, however, all traces of completely collapsed buildings and by repairing in the original style those partially destroyed, the Government has been surprisingly successful in remedying matters and in preserving as far as possible unaltered the original appearance of the three principal cities. While here and there a temple will be lacking, and some of the buildings will have the appearance of having been "restored," a sufficiency of the original structures remains to delight the eye and make one rejoice that so much that is beautiful has escaped destruction.

At the same time there is no denying that, apart from vanished temples and the like, much else that charmed the visitor in the narrow streets and other parts of the valley cities has departed, never to return. For the opportunity has been taken, wisely enough no doubt on general grounds, to carry out "town-planning schemes" which have involved still further sacrifices of the older buildings; and so, as has happened so often nearer home, quaint gabled roofs have been replaced by corrugated iron, and the picturesque in general has been sacrificed to the practical.

The damage in the valley was enormous, and in the two towns of Bhatgaon and Patan there is still evidence of devastation on every hand, many of the streets being neatly lined with piled-up debris on either side. In both towns the Darbar Squares, celebrated for their architectural beauties and ancient monuments, suffered severely, several of the largest temples on one side of the Darbar Square at Patan having completely collapsed, although those on the other side remained comparatively intact. Again, although the Golden Gate itself fortunately escaped serious damage, the roofs of a number of the principal buildings in the Darbar Square at Bhatgaon were torn off, though even the earthquake failed to dislodge the little gilt monarch perched high on his pillar, who remained throughout in his attitude of pious devotion—a mute witness of the desolation that surrounded him. The famous "temple of the five stages" (Nyatpola Deval) at Bhatgaon was also badly damaged. It has now, however, been completely rebuilt, and from a recent photograph which I saw of it looks much as it did before.

In Kathmandu, the damage was equally severe, though wonders have been achieved here in the work of restoration—special efforts having naturally been exerted to this end in the case of the capital and nerve centre of the kingdom. Here, as in Bhatgaon and Patan, the Darbar Square suffered sadly, the Hanuman Dhoka, the temple of Talcju, and other important buildings all being considerably damaged. As regards other well-known buildings, the clock tower collapsed completely, as did also the upper half of the monument (Dharara) on the parade-ground, the latter itself being disfigured by a gaping fissure traversing nearly the entire length of the ground. The general post office, the town hall and the military hospital were other buildings likewise badly damaged, though all have now been completely repaired.

On the other hand, many of the best-known temples and religious shrines in the valley were spared. Thus the famous Changu Narayan escaped with very small damage, while the most important of all, Swayambhunath and Pasupati, were practically untouched, their immunity being shared (so General Krishna Shumshere tells me) by many other buildings and places—Kirtipur, for instance—lying on high ground. But naturally

[Photo by Mrs. Kilburn.

DESTRUCTION IN THE DARBAR SQUARE. PATAN.

[Photo by Major R. A. Briggs.

DARBAR SQUARE, BHATGAON, UNDER REPAIR.

[Photo by Mrs. Kilburn.

COLUMN OF BHIMSEN, AFTER THE EARTHQUAKE.

[Photo by Mrs. Kilburn.

FISSURES ON THE THUNI KHEL.

this was not the explanation accepted by the multitude. On the contrary, the fact that at any rate the largest and most important of their holy places had escaped destruction was naturally attributed to divine intervention, resulting, it is said, in a great revival of religious faith throughout the valley.

Less fortunate were the fine palaces of the members of the royal family and the nobility, most of which suffered considerable damage, to the extent of complete destruction indeed in the case of some, though others came off more lightly. Thus while the king's palace was severely damaged, General Sir Kaiser Shumshere had nothing more serious to lament than the collapse of the bandstand in his beautiful garden. On the other hand, at Thapathalli, the residence of Jung Bahadur, the Gole Baithak (Round Hall) was reduced to ruins, while General Krishna tells me that his own palace was so badly damaged that it had to be completely demolished. It is pleasant to be able to add, however, that even these palaces are now in a complete state of repair once again.

The imposing entrance to the grounds of the Singha Darbar, the official residence of H.H. the Prime Minister, was also badly damaged, although the main building itself suffered little harm. But the entrance has been completely rebuilt, and after the manner adopted in many European cities, the front of the palace is nowadays floodlit.

Infinitely more serious of course than the destruction of any architectural treasures, was the grievous loss of life incurred, no fewer than 4,296 being killed. Indeed, had it not been for the fact that the earthquake took place in the afternoon, at a time when the soldiers of the garrison were on parade instead of in their houses, the casualty list would probably have been vastly greater. His Highness the Maharaja, it may be added, was in camp in the western Terai at the time a big-game shoot was actually in progress when the first violent shock was felt.

It was indeed in every way a national disaster, redeemed only in retrospect by the fine behaviour of the population and the admirable energy and wisdom displayed by the Government both at the time and subsequently in handling the situation. The measures adopted were indeed a model of promptness and efficiency. Thus, among the earliest steps adopted, free medical aid was given to the sick and wounded, three lakhs of maunds of rice were distributed, while official control was established immediately over the distribution and price of foodstuffs. Then later, land and sufficient money to cover the rebuilding and restoration of their homes were given (not loaned) to people without resources, while a fund for the assistance of victims was opened by the Maharaja, to which he himself made a donation of fifty lakhs of rupees. It is indeed difficult to do full justice to His Highness's achievements on this occasion. By no means a rich country, Nepal was suddenly faced with a burden that even larger and wealthier states would find difficult to bear. And it was fortunate that in Maharaja Sir Joodha Shumshere it possessed a man capable of rising to the emergency in his country's hour of need. For it is entirely to His Highness's energy, his unsparing efforts and his constant personal supervision in the work of rescue and restoration, that Nepal has made so rapid a recovery from one of the greatest disasters in all its history.

As regards the work of restoration, the Government wisely concentrated at first on rebuilding the dwellings of the people, in conjunction with the repairing of the temples and shrines, and although it was thought at first that the whole work of reconstruction would take at least ten years, such progress has been made that it is now considered that by 1938 there will be little outward evidence of the disaster remaining to be seen —except in the form of the many improvements which reconstruction has rendered possible. Thus, fine modern thoroughfares are already replacing many of the old narrow streets—a notable example being the one named "New Street," which leads off the parade-ground, having a roadway sixty feet wide, flanked by modern buildings in some cases four or five storeys high, and lit by electricity.

I have not seen the valley myself since the earthquake, but

[Photo by Major R. A. Briggs.

DAMAGE TO H.M. THE KING'S PALACE.

[Photo by Mrs. Kilburn.

ENTRANCE TO SINGHA DARBAR.

[Photo by Mrs. Kilburn

NEAR PATAN, AFTER THE EARTHQUAKE.

[Photo by Major R. A. Briggs.

WRECKAGE IN BHATGAON.

Lieut.-General Krishna Shumshere, the Nepalese Minister in London, has been most kind in placing at my disposal all available information on the subject. Not only has he shown me his own photographs of the squares, streets and buildings which were most severely damaged, before and after the disaster, but he has also given me a book written in Nepali by one of his nephews which furnishes an authentic record of what actually took place. With information drawn from these sources, therefore, together with the photographs kindly lent me by my friend Major Briggs and Mrs. Kilburn, who have been in Kathmandu fairly recently, I have been able to give readers at any rate some idea of what the valley has been through.

CHAPTER XVIII

Central Nepal

I HAVE already shown, in Chapter VI, how the recruiting of Nepalese for the Gurkha regiments of the Indian army dates from the time of the war between the British and the Gurkhas in 1814–1816. But if in those early days there were enlisted enough men for the formation of some three regiments only, it is to-day a very different story, for there are now no fewer than twenty Gurkha battalions, and, in addition, a considerable number of Gurkhas are enlisted in the Kashmir State Forces, the Burma Military Police, the Assam Rifles and in the Indian Hospital Corps. It may be noted, however, that Nepal, being closed to Europeans, the recruiting officer for Gurkhas cannot, after the manner of his confrères who recruit for other races enlisted in the Indian army (Dogras, Sikhs, Mahrattas, Pathans, and so forth) himself scour the country for recruits, but sends instead recruiting parties from each regiment into the Nepal hills from his recruiting depôts in British territory, which lie conveniently close to the Nepal frontier. Before the year 1885 when, as previously stated, Maharaja Sir Bir Shumshere introduced measures which greatly facilitated the obtaining of recruits, regiments used to send out their own recruiting parties who brought the recruits back with them to their regimental headquarters as best they could, very often by smuggling them across the border. After this date, however, the whole system was centralised, and two main depôts were established for the reception of the recruits brought in—one at Gorakhpur in the United Provinces, and the other at Darjeeling.

Of the two thousand recruits, however, which approximately constituted our annual requirements, more than threequarters are brought into Gorakhpur. For as sixteen out of the twenty battalions are composed of men who come from the country

Recruits at the Recruiting Depôt, Gorakhpur.

Family Pensioners at Gorakhpur.

On the Way to Batauli. (Butwal.)

to the west of the actual Nepal valley, the geographical position of Gorakhpur is particularly favourable, especially as it is also an important junction on the Bengal and North-Western Railway, whose branch lines touch the frontier at many points.

The actual enlistment of recruits, it may be noted, forms but a small part of the recruiting officer's work, since he is also responsible for everything to do with pensions, and it is this which takes up most of his time. For although pensioners of the four battalions composed of eastern Nepal men attend the Darjeeling office and the civil treasuries at Purneah and Darbhanga, and again those who live in districts of Central Nepal nearest the Nepal valley draw their pensions and have their pension claims attended to at the British Envoy's office in Kathmandu, the great bulk of them come to Gorakhpur. And so, during the winter months—for owing to the Gurkhas's aversion to great heat it is closed during the summer—the depôt at Gorakhpur is a scene of great activity.

It is at its busiest between the middle of December and the middle of March, when there is a constant stream of pensioners of every sort and description—sturdy, well set up men who come to draw their pension for the first time, ancient dames travel-stained but garrulous, battle-scarred warriors lacking a limb or bearing some other mark of the Great War, comely young women with large gold earrings and shawls Italian draped, and last but not least, the charming children, Mongolian-featured and complete miniatures of their parents in the matter of dress, for whom provision is also made. The entire absence of any kind of servility which I have already mentioned as being one of the chief characteristics of the Nepalese and their comparative freedom from the shackles of caste are particularly noticeable in connection with this matter of their pensions, and make the recruiting officer's work so much the easier and more pleasant.

Although the Nepal Government has arranged with the British authorities to pay the pensions of very old and infirm people at the principal headquarters of the civil districts throughout Nepal, yet a certain number of men and women well advanced in years still prefer to make the journey to Gorakhpur, where they meet old friends, discover long-lost relations and so on; it is, in fact, a general gathering of the clans, which they greatly enjoy and think well worth while the trouble entailed. For not a few may come from remote villages fifteen or twenty marches distant, by tracks that are often stony and precipitous, and where mountain streams have to be forded on the way.

Although sad and pathetic cases naturally occur now and again, the pensioners are a very cheery crowd on the whole, while the naïve simplicity of some of the old folk is also at times very amusing. Thus great delight was caused in my office on one occasion when out of gratitude for some service we had been able to render her, an old lady flung her arms round my neck and warmly embraced me! I must admit, however, that this was an exceptional instance, since I cannot claim to have received a similar token of affection from any other member of her sex during the five years my duties brought me into contact with them!

Everything is done nowadays to make the pensioners as comfortable and contented as possible during their stay in Gorakhpur, after their long and often arduous trek from the hills. Whereas formerly they used to camp under the trees or against walls in any convenient spot in the vicinity of Kuraghat—the open grassy site where the depôt is situated two and a half miles away from the town of Gorakhpur—there is to-day available for them a spacious Dharmsala or rest-house, with water and every facility for cooking and so forth, where they can be much happier and live under far better conditions.

Of the many improvements of recent years, however, the extension of the railway as far as Nautanwa, the town on the Nepal border fifty miles north of Gorakhpur, through which the great bulk of the Nepalese who come from western Nepal must pass, has been probably the greatest boon to the Gurkha bound for Gorakhpur, be he pensioner, soldier or recruit. For he is thereby saved the twenty odd miles of foot-slogging along the tedious piece of road from Nautanwa to Bridgmanganj (the station on the Bengal and North-Western Railway formerly chiefly used as railhead) which, in the case of recruits and pensioners alike, usually proved the most trying part of their long journey. The improved transport conditions have not been confined moreover to the Indian side of the border, for in 1931 the Nepal Government established a motor service between Nautanwa and Batauli, the Nepalese town twenty miles inside the border at the edge of the foothills, thereby averting much of the danger of passing through the dreaded Terai.

I had heard so much about Batauli—so near and yet so far where the European is concerned—that I asked Sir Chandra Shumshere's permission to visit it in the winter of 1920, and thanks to His Highness's kindness, was able to spend an interesting three days there during Christmas of that year. My companion on that occasion was one Lieutenant Ganesh Bahadur Regmi, a Nepalese officer detailed for special duty at the recruiting depôt—a genial, happy-natured person, and my guide, philosopher and friend on more than one adventure in Nepalese territory. Large stone cairns painted white and spaced at longish intervals mark the actual frontier, which is about a mile distant from Nautanwa. The motor road between Nautanwa and Batauli did not exist in those days, and there was in fact no real road at all. The "Trespassers will be prosecuted" notices, however, that too often cramp the style of the English wayfarer are to all intents and purposes unknown in the east, and as the greater part of our journey lay through cultivated country dotted here and there with clumps of trees —typical northern Behar scenery—it really mattered little if we occasionally lost the track or not.

A large house, high and imposing, built in the orthodox Nepalese style with white-painted projecting eaves—so often a prominent feature in the Nepalese landscape—which we could see long before we reached it, proved to be the residence of the chief official of Baitheri, the first place of any importance after leaving British territory. Otherwise, for nearly fifteen miles, the country and its inhabitants differed not at all from what we had left behind. After this, however, the fields of corn and sugar-cane gave place to the high grass and scrub jungle of the Terai, which continued for five miles till we crossed the Tindho Khola and found ourselves in the long, straggling street that is the main thoroughfare of Batauli.

To the simple Nepalese villager there is something almost magical in the name Batauli. Its praises have been sung in a hundred Gurkha songs, for in far-off Gurkha villages the name conjures up visions of a bustling cosmopolitan town. And indeed it is a place of considerable importance, for not only do the hill people come to it in great numbers for purposes of trade and litigation—for it is an administrative and legal as well as a commercial centre—but it is also the headquarters, during the winter, of three regular battalions, with two large parade-grounds, barracks and offices, while just above the town is the residence of the Governor, an imposing house standing in its own grounds.

To the European traveller approaching it for the first time however there is nothing particularly striking about Batauli. And yet although many of its four hundred houses are merely temporary buildings of sun-baked brick with corrugated iron roofs, others are ornamented with old Nepalese carving, so that it at once seems different from an Indian town. In the streets, too, sturdy Mongols mingle with dark-skinned Biharis, while the shop-keepers are in some cases Marwaris, in others, Newars. Batauli looks, in fact, partly Indian, partly Nepalese.

Almost wholly Nepalese, however, is the part of Batauli known as Kasauli, the far side of the Tindho Khola, where my camp had been pitched, and where below the barracks which house the Palpa regiments during the winter, numbers of sturdy hillmen, the bearers of bales of merchandise for the Indian markets, make their camp, as one speedily realises. For the smoke of their fires can be seen in every direction, and the throbbing of the dumpo (oval drum) with occasional snatches of familiar Nepali songs, continues practically unceasing night and day.

To the eye, my camp was a perfect delight—a work of art in green brushwood with the neatest of huts as living and sleeping rooms, trim-cut paths and garden seats, and with a high fence to frustrate the inquisitive and curious, the whole the handiwork of a party of blue-clad soldiers from the local regiments.

Although the climate of Batauli cannot be said to be healthy, and epidemics of the dreaded awal ravage the town from time to time, it is said to be possible to live in it all the year round. It is, however, almost entirely deserted by the Nepalese during the hot weather, its only inhabitants then being Marwaris and Indian merchants, who continue to ply their trade in such articles as cotton-cloths, cooking-pots and—Batauli's chief commerce—the clarified butter known as ghi. The troops also are only there during the winter, for directly the hot weather starts they are moved up to the chief town of the province of Palpa, often itself called Palpa, but more commonly known as Tansing. The Palpa battalions are recruited very largely from the Magar tribe, as Magars predominate in this part of Nepal, and two of them, the Sabuj and Bhawanidal regiments, formed part of the second contingent which served in India during the Great War, these two battalions being stationed at Dehra Dun.

On my first visit to Batauli I did not go beyond the hamlet of Nawakot, perched some four or five hundred feet above it, on the road to Palpa. Two years later, however, Sir Chandra gave me permission to visit the Massiang ridge, in the Palpa hills, some twelve miles to the north-east of Batauli, and as at that time (save perhaps for an occasional Jesuit missionary in the dim past) no European had ever set foot in the Palpa country, it was for me a trip of exceptional pleasure and interest.

One leaves Batauli by a modern suspension bridge, and then begins at once to climb up to Nawakot—a somewhat toilsome proceeding, for the track is littered with huge stones and rocks, and the gradient is steep.

If the transition from the atmosphere of the plains, with their listless Aryan inhabitants, to a country people with sturdy Mongols strikes the traveller as he leaves rail-head at Siliguri for the ascent to Darjeeling, it is almost more remarkable here when one starts to climb the steep path which leads to Nawakot. For, whereas a fair number of plainsmen are always to be seen on the Darjeeling highway, and there is of course a not inconsiderable population of Indians—Bengali clerks, Marwari shopkeepers, and so on—in the town itself, on crossing the spur of the hill on which Nawakot stands, one bids farewell to India altogether, since there is no longer a trace of it to be seen.

Except on the occasion of the annual Shivatri pilgrimage when many outsiders, chiefly Indians, make pilgrimages to sacred centres in the hill country, Nepal is as closed to Asiatics as it is to Europeans. Thus it is only with the express permission of the Maharaja that representatives of Indian trade who wish to do business with the Nepalese, persons engaged on a special mission and so on, are allowed to travel in the country. Even so the total number of such visitors from the outer world who find their way to the interior of Nepal is very small, and on the few occasions when I have been allowed to leave the beaten track for a little I have never seen anybody but Nepalese.

At Nawakot there are only a few small huts, a guardhouse and the remains of an old fort. At a spot overlooking the plains below stands a small stone cairn, erected—so Ganeshbahadur told me—in memory of a Gurkha bugler who had performed some act of great gallantry in the war against the British in 1815. For being a place of great strategic importance, Batauli was the scene of considerable fighting in this campaign, and was, indeed, for some time in British hands, as the remains of an old British fort still testify. From Nawakot, the path descends steeply through pretty wooded scenery, and then passing through the village called Jhirdi comes out at the Dobhan river which is spanned, rather surprisingly, by a fine suspension bridge. The shop-keepers in the village shops are invariably Newars, the trade of the country being, as I have already said, almost exclusively in their hands. And they do plenty of business, for the stream of heavily-laden hill-folk on the Palpa road is

Bridge Over the Dobhan River. Palpa District.

Customs House at Morek.

well-nigh unceasing, and few who have the means can resist the opportunity of making some purchase or other.

The shopkeeper's stock-in-trade is never very pretentious. "Hurricane" lanterns, umbrellas, packets of "Gurkha" cigarettes are usually much in evidence, while for the fairer sex there are bright bead necklaces and bangles in great variety. It may be noted, however, that when requiring the more serious and expensive articles of jewellery—the heavy anklets, large gold earrings and so forth, which, as I have said elsewhere really represent money in the bank—the Gurkha women patronise the Sunar, or goldsmith—a gentleman who, despite his lucrative and artistic calling, belongs to the lowest or most menial caste. While on this subject I may add that others at the lowest point of the social scale are the tailors (who belong to a tribe known as Damais, from whom, curiously enough, musicians are also chiefly drawn), butchers, boatmen, carpenters, miners, pottery and leather workers, to mention some of the principal menial castes. Not only can these never be enlisted, but the men of the fighting classes cannot eat with them. They are outcasts in the truest sense of the word. All artists, by the way, seem to come off particularly badly, for classed with the musicians amongst the dregs of society are the Gains, or "singing bards"!

After crossing the suspension bridge the road runs beside a beautiful stream of clear water until one comes to the customs house at a tiny village called Morek. The imposing retinue, almost invariably including an officer, that accompanies the European traveller, absolves him as a rule from any form of examination at Nepalese custom houses, but inhabitants of the country are submitted to a fairly searching one, and it is amusing to see the official in charge—often a Brahman—questioning some group of long-haired wild men of the woods on their way to the plains for the first time, or to watch the resigned but bored expression of a "Lahoriya" (a Gurkha serving in India is called a "man of Lahore") as he reluctantly disgorges packets of contraband cigarettes.

As I was recruiting officer on the first occasion I did this trip to Massiang, I was an object of great interest, not to say veneration, to the various parties of recruits whom we met on the road on their way to Gorakhpur. In the first place, I was certainly the first European whom they had ever set eyes on; and secondly, it was pointed out to them by the recruiters who had brought them from their villages that their fate lay entirely in my hands! For of the many who set out on the long journey—some come from districts as many as sixteen days' marches away—full of hope, a great many return full of sorrow—rejected by the recruiting officer. The standard of physical fitness for the army is indeed high, and the supply always exceeds the demand. And for the rejected recruit there is not only the fatigue of the long trek home again to be faced, but also the humiliation of his position when he gets back to his village. "Hullo! Back again! You haven't served for long!" is the kind of remark with which he is greeted by his friends. In fact, owing to their inclination to take up any kind of employment in India rather than go home again if the army authorities reject them, it has been found necessary to adopt measures whereby rejected recruits are escorted back to their villages. Otherwise quite a number would probably not return to their homes at all.

But to return to the customs house at Morek. Besides the ordinary examination for customs purposes of goods in transit, taxes are also collected here, the receipt for payment being stamped in the palm of the hand! From Morek the path drops gently down to the Sisnu (Nettle) Khola, a stream known to the people of those parts for the coldness of its waters, and after following its left bank for several miles, ascends steeply to the Massiang ridge, on the near side of which is the village bearing that name.

Beautiful as the panorama is that unfolds itself from almost any point of vantage on the Massiang ridge, the picture is doubly alluring to anyone who has been closely associated with Gurkhas, and who is acquainted with the wealth of legends and historical episodes attached to so many places in the country spread out before him. From the most easterly part of the

A Powa or Rest-House. Palpa District.

View from Massiang Ridge, Looking towards Tansing.

ridge one can see the track as it drops suddenly to the Dumri Khola and then climbs up to the town of Tansing on the ridge opposite. Tansing lies high on the crest of fairly steep and undulating hills, and though some four miles distant, the Governor's palace, with some other prominent buildings and the large parade-ground, can be clearly seen from the ridge.

High up again on the wooded spur to the west of the city the white roofs of the famous Kal Bhairab shrine—containing a figure of Bhairab that is a replica of one in the palace square at Kathmandu—rise clear-cut against the sky. A small track that runs under the western flank of the ridge and disappears on the other side leads to Riri, a well-known market town on the banks of the Kali river, and a place said to have been visited during the fifteenth century by one of the Rajput kings who, according to legend, laid the foundations of the Gurkha race. Riri is, however, chiefly celebrated for its sanctity, being regarded by the Nepalese as being almost as holy as Benares, and, as at Pashupati in the Nepal valley, so here dying men are placed upon a ledge with their legs in the Kali river, their bodies being burnt after death and the ashes strewn upon the water. Together with Pashupati, Gosainthan and Muktinath, Riri ranks as one of the four great places of Hindu sanctity in Nepal.

There are many mango topes in the locality, and oranges and lemons are also said to be plentiful. Otherwise, generally speaking, the soil is rather poor in this part of the country, and save in the sheltered valleys of the Kali river, very little rice is grown. Round Massiang itself, some four thousand feet or so above sea-leavel, they grow chiefly Indian corn, wheat, buckwheat and barley.

The houses, with their thatched roofs and walls coloured with red clay, and surrounded by patches of cultivation, have a comfortable and cheerful appearance. The locality is in fact a prosperous-looking one, many of the inhabitants being Gurkha officers or soldiers, either pensioned or still serving in their regiments in India, who have acquired higher standards of cleanliness and civilisation than generally prevail in their village homes. Curiously enough, the first orderly I ever had in a Gurkha regiment came from a village quite close to the Massiang ridge, and he used to say what a pity it was I should never be able to see the part of the world he lived in, because unfortunately "Sahibs are never allowed in Nepal"!

He also furnished in his speech an example of what is so commonly found in Nepal, where the people of one village will often talk a totally different dialect from those living in another village but a short distance away. Thus though the great majority of the Magars in Palpa speak their own dialects, known as Magarkura, in this man's particular village no one spoke anything but the lingua franca, Nepali. The girl he married, however, who came from a village on the same side of the hill as his, spoke Magarkura, her mother tongue, her knowledge of Nepali—as is often the case with the women who speak their tribal dialect—being somewhat limited. Happily, however, their domestic relations seem to have been in no way impaired by these linguistic differences, for when I saw the man, now a pensioner, only a few years ago on the Palpa road, he told me that his knowledge of Magarkura was still practically nil, and that he had still the same wife!

There is an unceasing stream of wayfarers on the Palpa track, and nearly all, men and women alike, carry their belongings on their back. Among them practically every type of Mongolian is to be seen. Aryan-featured Chetris, Gurungs from Lamjung wearing their hood-shaped blankets, long-haired, wild-looking Puns from far-off Baglung, quite a few Tibetans, and, of course, many "Lahoriyas" (pensioners, leave-men and so on), pass in endless procession. From where we stand we can see the country over which they have to travel, and it is certainly fair to look on. But it is to be supposed that they hardly appreciate its beauty as we do, for in the first place it is not for pleasure that they are travelling many weary miles heavily laden; and secondly, scenery rarely has the same attraction for orientals that it possesses for Europeans—certainly where the less educated folk are concerned.

Village of Massiang. Palpa District.

Palpa Landscape. Central Nepal.

To the European traveller, however, the characteristic mountain scenery of Nepal—tier upon tier of lofty mountains, some crested with dark-coloured firs, others bleak and forbidding-looking—cannot fail to be impressive, especially when there is a background of snow. But unfortunately, for the reason which has been explained, this part of the world can only be visited on exceptional occasions, and the snows are not always very accommodating. Thus when I visited Massiang in 1922 they were not visible at all. And the few others who have been there since, such as Major Briggs of the 5th Gurkhas in 1930, and Major Morris in 1931, have had to take the same chances, though the former apparently was rewarded with a beautiful view. In December, 1932, however, when by the kindness of His Highness Sir Joodha Shumshere, the present Maharaja, we were allowed to stay a week at Massiang, Morris and I had a most wonderful view of them. From west to east in their pale-pink loveliness they fringed the entire horizon, making a picture such as few have been privileged to behold.

Three peaks, Maccha Pucchar (the fish's tail), Annapurna, and a third, to which the local people give the name Dhaulagiri (though experts question its correctness), all long known to me from Gurkha songs, but which I had never hoped to see, stood out from the range in the most striking manner. Rarely have I seen the "glory of Himachal" reveal itself as it did on that day. And it was fortunate that it did so, for we had had overcast skies and rain almost daily since our arrival, and it was not until our last day that our patience was rewarded and the primary object of our visit achieved. Unfortunately, it was quite early in the morning—a few minutes after dawn to be exact—when a clear view was finally obtained, and even then only for a very few minutes. Hence, although the snows themselves stood out clearly in the early morning sun, the hills in the foreground and middle distance were in deep shadow, thereby making it impossible to obtain a photograph in which both the snows and the rest of the landscape could be clearly seen.

And now having tried to give some description of the valley and of Central Nepal, that is, generally speaking, off the beaten track of Europeans, I will devote a little space to the extreme western border, where the Kali river represents the frontier line between Nepal and the British province of Kumaon.

CHAPTER XIX

The Western Border

THERE are three main approaches into western Nepal from British India—the large frontier town of Tanakpur on the west bank of the Kali river, in British territory, and the terminus of a small branch railway line; the bridge over the Kali at Jhula Ghat, a village that lies east of Pithoragarh in the Almora district; and lastly, the bridge at Dharchula some three days march above Jhula Ghat, across which runs the road to Bajhang and Bajura, the two most northerly provinces of western Nepal. I have never been to Dharchula, but Sir Chandra Shumshere kindly granted me permission to cross the river at both the other places and penetrate a few miles into the country on the further side, where one was struck at once by the contrast between this and the Darjeeling frontier five hundred miles away. It could, indeed, hardly be greater, for instead of the damp, misty climate and fertile soil of the eastern Himalayas, you have here a country where the rainfall is slight and the soil is that of the contiguous province of Kumaon—barren, rocky and dry.

And not less striking is the difference in the appearance of the Nepalese in this part of the country. Belonging chiefly to the Chetri tribe, the Dotials and Bajhangis, as the inhabitants of these districts are known, looked much rougher and more uncouth than any Gurkhas with whom I had ever been brought into contact before, giving the impression that existence in these extreme western districts was a good deal harder than that known elsewhere.

They bear, in fact, little resemblance to their sturdier neighbours in Central and Eastern Nepal, and in customs, appearance and even language—although they are conversant with the lingua franca, Nepali—they hardly differ at all from the Kumaonis who inhabit the country to the west of the river Kali. Their affinity with these last people is not to be wondered at, for prior to the Treaty of Segowli, in 1816, the present British provinces of Garwhal and Kumaon were both part of Nepal. Thus, living as they have been for many years on either side of this western border, and merging into each other by intermarriage and in other ways, the two races naturally have many characteristics in common. Hence the races inhabiting the extreme western districts of Nepal—Doti, Baitadi, Jumla, Bajhang and so on are often not classified as Gurkhas at all.

So, too, in the matter of religion. Just as the farther one goes eastwards in Nepal the races become more and more influenced by Mongolian ideas in the matter of customs and religion, so as one progresses in a westerly direction they become more and more disposed to Hinduism, until they eventually lose every trace of the Mongolian influence, and become as Hindu in culture as the Aryan-speaking tribes that are found in the adjacent districts of British India.

I went to Jhula Ghat by way of Almora and Pithoragarh. At Almora, which has been the permanent station of the 3rd Gurkhas since the regiment was raised in 1815, I stayed for two days with Mr. and Mrs. Hugh Ruttledge (the former, well known as the leader of two Mount Everest expeditions, being at the time Deputy Commissioner of Almora), in their beautifully situated bungalow with its wonderful view of the distant snows; and Mr. Ruttledge kindly helped me in the matter of transport for my journey to Jhula Ghat—some four marches in an easterly direction from Almora. The road lies through beautiful country, thickly wooded and with frequent glimpses of the snows, till one comes upon Pithoragarh, the last stopping place before Jhula Ghat, where there is a large settlement of Gurkhas.

The question of the line-boy, the term by which a Gurkha born and brought up in British India is generally known—although it should, strictly speaking, be confined to the sons of Gurkha soldiers born and brought up in the regiment—raises a rather difficult problem. Although in the first generation they deteriorate but little in the matter of physique, and thanks to educational advantages denied to their compatriots born and bred in Nepal, they usually grow up to be extremely intelligent, they are—certainly the second generation—as a rule hardly up to the standard of the hill-bred article as far as things like morals and dependability are concerned.

Being born and bred in India, they have a tendency to lack the characteristic associated with the Gurkhas of Nepal. Hence a line-boy, unless his claims are very exceptional, is rarely enlisted in the ranks of a Gurkha regiment, and when he is, it is usually as a clerk, signaller, bandsman or bugler, in which capacity his intelligence makes him a valuable recruit. Nevertheless, in view of the fact that the Government has in the past always encouraged the establishment of Gurkha colonies in the neighbourhood of Gurkha cantonments like Dharmsala, Almora and Dehra Dun, the claims of line-boys to be provided for in the Government service are undeniably just and cannot be disregarded.

Moreover, of those enlisted in the army as signallers, buglers, or indeed in any military capacity, not a few rise to commissioned rank, where their superior intelligence naturally stands them in good stead. During the Great War, when the replacing of officers in Indian regiments was a constant difficulty, the line-boy was often the obvious man to be promoted, and what is more, he rarely failed to make good. Since the war, the number of Gurkhas domiciled in British India has swollen to very considerable proportions, and though an accurate estimate is difficult to obtain, it is said to be at least 400,000, the odds being that it is really much higher.

If a tendency to deteriorate is to be noted even in the Gurkha colonies near cantonments where at any rate the children are brought up amongst people who are for the most part of their own kith and kin, it is easy to understand that it is no less evident in the case of those reared in a big Indian city like Calcutta where there are said to be some thirty thousand Gurkhas. Evil communications corrupt good manners, and the consequences are indeed only too apparent in the case of Gurkhas brought up in such surroundings. For it may be noted that the Gurkha deteriorates even more rapidly in such circumstances than the average Indian belonging to such tribes as Sikhs, Punjabis, Mahrattas, Pathans and so on, although in mentioning Calcutta I am referring chiefly to the Gurkhas who eke out an insecure existence there by some means or other, and not to those doing duty in the police or some other form of government service, where they are under proper supervision and control. Hence it is easy to understand that both the Nepal Government and the Government of India do all they can to encourage Gurkha soldiers to return to their own country upon pension or retirement, to which end steps are in fact being taken by the Nepal Government to provide land for those who own no property of their own.

Apart from one or two pensioned officers, I did not, as a matter of fact, come across many Gurkhas in Pithoragarh, and the few that I did hardly resembled Nepalese at all. For it seems that the Gurkhas in this district have for many years intermarried much with the local women, and consequence have now much more the characteristics of the Kumaonis than of the Nepalese.

From the last bend of the path that takes one from Pithoragarh to Jhula Ghat, and from where it descends steeply to the village, one can see the Kali river as it runs swift and impetuous between precipitous banks of rock and trees, and the suspension bridge with a white guard-house on the further side where Nepalese sentries are ready to deny passage to anyone who fails to produce a permit to enter Nepal.

Standing in its own grounds on the British side of the river and behind the few small shops that constitute the village of Jhula Ghat, is a tall white house in Nepalese style, the residence of a Nepalese official connected with the fort of Baitadi, to visit which Sir Chandra had kindly granted me a permit. Although I do not know if he still lives there, it was the occupant of that house—a Nepalese lieutenant—who was in charge of

GURKHA LINE-BOYS.

GURKHA LINE-GIRLS.

[Photo by Major C. J. Morris.

THE WESTERN BOUNDARY OF NEPAL—THE KALI RIVER.

[Photo by Major C. J. Morris.

VILLAGE OF SIMALGHAT. WESTERN NEPAL.

my small escort when I went to Baitadi in March, 1926, and, like every Nepalese official who has been my companion on such occasions, he was a most courteous and pleasant man. As we were crossing the bridge he incidentally told me that he did not think that any European had successfully run the gauntlet of the guard on the Nepal side before!

From the bridge the path ascends steeply for some three miles to the village of Baitadi, in itself not imposing in appearance, but a place of some importance as being the chief town of the district of that name, and as possessing a fort garrisoned by a company of infantry. I was most courteously received by the military governor, and sat with him for a long time in the chief room of the local court-house, where he held a sort of impromptu levee in my honour, at which I found myself naturally the centre of all attention.

In the course of such a short visit—we returned to Jhula Ghat after about an hour's stay in Baitadi—one naturally obtained only a superficial impression of the hill country of western Nepal, but it is undeniably less beautiful than the other parts of the country. From the character of the soil, too, which, like that of contiguous Kumaon, is dry and barren, the crops are obviously of a very inferior quality, which no doubt goes to explain why the Nepalese in these parts are so inferior in physique to the other races in Nepal.

From Jhula Ghat, four marches southward through beautiful Kumaon scenery took me to Tanakpur, where I found my friend Morris, who is at the time of writing on the Mount Everest Expedition, waiting for me in the dak bungalow. It was then the middle of March, and it was beginning to get hot in this part of the world. Only the Kali river separated us from Nepal.

The Kali is known as the Sarda in its lower reaches, and at Tanakpur bears little resemblance to the deep, swift-flowing stream that runs through Jhula Ghat. For here it is a broad and beautiful river, with waters icy cold from the melted snow brought down from the great mountains at its source. There being no bridge, primitive boats which are nothing more than hollowed tree trunks convey one to the further side. A guard-house and a few buildings comprising customs house and forest offices are the only permanent structures at Simalghat, the village on the Nepalese side. For, save for a few Government officials who have to remain throughout the year, no one lives there during the hot and rainy season when malaria is so rife.

The village was anything but deserted, however, at the time we were there, for, it being March, the annual exodus had not yet begun, and on the open ground near the offices Marwari shopkeepers from India were plying a busy trade in temporary booths, of which, a few weeks later, not one would be seen. But even during the hot weather, life in Simulghat seems to have its compensations from the sportsman's point of view, for the surrounding forests are full of small game. It was clear, too, that our escort—two Brahman Subadars with a couple of sturdy Magars—had a very tender spot in their hearts for "Ole Man River." Icy cold even in the sweltering heat of summer, and full of fish, it certainly must help considerably to make conditions more bearable for those who have to bear the heat and burden of the day throughout the year.

Our escort insisted that we should visit the temple of Baramdeo, some two miles away in the forest, and from the awe-struck way in which they spoke of it we were prepared to find something imposing in the way of a shrine. In appearance, however, it proved decidedly disappointing—being but a small, roughly constructed shrine in a clearing of the forest—but it is held in great veneration in those parts, and its peacefulness and seclusion seemed to invest it with a certain atmosphere of mystery and impressiveness.

For the rest, Simalghat is typical of Terai forest country in so far as it is a boundless wilderness of big trees. Such indeed are the extent and the quality of the Nepalese forests that her forest wealth can justly be described as the country's greatest material asset. For of the great Himalayan timber belt a thousand miles long, that stretches from Sikkim to the Indus, no fewer than five hundred are in Nepalese territory. "Not

[Photo by Major C. J. Morris.

The Temple of Baramdeo.

only are these Nepalese forests important on account of their extent, but conditions of climate and rainfall are most favourable to the vigorous growth of forest vegetation," records Mr. J. V. Collier, of the Indian Forest Service, whom Sir Chandra Shumshere entrusted with the direction of the forest department in Nepal, "and those favourable conditions are reflected in the very high reputation the Nepal forests enjoy for the size and quality of their timber."

Of the three main zones into which the Nepal forests can be roughly classified, namely, the tropical zone up to about 4,000 feet, containing trees like sal, shishan, semal and toon; the temperate zone, from 4,000 to 10,000 feet, with oaks, maples, pines, spruces, larches and firs; and the Alpine zone, above 10,000 feet, where rhododendrons and junipers are the characteristic trees, the first is, from a commercial point of view, by far the most important. The trees of the temperate zone certainly fulfil a most useful purpose in supplying the population of those parts with fuel and timber, but commercially this zone is of little importance, and the most valuable timber is found in the belt of forest that stretches out from the foothills into the plains of the Terai. Although in many places the deadliness of the climate for half of the year makes the replacing of the forest by cultivation—part of the afforestation policy of the Government—a practical impossibility, the chief timber trees in the Terai forests, such as the sal, asna and shisham, are conserved and treated as valuable State property, so that they form a valuable source of revenue.

The absence of railways and the mountainous nature of the country make it commercially impossible to develop much of the mineral wealth of Nepal, with the result that although there are large resources of copper, iron, lead and coal in various parts of the country, little has been done with them so far. The few mines in existence are worked in the most primitive way, without any attempt to use modern scientific methods, and it is only some of the more valuable minerals that repay the heavy cost of freight to the rail-heads on the Indian frontier.

It is hoped, however, that the new development board which, under the energetic chairmanship of H.E. Commanding-General Sir Bahadur Shumshere, the eldest son of the Maharaja, is directing the general development of the country, will effect improvements in this respect and turn to better account the natural riches of the country.

CHAPTER XX

The Eastern Border

ALTHOUGH a visit to Nepal, or even crossing the Nepalese frontier, may not be possible for everyone, it may be of interest to note for the benefit of those desirous of learning more of the Gurkha's cheerful and engaging personality that in Darjeeling there is what may be termed an Indian Gurkha-land, where he can be studied at first hand without let or hindrance. And the transition from India to Mongolia begins almost as soon as the toy-like train of the Darjeeling-Himalayan railway puffs out of the station at Siliguri, the terminus of the East Bengal Railway at the foot of the hills, and begins what is probably the grandest railway journey in the world. For the dark-complexioned, gloomy Indian who presides in the shops over his counter, where cigarettes, betal-nuts and curious-looking edibles are displayed in true Oriental confusion, has given place to the vivacious, much-bejewelled lady of Nepal, and on the road that runs by the side of the railway as the line runs through dense jungles of cane and grass, from now onwards only Mongolians are to be seen. Within the space of a few minutes the traveller has been transported into an entirely new world.

Up to the year 1878, tongas—the two-wheeled, four-seated carriage so well-known in India—were the only means of travelling the forty-nine miles that separate Siliguri from Darjeeling. That year, however, largely as the result of an agitation by the tea industry, a company was formed for the purpose of constructing a steam tramway to supersede the tonga, and the Government aiding the enterprise substantially by permitting the line to be laid along the cart-road, the construction was pushed forward very rapidly, and by the year 1881 the line was carried as far as Darjeeling. The steam tramway was then dignified with the name of a railway, and its designation changed to the Darjeeling-Himalayan railway, as it is called to-day. Yet the Darjeeling cart-road, that wonderful example of engineering work, constructed some twenty years earlier, in order to replace the old military road built by Lord Napier of Magdala in 1839, was an even greater achievement than the railway. And it was the previous existence of this road that made the alignment of the railway a comparatively easy task.

With an average breadth of twenty-five feet and with easy gradients throughout, it is one of the best mountain roads in India, yet the difficulties which the engineers had to contend with during its construction were colossal. Owing to malaria and the plague of insects there were constant outbreaks of sickness amongst the coolies which impeded progress in the lower valleys and levels, while when it came to clearing the virgin forest of the Terai, only the personal energy and example of the engineer in charge prevented the labourers from deserting *en masse.* In the hills again the work was obstructed by totally unexpected difficulties. The ground proved much more rocky and difficult than had been foreseen, and a few miles below Kurseong, the small hill-station twenty miles from Darjeeling, a cutting had to be made in the face of a solid mass of rock about 500 feet high and as many broad. No wonder that the supply of gunpowder for blasting frequently gave out and that a stretch of only six miles in that sector alone cost two and a half lakhs of rupees! Small wonder either that the whole road took eight years to build, or that it stands to-day as one of the finest monuments to the engineering skill of the public works department in the whole of India.

To-day every mile of the train journey is full of interest. The line winds in and out along the hill sides, often running along the edges of precipices and tremendous gorges, where the traveller from his carriage window looks down a dizzy drop of many hundred feet. At one spot the line describes a complete figure of eight, at another a hill is climbed in a series of zigzags, with the engine alternately in front and behind as it draws or pushes the train. The curves, too, are so sharp that the train is in the shape of the letter S for most of the way. The travelling is nevertheless smooth and steady, and I have always thought the train journey more comfortable than doing it by car, when the incessant turns of the road, taken at high speed, make one positively giddy.

Except where spurs of wooded hills have been cleared for tea gardens, and where the red-roofed factories and managers' bungalows make a pleasant break in the landscape, the line runs through dense primeval forest practically the whole way, with fresh beauty revealing itself at every turn. To the south, stretching as far as the eye can see and streaked by the rivers that meander out from the mountain gorges, the vast plains of Bengal shimmer faintly under an Indian sun. In front rise the first ranges of the Himalayas, thickly wooded to their summits and 5,000 to 8,000 feet above the plain. The vegetation varies as the train ascends. Thus for the first few miles after leaving Siliguri the line runs through dense jungle of cane and grass, impenetrable wildernesses which are the haunts of tigers, bears, sambhar deer, rhinoceros and other game.

As the train climbs still higher, the jungle gives place to forest, where clumps of bamboo often sixty feet high can be seen amongst the oaks, mimosas, acacias, India-rubber and mulberry trees that flourish in this zone. Just below 4,000 feet, peach and almond trees can be seen in full blossom in January, and some five hundred feet higher are fine spreading chestnuts such as one might see in some English park. At 5,000 feet appear the first of the beautiful Himalayan tree ferns, fifteen or twenty feet high, and over 6,000 feet again comes the region of such trees as oaks, maples, laurels, magnolias and birches—trees that characterise what may best be described as the temperate zone.

Darjeeling comes comparatively late into the history of British rule in India, for it was not until the beginning of the nineteenth century that the Government, represented in those days by the East India Company, was brought into direct relations with the tract of country which now bears its name. In those days it formed part of the dominions of the Raja of Sikkim, a petty chieftain whose time was chiefly—though somewhat unsuccessfully—employed in trying to stem the growing power of the Gurkhas, who by the year 1810 had indeed overrun Sikkim as far eastward as the Tista river, and conquered and annexed the Terai country lying between the Tista and the Mechi river—now a region of valuable tea-gardens owned by Darjeeling planters. The aggressions of the Nepalese on the northern frontier of India however invoked a sterner retribution than any which the Sikkimese chieftain could impose, and at the close of the war of 1814, to which I have referred elsewhere, the tract of country which they had wrested from the Raja of Sikkim was ceded to the East India Company and the Raja reinstated. Further, in 1817, the territory in the Terai between the two rivers just mentioned was restored to him and his sovereignty guaranteed.

Thus did British intervention check the Nepalese encroachment in this direction and in fact prevent Sikkim from being turned into an outlying province of Nepal. Under the treaty of 1817 the Company assumed the position of paramount power in Sikkim, and any disputes between the Raja's subjects and those of such neighbouring states as Bhutan and Nepal had to be referred by him to the British Government for arbitration. And it was the settlement of such a dispute that led to the acquisition of Darjeeling by the British authorities and its adoption as a hill sanitorium as it exists to-day. For when, in 1828, General (then Captain) Lloyd was deputed to effect a settlement in disputes that had arisen on the Sikkim and Nepal frontier, he sent such enthusiastic reports on "the old Goorkha station called Dorjeling," where he stayed for six days in February, 1829, and which he described as being "well adapted for the purpose of a sanitarium," that negotiations were opened with the Raja of Sikkim for the cession of Darjeeling in return for the equivalent in money or land.

And so on the 1st of February, 1835, a deed of grant in which

"I, the Sikkimputtee Rajah, out of friendship for the Governor-General, who has expressed his desire for the possession of the hill of Darjeeling on account of its cool climate, for the purpose of enabling the servants of his Government, suffering from sickness, to avail themselves of its advantages, hereby present Darjeeling to the East India Company . . ." was executed by the Raja of Sikkim, and what was then a worthless uninhabited mountain became British territory. It was, as a matter of fact, ceded unconditionally at the time, although subsequently the Government granted the Raja an allowance of 3,000 rupees, later raised to 6,000, as compensation. Thus was Darjeeling acquired by Great Britain after its discovery by General Lloyd, whose grave (he died in 1865) can be seen in the cemetery below Birch Hill Park, exactly a hundred years ago.

Beyond a few Lepchas—the original inhabitants of the country—and Limbus, an eastern Nepal tribe, occasional raiders from Nepal and a stray Tibetan or two, the Darjeeling hills were at the time of their cession to the Indian Government practically uninhabited. And the first great immigration of Nepalese from the west dates from the appointment of Dr. Campbell, at that time resident in Nepal, who was transferred to Darjeeling with the title of Superintendent in 1839. For if Darjeeling is much indebted to Lloyd, to whose personal influence with the Raja of Sikkim the cession of the territory was mainly due, no less is it indebted to Campbell for his unceasing and successful efforts to develop its resources, and above all for his introduction of the tea plant.

Campbell found Darjeeling an inaccessible tract of forest, with but a handful of inhabitants. With such energy, however, did he apply himself to the task of developing the station, stimulating trade and commerce, and attracting immigrants to cultivate the mountain slopes, that within ten years the population had risen from 100 to about 10,000, chiefly as the result of immigration from the neighbouring states of Bhutan, Sikkim and Nepal, in all of which slavery was prevalent at this time. By 1852, there were no fewer than seventy European houses, an excellent sanitorium for troops and others, well-made roads, a hospital, a jail, and a simple system of administration in such matters as justice and revenue which was well adapted to the unsophisticated Mongolians with whom Campbell had to deal. The subsequent planting of tea in the hills, as the result of which Darjeeling tea has become known throughout the world, I will come to later on.

The rapid development and ever-increasing importance of Darjeeling at this time were, however, to become a source of much jealousy and annoyance to the Prime Minister of Sikkim, Namguay, who, in consequence of the great age and infirmity of the Raja, had taken the administration of the State virtually into his own hands. This man, popularly known as the Mad Diwan, was notoriously corrupt and ambitious, threw every possible obstacle in the way of friendly relations between Sikkim and the British Government. His own conduct towards the British was studiously insolent and aggressive; British subjects of good character were rigorously excluded from Sikkim, while notorious offenders and political refugees were, on the other hand, granted sanctuary. At the same time all attempts to trade and any efforts to further mutual intercourse between the two governments only met with insults and rebuffs from the Sikkimese officials, who seemed indeed to have been specially chosen for their incapacity and insolent manners.

The climax was reached in the winter of 1849 when Sir Joseph Hooker, the eminent botanist, and Dr. Campbell, both of whom were travelling in Sikkim with the permission of both governments, were on some flimsy pretext arrested and made prisoners. They were released after six weeks' imprisonment, during which they were subjected to much violence and indignity, but by this time the patience of the long-suffering authorities at Calcutta had become exhausted, and a punitive expedition was despatched into Sikkim to exact a much belated retribution. As the result of this, the grant of 6,000 rupees which the Raja had received since 1846 was withdrawn, and the Sikkim Terai—originally a gift from the British and the most fertile piece of land in the State—was annexed, together with a tract of hill country with a population of some 5,000 inhabitants. The Raja was now entirely confined to the mountainous hinterland, without any access to the plains except through British territory.

To Darjeeling, the new territory, covering as it did an area of 640 square miles, formed a most important addition. For whereas the district had up to that time comprised a small area in Sikkim territory, to reach which the British had to pass through territory that was governed by a foreign, though dependent ruler, it was now directly connected with the British districts of Purnea and Jalpaiguri in the south, while the British boundary on the west marched with Nepal, and on the east with Bhutan. All this had been accomplished by the mere moral effect of the Government forces upon the inhabitants, for of actual fighting there was none. The force was recalled without any "incidents" after remaining a few weeks in the country, and the formal acquisition of the territory was effected by the dispatch of four policemen to take possession of the treasury which, it is said, contained exactly six rupees! The villagers were then informed that the territory had been confiscated by the British Government, and the annexation was an accomplished fact.

After this, relations between Sikkim and the British Government proceeded smoothly enough for some years, but with the advent to power again of the Diwan Namguay, who had retired from the scene at the time of the annexation, trouble in the shape of raids into British territory, the plundering of property and so on, broke out anew. By this time, the Raja, now approaching his eightieth year, had retired to Chumbi in Tibet, after entrusting the affairs of state to the tender mercies of Namguay—the man chiefly responsible for the raids, and the captor of Hooker and Campbell in 1849. In the punitive measures which followed, Dr. Campbell himself advanced with a small force as far as Rinchinpong, but was obliged to fall back on Darjeeling for want of ammunition. In March, 1861, however, a force of 2,600 men, with mountain howitzers and a detachment of artillery under Colonel Gawler, accompanied by Sir Ashley Eden as Envoy and Special Commissioner, entered Tumlong, the capital of Sikkim, without serious opposition. The forts were dismantled, the old Raja abdicated in favour of his son, and the Diwan fled.

The treaty which Sir Ashley Eden subsequently effected with the new Raja was of the greatest importance to Darjeeling, for with the guarantee of such things as facilities for trade, the removal of all restrictions on merchants and travellers, the construction of roads, compensation for losses in cases of robbery or raids and so on, its inhabitants were now free from the constant annoyances to which they had been exposed, and all obstacles in the way of trading with Sikkim had been permanently removed. Another important result of this treaty was that steps were now taken for the first time to tap the Tibetan trade, for during their occupation of Sikkim, the British constructed a road from Darjeeling to the Tista river, the Sikkim authorities undertaking to complete the remaining portion from the Chola Pass to Tibet.

It was not until 1866, however—five years later—that the Darjeeling district attained its present dimensions, for in that year was added some further territory—this time in consequence of trouble with the adjoining state of Bhutan. The events which led up to the Bhutan war did not differ greatly from those which had precipitated the crisis with Sikkim, for the Bhutanese had for some time been engaged in acts of aggression, robbery and kidnapping on the frontier in much the same way as the Sikkimese. Rumours in 1862 that they were actually contemplating entering British territory, and possibly even attacking Darjeeling, led to the dispatch of troops from Dinapore, whereby confidence on the frontier was restored. The dispatch of a special mission the following year under Sir Ashley Eden, however, aggravated rather than improved the situation, for although the British proposals were of a conciliatory nature, they were rejected by the Bhutan Government in the most insolent manner, and Sir Ashley Eden, who had been treated throughout with great indignity, even experienced some difficulty in getting away.

As the result of the campaign which followed, in which the Bhutanese showed themselves incapable of offering anything but the slenderest resistance, the Bhutan Duars, with the passes leading into the hills, were ceded to the British in return for an annual subsidy. Thus the Bhutia possessions in the plains were now entirely British, while a tract of British hill country on the eastern bank of the Tista was interposed between Bhutan and Sikkim. The addition in 1866 of this tract—which now forms the Kalimpong police circle—was the last that was made to the Darjeeling district. That year in fact marked an epoch in the history of Darjeeling. For with peace at last established within its borders, the civil and commercial development of the district could begin.

CHAPTER XXI

Darjeeling and its Surroundings

In this development the advantages offered by Darjeeling as a health resort constituted an all-important factor, and in an attempt to make it the home of European education in India several hill schools were established, the first of these being St. Paul's School, which was transferred from Calcutta in 1864. The Roman Catholic St. Joseph's College at North Point came later in 1888, but since its establishment has always had the larger number of pupils. Apart from its excessive humidity, the climate of Darjeeling is very similar to that of Europe. Anyone who has met the boys of St. Paul's or St. Joseph's on the hockey or football field can testify to their physical fitness, while very young children seem in particular to thrive in Darjeeling, regaining health, strength and colour in a surprising manner when sent there after illness or prolonged residence in the plains.

Very little rain falls in the Darjeeling hills from the beginning of October to the end of February, and although there is snow occasionally in January and February, heavy falls are the exception rather than the rule. During these months the air is usually cloudless, dry and bracing, with bright sunshine in the day and nights clear and starry but bitterly cold. There is a brief spring lasting only till the end of March and a short-lived summer, accompanied by showers, which become heavier and more frequent until the rains set in in earnest in the beginning of June. During June, July and August the rains continue unabated, and only in September does the incessant downfall give place again to showers, and the sun condescend to show itself more often and for longer intervals, until towards the end of the month or the beginning of October it ceases altogether and normal existence can be resumed.

During the actual rains Darjeeling is one of the wettest

DARJEELING.

[Photo by Major C. J. Morris

KANGCHENJUNGA, FROM EASTERN NEPAL.

stations in the whole of India, being enshrouded by almost constant cloud and fog that rise from the deep humid valleys and hang over it like a pall for days on end, while, to make matters worse, it is also shut in by a screen of mountains which, though they certainly shelter it from the wind, yet prevent the dissipation of the masses of mist that rise from the ravines like steam from a cauldron. Out of the 115 to 120 inches that constitute the average rainfall for the year in Darjeeling, all but some 15 inches or so fall during the rainy season. Unfortunately, however, even during the drier months it is only for brief periods in the summer, after the rains and in the beginning of the cold weather, that anything more than fleeting glimpses can be obtained of the glorious surrounding panorama of snow-clad mountains and sunlit sky. For the prevailing wind throughout the greater part of the year is from the south-east and comes laden with moisture from the Bay of Bengal, with the result that masses of mist are unceasingly rolling over the ridges and filling up the valleys until not infrequently the whole station is enveloped in blinding mist and fog.

Yet when the weather is clear and its surrounding glories stand revealed, few towns surely can compare with Darjeeling. For its situation is singularly beautiful, standing as it does on a narrow ridge that juts out into a vast basin in the heart of the Himalayas. To the west and the south it is enclosed by higher mountains, but to the north and north-east the view is more open, and behind the well-cultivated slopes of the nearer Sikkim hills the eye travels over range upon range, rising in ascending waves to a background of snowy mountains with towering peaks. One stands as it were on the stage of a vast amphitheatre of mountains in which the Singalila ridge that forms the boundary between British territory and Nepal forms the western and loftier Chola range, twice as far again away, the eastern side. And some of the mightiest giants in the Himalayas are represented by those distant peaks. Straight in front, for instance, and only forty-five miles away, tower the twin peaks of Kangchenjunga, over 28,000 feet high.

Nor are the mountains that flank it much less imposing than the giant itself, for to the west the sharp horn-like peak of Jano is 25,300 feet, and the tent-shaped crest of Kabru, 24,000 feet, while on the east again Pandim—"the King's Minister," so called because it stands by the side of the king of mountains, Kangchenjunga—is 22,000 feet high. Further to the east again rise other great mountains, of which Narsing (18,200 feet) with its sharp conical peak, and Siniolchu or D2 with its graceful snow-mantled crest, are perhaps the most beautiful, while the great mass of Dongkya (23,200 feet) stands out furthest away amongst the distant mountains of Bhutan. Even their fine sonorous names seem to express something of the majesty and the grandeur of these monarchs of the Himalayas.

Unfortunately, no pen—certainly not mine—can adequately describe the stupendous magnificence of the snows from Darjeeling, though some of Sir Joseph Hooker's word-pictures are admirable as far as they go. "On viewing this glorious panorama, the impression produced on the imagination by their prodigious elevation is that the peaks tower in the air and pierce the clouds," he says, in describing one particular view. Yet even he professed himself incapable of conveying to his readers a true impression of the wonderful play of colours reflected on the snow by the sinking or rising sun, for here he writes, "Such dissolving views elude all attempt at description, they are far too aerial to be chained to the memory, and fade from it so fast as to be gazed upon day after day, with undiminished admiration and pleasure, long after the mountains themselves have lost their sublimity and apparent height."

For the pages of this book, Hooker's description must suffice. This much only will I add, that when the mists do lift, so clear and rare is the air of this region that the mountains stand out with a distinctness that I, at any rate, have never seen elsewhere, though at Dharmsala in the lovely Kangra valley, and at similar Gurkha stations, I have spent many years amid the grandest Himalayan scenery. I may add that on my first visit I had been nearly two months in Darjeeling before seeing the hills across even the nearest valleys, to say nothing of the more distant snows; but the sight of Kangchenjunga, when the mist ultimately lifted, left an impression on me that I am never likely to forget. For although, as the crow flies, the summit of Kangchenjunga is forty-five miles away, it seemed to appear quite suddenly in the sky almost above my head.

To anyone interested in the Gurkhas and their country an expedition along the Singalila ridge as far as Phalut is a trip never to be forgotten, for this immense ridge sixty miles long, that stretches from Kangchenjunga southwards to the Indian plains, forms the boundary between Darjeeling and the forbidden land—Nepal. The road runs right along the sky line at an average altitude of 11,000 feet, until one reaches Phalut 11,800 feet high, where the boundaries of Nepal, Darjeeling and Sikkim meet. The views are magnificent, for not only is the great Kangchenjunga range visible the whole way, but from Sandakphu and Phalut, the two highest peaks on the ridge, the whole of the vast Nepalese snowy range, including Chunlang (24,000 feet) and Everest itself (29,002 feet) is revealed in all its matchless beauty to the traveller's gaze.

There is more than the actual magnificence of the scenery however to attract one on this particular journey, for throughout you are looking down on one side into the deep valleys and forests of a country that is inexorably barred to you—unknown Nepal.

I had made this trip several times before I summoned up courage—I think in 1920—to ask Sir Chandra Shumshere to grant me the great privilege of making a small tour in eastern Nepal, and in the result was enabled to enjoy the memorable experience of walking through that very same country that had so often tantalised me when I looked down into it from the Singalila ridge. And I can call the experience memorable with justice, for at that time only one other European—Sir Joseph Hooker—had ever set foot in that country before. My joy on the day when, accompanied by the escort sent to Tonglu—the first halting-stage on the road to Phalut situated just inside

British territory—I found myself walking down the rocky uneven path that led straight into Nepalese territory, can I think only be fully realised by those who have also had the fascinating experience of travelling into country forbidden and unknown.

It is sad to relate, however, that on this particular occasion, although I had selected the middle of May as being a fairly reliable time of the year, even for the fickle climate in that part of the world, the elements were unfortunately on their very worst behaviour. Mist I could have put up with, and indeed expected, but rain set in relentless and unceasing the very evening of the first day, with the result that, the object of my trip being largely photographic, and no sign of any abatement of the downpour being forthcoming, I was compelled to retrace my steps and return to the Singalila ridge on the third day. It was a bitter disappointment at the time, but fortunately I was to have another opportunity of seeing the promised land, for in the winter of 1926 the Maharaja kindly allowed me—this time in company with Major C. J. Morris—to make the trip again. This time I was determined to take no chance with the weather, and so we chose the middle of November, a month when, as I have already said, there is very little fear of rain even in Darjeeling. Mist was another matter, however, but in this respect, too, we were exceptionally lucky, for though there had been plenty of it up to the very day of our departure, and again immediately after our return, we enjoyed cloudless, sunlit days throughout the whole time we were away. Had we made the trip ten days sooner or ten days later, we should have seen very little—perhaps even nothing at all.

The Maharaja very kindly gave us permission to enter Nepalese territory at Tonglu, and, striking west, to take a route which ran by way of the villages of Ingla, Jamuna and Maimajua as far as Banduki, whence we rejoined the road on the Singalila ridge at Sandakphu. A channel cut in the side of the hill by one of the streams that gush down its side during the rains was

[Photo by Major C. J. Morris.

BRIDGE OVER THE MAI KHOLA, NEAR INGLA, EASTERN NEPAL.

[Photo by Major C. J. Morris.

A Village in Eastern Nepal.

our path during much of our journey on the first day, but we had been warned that the going was likely to be rough, and so considered ourselves lucky to find a path at all. Ingla itself—a collection of small houses sprawling over the hillside—lies in a valley, and as is the case with most Himalayan valleys similarly situated, rice is here the staple crop. Long white strips that flapped in the breeze in several homesteads signified the presence of followers of the Buddhist faith in the neighbourhood, although more than one religion is represented in the village—Bhotiyas, Rais, Limbus (these last being the two best known eastern Nepal tribes) and even Brahmans living peaceably side by side.

Although—certainly to the initiated—the Nepalese of eastern Nepal differ but little in appearance, manners and so forth from those of other parts of Nepal, there is at any rate one divergency of dress that is very noticeable, namely, the almost universal wearing of loosely-fitting trousers in place of the thin "kilt" that is always worn in Central and Western Nepal.

Here too we discovered another unusual method of catching fish. A dam composed of large stones having been made across a stream, the fishermen proceed a hundred yards or so upstream—having left a few at the dam to see that no fish pass the obstruction—and then walk slowly back through the water, driving the fish before them as they go. As they approach the dam they close in and scoop the fish out of the water with their hands. Though, as might be expected, a considerable number manage to escape during the process, yet at the same time quite good catches are often secured in this primitive way. Science has as yet left untouched these villages in Nepal.

Distractions for those who live in these far-off Himalayan villages are, of course, few and far between. The large fairs, however, that are held from time to time at various centres—usually at the junction of two rivers—do not a little to bring a touch of colour into their drab, though by no means unhappy lives. A primitive structure that does duty as a swing takes the place of the galloping horses and strident steam organs of

Europe in this part of the world, but the screams of delight of those who sample it are just the same. Wild-looking Bhotiyas from the Tibetan border vie with the more shrewd and intelligent Newars from the bazaars of Ilam in their efforts to attract the passers-by to their brightly-laden stalls, and for a few days at any rate, all is bustle and animation.

Our route lying as it did in a northerly direction, the cultivation and scenery generally of the country through which we passed changed, as was to be expected, as we started to ascend. Thus after leaving Jamuna—a village of one small street—our path took us through beautiful rock-strewn woods to the village of Mahbu, where the rice-fields of Ingla had given place to mustard of the brightest yellow, making, with the red roofs of the houses, a delightful picture as we approached it in the morning sun. Again beyond Maimajua we passed through pretty undulating country, dotted here and there with prosperous looking houses—the whole scene, with the green of the grass and the blue of the sky, being strangely reminiscent of Switzerland.

Our quarters at night were varied and unconventional. At Jamuna, for instance, we enjoyed comparative luxury on the ground floor of an empty shop. At Maimajua, on the other hand, a cow was evicted to give us lodging in its shed. Here again our Nepalese escort were invaluable. They had but to command and the order was instantly obeyed. Yet, as I have always noticed in Nepal, relations between them and the villagers were always of the friendliest. Perhaps, too, the latter were not displeased at being asked to bestir themselves for such strange and exciting visitants from another world; for though not far, as the crow flies, from civilisation, as represented by Darjeeling, quite a number had never been there, and we were probably the first Europeans they had ever seen.

And so, ascending higher and higher, we finally reached Banduki, situated in a clearing of the forest and consisting apparently of but one house and a few sheds. What Banduki lacked in size, however, it made up for in importance, for it

Escort and Village Headman (Brahman). Eastern Nepal.

LIMBU WOMEN OF EASTERN NEPAL.

is a customs house station, and many travellers pass it every day. Toll is levied here on many things which are brought in from across the border. Cloth, animals and salt, to mention only a few, are all liable to duty, while certain articles like cigarettes, not to mention the domestic cow, are prohibited altogether without special permission. The life of the solitary customs house official at Banduki could hardly by any stretch of imagination be called a gay one, but he was perfectly cheerful and philosophical about it, explaining that "it isn't really so bad."

It was not far from Banduki that, across a mass of beautiful hills, we saw the distant snow mountains from a point of view that probably none save Hooker had before been privileged to observe them from—a dazzling array of snowy peaks with the majestic Kangchenjunga raising its mighty head above them all. We had now passed into the country of the Limbus, known in their history as the "land of the five tribes." Here the bamboos and tree-ferns of the lower valleys had given place to the oaks, maples and magnolias of the higher elevations, while the fields of rice and mustard had been replaced by buckwheat and Indian corn. As we climbed slowly up the spur that led to the Singalila ridge, at times through thick verdant forest, at times over ridges crowned with stunted pines, often lightning-blasted, to where the rhododendrons became plentiful, the thought was again brought home to us—that not in the majesty of its snowy mountains, in its rushing torrents or its deep forest-clad valleys, but rather in the hardiness and valour of its open-hearted inhabitants was to be found the greatest charm of Nepal.

CHAPTER XXII

Darjeeling To-day

THE district of Darjeeling, extending as it does as far eastward as Bhutan and connecting with the British districts of Purnea and Jalpaiguri on the south, contains an extremely heterogeneous population of some 320,000 souls. It has in fact been described as a "Babel of tribes and nations," for together with the Mongolian hillmen, there are Bengalis, Marwari merchants, Punjabi traders and even some Chinese (usually carpenters), while in the Terai are tribes like the Rajbansis and settlers—attracted by the tea-garden wages—from such places as the Santal Parganas and Chota Nagpur. And of this population the greater proportion is due to immigration, mostly from Nepal. The people in the hills include a large number of Bhotiyas, Lepchas (the original inhabitants of the country) and Tibetans, but, the dominant race is undeniably the Nepalese, who account for more than half the total number. More resourceful, thrifty and industrious than the others, and at the same time born cultivators, it is they who have managed to secure most of the best agricultural land in the district, while the labourers employed on the tea estates in the hills are also almost without exception Nepalese. The fascination of Darjeeling, therefore, with such a medley of races to be seen in its shops and its streets, will be readily understood. Otherwise, however, so far as the European is concerned, life in Darjeeling differs not a whit from that of any other hill station in India. There are the same big hotels, the same large clubs (two) with their dances and entertainments, there are the British garrisons in Lebong and Jalapahar to contribute to the social and sporting activities of the community; there is the inevitable Mall with shops bearing such well-known names as Hall and Anderson, and Whiteaway and

Laidlaw; there is even the usual Italian confectioner with afternoon teas at one rupee. In a word, everything of this kind can be seen equally well in places like Simla, Murree or Dalhousie. To which it may be added that, owing possibly to its excessive mist and rain, Darjeeling, considered solely from a social point of view, is perhaps less popular with most people than some of the other hill stations such as I have mentioned. Yet for those whose interests are not confined entirely to the ordinary round of hill-station amusements, Darjeeling has characteristics and attractions all its own, and not least among them its fascinating Mongolian inhabitants. Indeed for some people—amongst whom I would venture to include myself—it is they who provide the chief interest of the place. True the actual bazaar with its closely-packed huts and shops, and all-too-frequent corrugated-iron roofs has little enough to recommend it in the way of the picturesque or otherwise, but of its swarming inhabitants the tale is very different.

The tenants of the shops are usually Indians. Sleek, black-bearded Marwaris sit cross-legged in the cloth shops, seemingly ever absorbed in mysterious account-books—a small door at the back concealing an image of Ganesh, their favourite god. Presiding at other shops are smooth-tongued but rapacious merchants from Punjab and Kashmir, while petty Hindustani shopkeepers from the plains add to the din with their strident, unmelodious voices—for the noise of the bazaar at noon can be heard a mile. All these, however, form but a small and that not the most interesting part of the medley of races and kaleidoscope of colour that go to make up the Darjeeling bazaar. For the crowds that throng the streets, no less than the keepers of the open stalls that, particularly on Sundays, take up the whole of the big open square, are almost entirely Mongolian—Bhotiyas from Sikkim, Lepchas, Tibetans and, most numerous of all, Nepalese. In addition to the ordinary shops and stalls, quaint "side-shows" of various kinds also attract attention. Here, for instance, along a sunny wall are some twenty barbers plying a brisk trade, their customers being for the most part uncouth and unkempt traders from Tibet, in the case of whom one feels a good shampoo would be even more salutary than a haircut. Here again Bhotiya women, their broad, good-humoured faces beaming like the rising sun, preside over great bowls of snow-white curds, a favourite local dainty, which they serve out in square vessels ingeniously twisted out of plantain leaves. Elsewhere others dispense tea, a somewhat gruesome compound boiled up with molasses, yet evidently much appreciated in this part of the world.

In the open market, where, as I have said, there is great activity on certain days, the salespeople, mostly hailing from outlying villages, squat in front of the most heterogeneous assortment of wares imaginable. For besides the goats, chickens, eggs, grain, fruit, oil and the like, you find also such things as yaks' tails, brass Buddhas, ironmongery, old bottles, umbrellas, feeding-bottles, together with piles of cotton and woollen goods, all making up the most glorious and amusing medley imaginable of what a famous London purveyor so proudly labels "merchandise."

From the scenic point of view it is perhaps the Bhotiya women who contribute most notably to the colour scheme and generally attract most attention. From their ears dangle enormous gold earrings, four or five inches long; necklaces of amber, coral, agate or large course turquoises adorn their necks, while massive silver girdles with hanging ornaments encircle their waists. Round their heads again are great circlets formed of large beads of turquoise and coral, set alternately on a frame, the blue and the red showing up strikingly against their thick black hair. With ornaments such as these embellishing dresses of bright but not inharmoniously blended colours, the well-to-do Bhotiya ladies have, indeed, just reason to be proud of their appearance. In point of looks, too, many of the younger ones are by no means uncomely, though unfortunately the faces of too many—especially of the elder women—are embellished by dabs of brown paint and the even more freely employed pigs' blood!

Less vividly attired but hardly less picturesque are the Nepalese women, for Darjeeling bazaar is the Bond Street of Gurkha-land, and here the shawls and veils which the women wear over their heads, Italian-fashion, are of a texture and a colour rarely seen in Nepal proper, while some of the ultra-smart even affect silk stockings, to which high-heeled shoes will possibly be added in due course. Indeed, with the modern craze for beauty competitions and "queens", of every conceivable profession and community, there may yet be a "Miss Darjeeling" at no distant date!

Not to be overlooked in the crowd either are the Lepchas. Distinctly Mongolian in feature with high cheek-bones and eyes set wide apart, they are distinguished by magnificent heads of coal-black hair—though they have none on their faces—thick and abundant as a horse's mane and worn in a long pig-tail. Their women-folk, as strong and lusty as the men, and usually carrying enormous loads on their backs, are often only distinguishable by their jewellery and their two pig-tails, for their dress—a loose robe of course cotton cloth which leaves the arms free and comes down below the knee—is much the same as that of the men.

At one time the possessors of all the hill country of Darjeeling and Sikkim, the Lepchas have been to a great extent supplanted by the more self-assertive and pushing Nepalese. Yet placid, somewhat indolent and unenterprising though they may be, the Lepchas in reality possess qualities for which perhaps they are not always given sufficient credit. They often make, for instance, admirable servants, while, being born naturalists with an almost uncanny knowledge of forest and jungle craft, not a few have gone far afield and done valuable biological work in countries such as the Malay Archipelago, Sumatra, Borneo, Burma and the Celebes. Intermarriage with other races, especially with the Limbus of eastern Nepal and the Bhotiyas of Sikkim has contributed to the gradual effacement of the Lepchas, but statistics taken from census figures do not show them to be actually declining in numbers.

Another picturesque figure to be frequently encountered in the Darjeeling bazaar is the Buddhist Lama, who, followed by an acolyte as unwashed as himself, walks slowly through the crowd bellowing aloud for alms.

Tibetans, Bhotiyas and Lepchas have a great weakness for the European Homburg hat, and it is highly amusing to see this form of head-gear—usually much too small in size—perched rakishly on the pig-tailed heads of uncouth Tibetan traders, or Bhotiya rickshaw coolies from the Darjeeling Mall.

It is a jovial, good-natured crowd which fills the bazaar on a Darjeeling market day. Though nearly every man carries a knife that would disembowel an elephant, and although there are shops selling beverages that are much more potent than tea, the utmost good humour prevails, and smiles not scowls are the order of the day. And so, it is with the pleasantest recollections that we will take leave of the cheery Mongolian friends that we have met there—of the pig-tailed, Homburg-hatted Tibetans, of the buxom Bhotiya women with their bowls of curds and tea, of the spruce khaki-clad soldiers of the 7th and 10th Gurkhas from the recruiting depôt at Ghum and of the ladies they flirt with (Nepalese and Lepcha ayahs, white-clad and rosy-cheeked), of the giant shaven-headed Lama with his stentorian supplications for alms, of the vivacious women from the tea-gardens with their gaily coloured shawls and their bright-eyed babies on their backs, and all the rest. Certainly one and all, with others too numerous to mention, will linger in the memory long after Darjeeling itself has been left behind as the component members of one of the most charming and good-natured races on the face of the earth.

If in the early history of Darjeeling its climatic advantages contributed in no small degree to its rapid development, another and hardly less important factor was the planting of tea in the hills. For the planting of tea, involving as it did so many other activities, such as the opening up of the land, the clearing of forest, and, last but not least, the running of the necessary machinery employed, caused an enormous demand for labour,

Darjeeling Bazaar on a Festival Day.

HAVILDAR DHANSAR, MANBAHADUR AND SAILA.

to say nothing of that required in connection with the feeding, clothing and housing of the large number of workers thus attracted. It is thus easy to understand how predominant a part tea was to play in the economic and industrial development of Darjeeling, and how the introduction of this industry has been primarily responsible for the large numbers of Nepalese to be found in the district to-day. Bordering as it did on their own country, and with climatic and general conditions differing but little, if indeed at all, from those obtaining in Nepal, Darjeeling was indeed obviously well calculated to attract the hard-working and resourceful Nepalese, and so it was not surprising that from the first they furnished, as indeed they have continued to do ever since, the bulk of the newcomers.

Except in the Terai, where owing to the extremely unhealthy climate the Nepalese are less disposed to settle, most of the labourers employed on these estates coming from the Santal Parganas and Chota Nagpur, the tea-garden labour in the Darjeeling district is almost entirely Nepalese. And if you ask any planter who has had wide experience, whether in Darjeeling itself, Assam, Ceylon, or even further afield, his opinion of the Nepalese as workers, you will almost invariably be told that there are none finer in the world. So long as they are treated fairly and with consideration, the cheerful, hard-working Nepalese labourers are indeed hard to beat. Unlike a regiment where there are many factors—tradition, numerous officers, commissioned and non-commissioned, and so on—to enforce and maintain discipline, a tea-garden depends usually for its harmonious and efficient working upon the personality of one man—the manager. It is true that he has generally one or more assistants, but when, as often happens, these are young and lacking in experience and knowledge of the language, the main responsibility rests upon his shoulders alone.

The working strength on an average-sized garden amounts to about eight hundred, half men and half women, this being about the usual proportion in this district. The women, it may be added, are excellent workers; indeed, in work that lies within their physical capacity, such as the plucking of the leaves, they are usually considered better than the men.

In this connection by the way it is remarkable how adaptable the Nepalese in general are in getting the hang of entirely unfamiliar kinds of work. Thus the Nepalese lads on the gardens learn the mysteries of the engine-room and the other purely technical sides of the business with amazing rapidity. And, similarly, in the railway shops of the Darjeeling-Himalayan railway at Tindharia, as well as in the electric-light works at Darjeeling, the personnel is very largely Nepalese.

The planters' servants are invariably Nepalese and come usually from families who have been long resident on the estate. They make almost always admirable servants—quick, honest, capable and willing. I had one myself for many years, who rejoiced in the name of "Saila," meaning "the third son." For it may be noted that though the Nepalese have names just like other people, these names are very rarely used in the family circle, the owners being almost invariably addressed in such terms as "elder brother," "eldest sister," "youngest brother" and so on, signifying the degree of relationship between themselves and the speaker. Nor is this rather charming mode of address confined to members of the family, since even total strangers encountered on the road or elsewhere will also be invariably addressed as "Daju," meaning "eldest brother," or "didi," "eldest sister," according to their sex.

To return however to Saila. Although the possessor of many virtues, he had a very quick temper that used to break out somewhat inconveniently at times. "Saila has had a slight altercation with the old one-legged chowkidar (watchman) and has a black eye and a bruised shin-bone, he asks therefore to be excused," was the type of communication occasionally whispered into my ear at the mess table of the recruiting depôt —usually, of course, when some especially distinguished guest was present, and Saila's services were particularly required! As he grew older, however, these outbursts became less and less frequent, and it was with genuine regret that, on my last visit to Darjeeling a few years ago, I learnt that Saila had died of influenza at his home on Dooteriah Tea Estate in his thirtieth year.

In selecting a Darjeeling boy as a servant one should always be careful to take one who comes from a tea-garden, and to avoid anyone from Darjeeling itself. For though I have sung the praises of Darjeeling on a market day, it must be noted that those who produce such a favourable impression—stall-holders, Bhotiya women and so on—are mostly visitors for the day only who have come in from the surrounding district to buy or sell their wares, and are not to be confused with the Nepalese domiciled in the town, of whom it is not so easy to speak in unqualified terms. Far be it from me to say that every Gurkha who lives in Darjeeling is a shady character; for I have myself been brought into contact with many to whom such a sweeping assertion could certainly not apply. But the fact remains that the lives they lead are entirely different from those of other Gurkhas and that they are in consequence sophisticated to a degree unknown amongst Nepalese elsewhere.

Another circumstance having an important bearing on the matter is the fact that the caste system is so lax amongst many of them as to be practically non-existent. Men of the highest caste are to be found in quite lowly occupations or doing work that they could never perform in their own country. Thus the syce (groom) of the pony that you hire on the Mall may as likely as not be a Chetri or even a Brahman, while the fact that a man of good caste marries a woman of low caste, or vice versa, seems to matter very little if at all here. There are temptations in the town too that are not to be found in the country districts or on the tea-gardens. In short, too close proximity to Darjeeling, even though it make life pleasanter for the Europeans, has its distinct handicaps where Nepalese labour is concerned, and therefore I do not hesitate to repeat that you are unlikely to get a really good servant from the Darjeeling bazaar.

Unlike the Nepalese of the Darjeeling tea-gardens who, from environment and long association with Europeans take readily to domestic service, the Gurkhas of Central Nepal who make good and reliable servants are few and far between. To begin with, unlike the Darjeeling boys, whose religious observances are less orthodox and who are thus less hampered by questions of caste, a Central Nepal man will not wait at table, but will only do valeting pure and simple—or what is known in India as "bearer's" work. This in itself renders him an expensive luxury to persons of slender purse. In other respects, too, servants from Central Nepal—they are usually discharged or pensioned soldiers—are seldom very satisfactory. There are, of course, exceptions, but generally they are inclined to be somewhat slow and stolid, and to lack the initiative and alertness of the tea-garden boys. Their honesty and frankness, however, go a long way to compensate for their other failings.

For several years I had an ex-colour havildar (sergeant) of my own regiment as a bearer. His methods of looking after one's clothes in the early stages of his new profession were hardly those to win the approval of a European valet. He used, for instance, on coming into my room in the morning, to throw any clothes of the night before on to the floor, quite regardless of what the garment might be. Thus a practically new dress suit would be flung into a corner of the room or anywhere on the floor with the same cheerful abandon as a soiled handkerchief —the idea being apparently that as it would be properly attended to in due course it mattered not in the meantime whether it reposed on a chair or on the floor!

During the winter season at Gorakhpur the good havildar used to be assisted in his ministrations by a delightful Magar youth called Manbahadur—a relation of his, who came down to the depôt every year from his village in the hills. What exactly Manbahadur did, or indeed was even supposed to do, I could never quite discover. Occasional glances at his handiwork made me wonder if he quite knew himself! But he was utterly unsophisticated and absolutely truthful, and certainly added to the brightness, if not to the general efficiency, of the establishment. Yet, despite their failings—the havildar I may say subsequently became a first-class servant—I never regretted employing only Nepalese.

To return however to Darjeeling. The labourers on the tea-estates belong to well-known tribes of eastern Nepal such as Rais, Limbus, Gurungs, Magars and Tamangs, and unlike those domiciled in Darjeeling, observe the ritual and ceremonial of their respective tribes in the orthodox—if never very rigid—manner. Like all Nepalese, they are intensely superstitious, and wizards, witches and all kinds of witchcraft play an important part in their lives. Above all things, they have the most child-like belief in ghosts, or, as they are called in their language, *bhuts*. Not only are these supposed to haunt rivers and streams, but they are constantly to be met with in everyday life. "It is not my fault. The *bhut* will push into me so violently from behind that my basket naturally gets damaged," explains Maili, a tea-garden girl, when her manager reproaches her for breaking her basket for the third or fourth time. So also they will never walk alone in the dark, if they can possibly help it, owing to fear of *bhuts*.

I have even been taken for a *bhut* myself. For when on one occasion I was walking back to Ghum from Darjeeling late at night, my aspect seemed so terrible apparently to a party of Mongolians who were coming towards me from the other direction that they stopped suddenly, and then, terrified out of their wits, ran shrieking down the khud. "It is perfectly simple. They thought you were a *bhut*," was Saila's comment when I told him of the incident on the following day. But my domestic staff's interest did not end there, for, on my telling them that, the night being cold, I had muffled myself up until my face, if not my head itself, was almost hidden and that I was carrying a parcel containing my evening shoes, the whole matter became more clear, since it now seemed evident that I had been mistaken for the much-dreaded *Mathkata*—the ghost who carries his head under his arm!

Such are the people, then, among whom the Darjeeling planter lives and moves and has his being; and they certainly do much to brighten his existence. For even if a planter's life is usually too full and varied to be called monotonous, yet it is naturally rather lonely at times—especially in the case of the younger men and those unmarried—and in such circumstances the cheerful, willing Mongolians all round him make a lot of difference.

At the same time, by being brought into such close and intimate contact with his servants and labour, he acquires a knowledge and understanding of the Nepalese character such as an officer in a Gurkha regiment is rarely likely to obtain. And so it came about that among the host of men from every profession who rushed to answer their country's call at the time of the Great War the planters from Darjeeling proved an invaluable asset to the Indian army. For the replacing of the European officers in the Indian regiments, whose numbers from casualties and other causes dwindled so rapidly, was one of the greatest difficulties with which the Government had to contend. Especially was this so in the case of the Gurkha regiments, where officers were required who knew the language and the rather special characteristics of the men, and it is easy to understand how invaluable the Darjeeling planters were to fill these vacancies. For they joined their regiments with a knowledge of the language and of the ways and customs of the rank and file greater often than that of the original officers themselves, while in such matters as recruiting their knowledge and experience were, of course, of inestimable service. It is hardly necessary to add that the planters play an all-important part also in times of peace in the administration and direction of the district.

The future of Darjeeling[1] is not easy to foresee at the moment. It may indeed almost be said to be standing at present at the crossroads, for it is as yet uncertain whether it is to remain an "excluded area," as it has been hitherto, or become part of Bengal. In the case of Darjeeling, the term "excluded area" rather than "backward tract" has been applied, although the

[1] Since these lines were written, Darjeeling has become a "partially excluded area" under the 1935 Government of India Act.

official terms defining both are much the same. For in both cases regulations "prescribed under special laws to suit the primitive character of the inhabitants," or again "simple and elastic regulations" have been now in force for many years. The term "backward tract" was, however, adopted in the first instance to designate certain places in India where the inhabitants could really be considered backward (the Santals, for example), and was therefore hardly applicable in the case of Darjeeling, where, certainly in the hills, the inhabitants are anything but backward. In the result, however, Darjeeling has been run on somewhat independent lines for a good many years, and to the apparent satisfaction of all concerned.

But now has arisen the question of its affiliation with Bengal. Many of the more prominent members of what is known as the Hillmens' Association, representing the Nepalese, Bhutia and Mongolian communities in general on the ground that by the election of some of their countrymen to the legislative council they would have a voice in the government, are in favour of it. The planters and European community in general on the other hand are for the most part opposed to it. They argue, not without force, that the Hillmens' representatives even if elected would be so few in number that they would carry little weight, and, not less cogently, that the existing system of administration has been so entirely satisfactory that no change is called for. It remains to be seen, therefore, what the outcome will be. In any case, whatever is eventually decided, it is certain that the planters will always play an important part in the public life of the district.

As regards life in Darjeeling there is much that is attractive and even enviable in the tea-planter's existence. Just at present the industry is suffering from the universal disease of over-production, but with the introduction, by international agreement, of a restricted output, conditions have undeniably improved during the last few years, and the outlook is much more cheerful. In other respects, too, the planter's lot is continually improving. During recent years especially motor cars and better roads have made a tremendous difference, bringing Darjeeling within comparatively easy reach of even the remotest gardens—in some cases nearly thirty miles away. In the matter of sport, there are few who cannot get quite good shooting, even on their own estates, in the shape of leopards, barking-deer, bears, woodcock, jungle fowl and even sambhar and thar, while it is hardly necessary to add that in the way of milder outdoor amusements tennis is a great standby here as all the world over. The bungalows, almost invariably red-roofed, and making, with the factories, gay splashes of colour amid the green of the tea-bushes, are usually charming, as also are the flower-gardens that invariably surround them.

It is a life in which a man learns at an early age to take responsibility and to act on his own initiative, while there are few professions where the duties are so multifarious, for besides being an agriculturist, the planter is also engineer, architect and even on occasions doctor. Yet, although, like most people whose business is concerned with mother earth, he has good reasons for grumbling at times, his work is always interesting and of a varied nature. Finally, to help him through his job he has in his Nepalese labourers what has been not unjustly described as the "finest labour in the world."

Bibliography

BELL, SIR CHARLES. *Tibet: Past and Present.* London, 1924.

BENDALL, C. A. *A Journey of Literary and Archæological Research in Nepal and Northern India.* Cambridge, 1886.

BROWN, PERCY. *Picturesque Nepal.* London, 1912.

BRUCE, MAJOR (now Brig.-Gen.) The Hon. C. J. *Twenty Years in the Himalayas.* London, 1910. *Himalayan Wanderer.* London, 1934.

BRUCE, BRIG.-GEN., The Hon. C. J., and NORTHEY, MAJOR W. BROOK. *Geographical Journal,* Vol. LXV, No. 4. London, 1924.

DAS, SARAT CHANDRA. *Journey to Lhasa and Central Tibet.* London, 1904.

DEKOBRA, MAURICE. *Les Tigres Parfumés.* Paris, 1927. *Perfumed Tigers.* London, 1931.

ELIOT, SIR CHARLES. *Hinduism and Buddhism.* 3 vols. London, 1921.

ELWES, J. H. *Memoirs of Travel, Sport and Natural History.* London, 1930.

"ENCYCLOPÆDIA BRITANNICA." All Editions. Darjeeling and Nepal.

FRESHFIELD, D. W. *Round Kangchenjunga.* London, 1903.

HAMILTON, B. *An Account of the Kingdom of Nepal.* Edinburgh, 1819.

HODGSON, B. H. *Essays on the Language, etc. of Nepal and Tibet.* London, 1874. *Miscellaneous Essays.* London, 1880.

HOERNLE, R. *Inscribed Seal of Gupta.* 1889.

HOOKER, J. D. *Himalayan Journals.* London, 1854.

HUC, E. R. *Travels in Tartary.* London, 1927. (Reprint.)

HUNTER, SIR W. A. *Life of Brian Hodgson.* London, 1896.

KIRKPATRICK, W. *An Account of the Kingdom of Nepal.* London, 1811.

LANDON, PERCEVAL. *Nepal.* 2 vols. London, 1928.

LANDOR, A. H. SAVAGE. *Tibet and Nepal Painted and Described.* N.d.

LEVI, SYLVAIN. *Le Népal.* 3 vols. Paris, 1905.

MASSIEU, ISABELLE. *Népal et Pays Himalayens.* Paris, 1904.

MORRIS, MAJOR C. J. *Handbooks for the Indian Army Gurkhas.* Calcutta, 1933.

NORTHEY, MAJOR W. BROOK, and MORRIS, CAPTAIN C. J. *The Gurkhas: Their Manners, Customs and Country.* London, 1928.

O'CONNOR, SIR FREDERICK. *On the Frontier and Beyond.* London, 1931.

O'MALLEY, L. S. S. *Darjeeling, Bengal District Gazetteers.* Calcutta, 1907.

OLDFIELD, H. A. *Sketches from Nepal.* London, 1880.

OLIPHANT, L. A. *A Journey to Kathmandu.* London, 1852.

RISLEY, H. H. *Tribes and Castes of Bengal.* Calcutta, 1891.

SMITH, CAPTAIN T. *Five Years' Residence at Nepal*, 1841–45. London, 1852.

TEMPLE, SIR RICHARD. *Journal kept at Hyderabad, Kashmir, Sikkim and Nepal.* London, 1887.

TURNER, DR. R. L. *Nepali Dictionary, Comparative and Etymological.* London, 1931. *The Infinitive in Nepali*, Philologica, Vol. I. London, 1921. *Specimens of Nepali*, Indian Antiquary, Vol. I. Bombay, 1921. *Further Specimens of Nepali*, Indian Antiquary, Vol. II. Bombay, 1922.

WHEELER, J. T. *Short History of India and the Frontier States of Afghanistan, Nepal and Burma.* London, 1880.

WRIGHT, D. *History of Nepal.* Cambridge, 1887.

Index

ALBERT, Prince Consort, 73
Allahabad, 31, 74
Almora, station of 3rd Gurkhas, a visit to, 194; Gurkha colony near, 195
Almora district, 193
Alps, the, 1
Amar Sing Thapa, General, 56, 58
Amlekhganj, motor road beyond, 27
Amsu Varman, King, 33, 35, 37.
Animal sacrifice, Gurung, 10
Annapurna massif, 3, 7
  Peak, 191
Api, Peak, 3
Arghun rites of the Gurung, 9–10
Arun River, 13
Asoka, in Nepal, 11, 34, 146–7; city founded by, 161; an inscription by, at Rummindei, 147; stupas built by, at Patan, 11, 35, 162–3
Assam Rifles, Gurkhas in, 180
Ata-ud-din Khilji, Chitor taken by, 42
Awal, *see* Malaria

BABER SHUMSHERE, General Sir, 85; service of, in the Great War, 89
Badri Narsing, conspiracy of, against Jung Bahadur, 73, 79
Badri Sing, 73
Baghini, goddess, 169
Baglung, Puns from, 190
Baghmati river, 23–4, 34, 136, 154, 168; gorge of, 25; shrine on, 153
Bahadur Sah, regent, successes of 51; British aid requested by, 53; at Nayakot, 173
Bahadur Shumshere, General, Chairman of the Development Board, 89, 200
Baitadi, inhabitants of, 194
Baitadi, 29; fort of, visited, 196–7
Baitheri, 183
Bajhangis of the Western border, 193, 194
Bajra, the, 150–1
Bal Nar Sing Kunwar, 66, 67
Balaji, festival at, 163; "makaras" at, 158; pilgrims at, 159
Bam Bahadur, General, 72, 73; Prime Ministership of, and death, 75
Banduki, 214; customs station at, 216–17
Banepa, kingdom of, 40
Banepa valley, 23
Banhra priests and the Indrajatra, 163
Bara Nilkantha, shrine, 159–60; festival at, 163
Baramdeo, temple of, 198
Bartijai River, 8
Batauli, a visit to, camp at, description of, malaria at, and ghi trade of, 183, 184, 185; populace at, 184
Benares, exiled Nepalese royalties at, 54, 55, 70, 71; sanctity of, 189
Bhabar (jungle), the, 25, 26
Bhairab, images of, 189
Bhairabjatra festival, 163
Bhairavi, temple of, 172, 173
Bhartpur, battle of, 97
Bhatgaon, 29, 37, 44, 45, 71, 136; alleged founder of, 38; atmosphere of, 169; beauties, of, 168; the Darbar at, 172, 173, 174, 176; earthquake devastation at, 175–6; the Golden Gate at, 168, 176; the King of, 47; taken by treachery, 49; the Temple of five stages at, 168–9; damaged by earthquake, 176; other temples in, 141
Bhatgaon Raha, athletes of, 169
Bhawanidal regiment, 185
Bheri Ganga River, 7

Bhim Sen Thapa, Prime Minister, 55, 56, 89; invasion by, of India, 37–8; later career of, downfall and death of, 60–1; Hodgson on, 61–2; monument of, 123; Nepal's debt to, 53
Bhim Sen's Folly or Dharara, and Jung Bahadur's daring, 145; damaged by earthquake, 176
Bhim Shumshere, Premiership of, 86
Bhimphedi, 28; architecture of, 131; the road to, 128
Bhirbandi, Mount, height of, 24
Bhot, *see* Tibet.
Bhotiya girl, the photograph of, 138, 139
Bhotiya men, liking of, for Homburg hats, 222
Bhotiya women at Darjeeling, 220, 222; ornaments of, 220
Bhotiyas visiting Bodnath, 153; at Darjeeling, 218, 219; at Ingla, 215; at Kathmandu, 142
Bhupatindra Malla, temple built by, 169
Bhutan, mountains of, 212; slavery in, 205
Bhutan Duars, cession of, 209
Bhutan war, the, 208, 209
Bhuts, ghosts and spirits, 227
Bibliography, 231–2
Bihar, earthquake in, of 1933, 175
Bihari palanquin bearers, 128–9
Bilauri, 29
Bir Shumshere, Maharaja Sir, the Premiership assumed by, 80; plot against, visits to India, and death of, 81; and recruiting, 180
Bird of paradise plumes worn by kings and other royalties, 104
Bishnumati river, 24, 136
"Blessing of the Colours" in the Dasehra festival, 166
Bod, *see* Tibet
Bodhnath, temple at, 152; pilgrims to, 153
Brahmans in Nepal, 215; arrival of, 39; results of, 43; persecution of (1807), 56; status of, 51, 93, 109; supporters of Prithwi Naryan, 47, 48
Brahmaputra river, 13; source of, 7
Bri-btsun, Princess, fateful marriage of, 37
Bridgmanganj, 29, 182
Bridges, improved, suspension and other, 28, 172, 173, 185, 186, 187, 193, 196
Briggs, Major, 191; photographs by, 179
British force sent to Nepal (1765), 48 (1815), 58–9
British India, area contiguous with Nepal, 17, 18, 22, 207
Gurkhas in, number of, 195
British mission to Nepal (1792), 53
British representative at Kathmandu, 54; duties, and position of, 59–60
Brown, Percy, on Nepalese art, 154; on the road to Kathmandu, 128
Bruce, Brig.-Gen. the Hon. C. G., A General Survey of Nepal, 1
Buddha, alleged Nepalese birthplace of, 147; alleged visit of, to Nepal, 149, 150; eyes of, at Swayambhunath, 150; statues of, 150
Buddhism, lamaistic, of the Kirantis, 13–14; of the Tibetans, 149; Nepalese, 11; decay of, 109; modification of, by Hinduism, 149
Buddhist Lamas, at Darjeeling, 222
Buddhist revivalist, a, 45
Buffalo-decapitation by the khukri, 99
Buffalo, eaten in Nepal, 109
Brahman, wife of Rana Bahadur, 54
Buria Gandak river, 8
Burial Customs, Gurkha, 112; Gurung, 9
Burma Military Police, Gurkhas in, 180
Butwal or Batauli, 29; road to, 28

CALCUTTA, Gurkhas in, 195, 196
Campbell, Dr., and Darjeeling, the tea plant introduced by, 205–6; imprisoned in Sikkim, 206, 207
Canning, Earl, Nepalese troops invited by, in 1857, 76
Capuchin missionaries, expulsion of, 51
Cassion, Father, and the Kuti-Lhasa route, 19
Chaepi river, 8
Chanda, 76
Chalitra, songs of, used in Nepal, 123
Chandra Shumshere, Maharaja, Sir, Prime Minister, 55, 145, 170, 199; accession of, and reforms fostered by, 82, 83, 87, 106, 107; co-operation of, during the great war, 84–5; diplomatic sagacity of, 84; impression made by, on the author, 86; kindness of, to the author, 171, 185, 193, 196, 213, 214; and the railway, 128; shooting camps of, for the late King and the Prince of Wales, 116, 118; visit of, to England, 86, 87; death of, 86
Chandragiri, Mount, 24
  Pass, 24, 28, 132; view from, 135
Changu Narayan, Hindu shrine, 154; the Dharmsala of, 185; and the earthquake, 176
Charjat division, Gurung tribe, 9, 10; Arghun rite of, 9
Chaubandi, the, 103, 104
Chaubisia Raj, the 8; mountain tribes of, 51; surrender of, 52
  States, Gurkhas annexation of, 45, 55
Chepang tribe, 16
Chetriya or Chetri or Khas tribe, 8, 172, 193; aspect of, 93–4, 190; importance of, 14, 39; language (Khas), 39; origin of the name, 38; Rajput blood of, 42, 43, 93
  rank and honour bestowed on, 39
  religion of, 109
China, Gurkha quinquennial mission to, 52–3; trade routes to, 5; treaty of, with Nepal, 6
Chinese, the, Gurkha likeness to, 96
Chinese at Darjeeling, 218
Chinese invasions of Nepal, 6, 8, 52
Chinese missions to Nepal, 36
Chinese pilgrims to Nepal, 36
Chisapani Pass, the snows seen from, 133
Chitawan district, rhinoceros in, 115; shooting camps in, 116
Chitlong Valley, or Little Nepal, 23, 135, 137
Chitor, capture of, 42
Chola Pass, road from, to Tibet, 208
Chola range, the, 211
Chota Nagpur, coolies from, 218, 223
Chumbi, 207
Chunlang, Mount, height of, 213
Churia Pass road, route W. of, 59
Churia Ridge, importance of, 130
Churia river, rest house on, 129, 130
Churyaghati range, 27
Coins used in Nepal, 134
Collier, J. V., on Nepalese forests, 199
Commandership in Chief in Nepal, scope of duties of, 82
Conjecvram, 38
Cornwallis, Marquis, and Nepal, 53
Cowrie shells used in gambling, 107–8
Curds in marriage ceremonial, 110; sold by Bhotiya women, 220
Curzon of Kedlestone, Marquis of, and Bir Shumshere, 81

DAELEKH, 29
Damais, the, 187
Ḍamodar Panre, Regent, 54; fate of, 55, 61
Dancing, Gurkha, 15, 110, 121, 122; Tibetan, 134

Darbar Square in cities, temples in, 145–6
Darbhanga, 181
Darjeeling, 29, 186, 216; ascent to, 286; British acquisition of, 204–5; climate of, 210–11; debt of, to Campbell, 205; possible affiliation of, with Bengal, future of, 228–9; history of, 203 ff.; market and bazaar of, 220; Mongolians of, 218,219; present day, 218 ff.; recruiting and pension, depot at, 180, 181; schools at, 210; shops and shopkeepers of, 218, 219; situation and surroundings of, 210 ff.; the snows seen from, Hooker's description quoted, 212; tea planting at, introduction of, 204, 205, 206, Nepalese labour in, 218, 223 ff.
Darjeeling, District of, 17; British acquisition of, 204; further territory added to, 208–9; frontier of, a contrast to, 193; immigration into, and heterogeneous population of, 205, 218 ff.
Darjeeling cart-road, the, 202
Darjeeling tea-planters, as officers in the Great War, 228
Darjeeling-Himalayan railway, the, 201 ff.
Darjeeling-Pithoragarh road, 28–9
Dasehra festival, the 163; the khukri in, 99–100; review during and slaughter of animals, 165-6; singing during, 122
Death, burial and mourning customs, Gurkha, 112; Gurung, 9
Dehra Dun, 85, 186; Gurkha colony near, 195
Desideri, Father Ippolito, 19
Devapatan, *see* Patan
Deva Shumshere, Prime Minister, 81; abdication of, 82
Devi Ghat, scenery at, 173
Devi Sitla, temple of, in a Buddhist temple, 151
Dhaibung or Jibjibia Mount, 25, 172
Dhankuta, 12, 29
Dharara or Bhim Sen's Folly, 145, 176
Dharchula, bridge at, 193
Dharma Datta, king, 38
Dharmsala, 212; Gurkha colony near, 195
Dhaulagiri massif, 2, 3, 7, 8, 18, 22; Peak, 171
Dhir Shumshere, Commander-in-Chief, 79; death of, 83
Dinapore, 208
Diwali festival, 163; gambling during, 107–8, 167; illuminations at, 167, 174–5
Dobhan river, 186
Donaldson, 2nd Gurkhas, 172
Dongkya, Mount, height of, 212
Dorville, Father, S.J., 19
Dotiwals, the, 6–7, 193, 194
Dudh Kosi river, 13
Dumri Khola, the, 189
Durga, propitiation of, 167; sacrifice to, in the Kot, 166–7; temple of, 159

Earthquake in Bihar and Nepal (1933), 141 *n.*, 175 ff.
Eden, Sir Ashley, and the Sikkim treaty, 208
Edward VII, when Prince of Wales in a big-game shoot in the Terai, 78
Elephant-catching methods, 78, 118–19
Elephant-sagacity, 119
Elephants, duels between, 119; Jung Bahadur's exploits with, 67, 68, 119; used in tiger and rhinoceros hunting, 116–17, 118, 119 ff.
England, visits to, of Jung Bahadur 72–3, 86; and of Sir Chandra Shumshere, 86, 87

Everest, Mount, country round, knowledge of, 4–5; expeditions to, 1, 21, 197, flight over summit, 5, Sherpa porters used, 21; height of, 12, 13, 18, 22, 213; location of, 12; a view of, 170

FRIENDSHIP, Treaty of, 91
Führer, Dr., 147

GAGAN SING, murder of, massacre after, 65–6, 69
Gaijatra festival, 163
Gains, Gainis, 123, 187
Gandak mountain basin of, 22
Gandak, Gandaki or Tirsul river (*see also* Tirsul), 7, 8, pass of, 27
Gandakis, the Seven, 7, 23, 43
Gandi river, 8
Ganeshbahadur, 186
Gardner, Captain, 60
Garuda, the, 156, 158
Garwhal, annexed by Nepal, 53, 194; ceded, 58, 59
Gauri Sankar, Mount, 13
Gautama Buddha, visit of, to Nepal, 11, 35
Gawler, Colonel, R.A., at Tumlong, 208
Gaya, 40
George V, King, shooting expedition in the Terai, 116, 118
Ghandrung district, 9
Gheyas-ud-din Tuglak, 40
Girvan Juddha Vikram Sahi, King of Nepal, 54, 56, death of, 60
Gole Baithak, the, ruined by earthquake, 177
Gopala dynasty, the, 34
Gorades, Raja, 152
Gorakhpur, 28; captured by Jung Bahadur, 76; recruiting and pension paying office at, 180 ff.
Gosainthan, holy mountain, 4, 23, 25, 171, 189
Great Britain and the friendship of Nepal, cemented by Jung Bahadur, 69, 72, and by Sir Chandra Shumshere, 85; Treaty of 1923, 91
Great War, the, Nepalese troops supplied for service in, 85, 87, 144–5, 185
Grueber, Father, S.J., 19
Gurkha, old capital of Nepal, 45, 173
Gurkha aggressions early nineteenth century, 55 ff., checked, 68, 204; defeat in the Kangra valley, 56; invasions of Nepal, 40, 41, 44, and conquest of Nepal, etc., 5, 11–12, 40, 41, 45, 51–2, 53, 55–6; incursion into India, 57, defeat and treaty after, 59, 194; incursions into Sikkim, 52, 53, 204; invasions of Tibet, 52, 56
Gurkha ceremonials, 109–10; colonies, children born in, 194–5
Gurkha, kingdom of and provinces of, 23, 53; conquered by Yaksha Malla, 40
Gurkha line-boys, question of, 194–5
Gurkha men, dress of, 103, 104, 133–4
Gurkha military men at Massiang, 189–90; quinquennial mission to China, 52–3; soldiers at Darjeeling, 222; tribes and clans, 8, 13, 93–4; weapons, kukhri, uses of, errors on and mode of wearing, 99–100, 104, 133, 166; pellet-bow, 101; women, dress and jewellery of, and freedom of, 105, 122, 124–5, 181, 187, 221; Gurkhali, title, and race, 12, 42
Gurkhas, the, amusements of, 15, 102, 105, 106, 107, 110, 112, 121 ff., 167
  Characteristics of, addiction to gambling, 107 ff., 167; amenability to discipline, 105; aversion

Gurkhas, characteristics of—*contd.*
to great heat, 181; bonhomie, 121; camaraderie of, with the British soldier, 97; cheerfulness, 97, 174, 201, 217, 223, 228; devotion to British officers, 98; hard-workingness, 223, 230; honesty and truthfulness, 104, 105; independence, 98, 181; lack of cleanliness, 104–5; manner and manners of, 97–8; military qualities, 98–9; outlook on money, 143; peaceful tastes, 99; sense of humour, 135; superstitiousness, 110; tendency to drunkenness, 15, 105–6; vanity, 725
Customs of, birth, 112; death and mourning, 102; marriage and marital infidelity, 99, 100, 105, 110, 111
Deterioration of, in city life, 196, 225; domiciled in British India, number of, 195; food of, monotony of, 108–9; languages used by, 92; music and musical instruments of, 106, 107, 122, 124, 164, 165, 184; origin of, probably Mongolian, 92 ff.; origin of their name, 42
physical characteristics and appearance, 93 ff., 98, 104, 125–6, skin colour, 95–6, stature, 95; Rajput ancestry claimed by, 42, 43, 126, 189
Serving in the Indian army, 6, 8, 14, 77, 94, 98, 100, 144, 187, 190, 196, the first, 58, 180; pensioners, 181 ff., 196; pipers of, 106; recruits, rejections among, 188; war casualties of, 85
Singing habits, 110, 121 ff., singing for a bride, 112; sporting methods of, 100 ff., 115 ff.; of to-day, 42–3; the true (Chetriya), 14; umbrellas prized by, 111, 148, 187

Gurung tribe, caste divisions of, 10
Gurung tribe, 8, 93, 94, 173, 190; origin, language and customs of, 9–10; regiment composed of, 144
Gyabrings, a story on, 10

HAMILTON, B., on honours for Jung Bahadur, 75
Hanuman Dhoka, the, 146; damaged by earthquake, 176
Harisinha Deva, King of Simraun, conqueror of Nepal, 40, 42
Hastings, Marquis of, and the war with Nepal, 57; and the Treaty of Segowli, 59
Hatia Pass, 18
Headdress of the King and Prime Minister, 103–4
Hill Territory, the, 7 ff., 17
Hillmen's Association, the, views of, 229
Himachal, the glory of, unveiled, 191
Himalayas, the, Central, as seen from Kakani, 170–1; Eastern, climate and soil of, 193; expeditions and exploration in, 1; gorges, passes and heights on, 2, 3, 4, 5, 6, 8, 10, 13, 17, 18; in Nepal, 2 ff., 22, and bounding it, 17, 18, seen from Darjeeling, 211; seen after the monsoon, 136–7; snows of, failure to photograph, 137 ff., seen from Darjeeling, 212, other views of, 191; terror felt for in Nepal and Tibet, 16; timber belt of, 198–9; under-features of, 29
Hindu clans, 8
Hindu epics, Nepal unmentioned in, 32
Hindu festivals observed in Nepal, 163
Hindu sanctity, places of, 189
Hindu shrines and temples, 153–4; a Hindu temple within a Buddhist temple, 150–1

Hinduism, 11, 43, 94; spread of, 109, 110, 149
Hiuen Tsang on the Nepalese in the seventh century, 35, 36
Hodgson, Brian, 16; on Bhim Sen Thapa, 61–2; war averted by, 63
Holi festival, the, 163, singing during, 122
Honourable East India Company, the, and the Darjeeling district, 204; Nepalese commercial treaty with, 54; troops sent by, to Nepal, 48, 57–8
Hooker, Sir Joseph, and Eastern Nepal, 213, 217; made prisoner, 206; on the snows, as seen from Darjeeling, 212; and the Wallanchen Pass, 20, 21
Horinje, Pagoda of, Nepalese counterpart of, 168
Horoscopes, importance of, 112

Ilam, 12, 29, 216
India, Gurkha invasions of, 57, 63; Gurkha troops in, during the mutiny and the Great War, 77, 85; the Mallas of, 38; Mohammedan invasion of, 39, 40, 42, 44; Nepalese contacts with, 34, 37 ff., *and see* British India; Southern, link of, with Nepal, 37–8; visits to, of Maharajah Bir Shumshere, 81
Indian Army, the, Gurkhas in, 6, 8, 14, 77, 94, 98, 100, 144, 187, 190, 194, 196; the first, 58, 180; pensioners, 181 ff., war-casualties among, 85; other races in, 180
Indian Hospital Corps, Gurkhas in, 180
Indian Gurkha-land, an, 201
Indo-Aryan languages, 92
Indo-Tibetan troubles, peace terms made by Sir Chandra Shumshere, 84
Indra, 16; thunderbolt of, 150
Indrajatra festival, the, 48, 163
Indrathan, Mount, 25
Indus River, source of, 7
Ingla, 214, various religions at, 215

Jagat Jang, plot connived at, by, 79; fate of, 80
Jai Bahadur, 55, 74
Jamuna village, 214, 216
Jano, Peak, height of, 212
Jalpaiguri, 207
Japanese, the, Gurkha likeness to, 96
Jaya Malla, 169
Jaya Prakasha, king of Kathmandu, defeat of the Gurkhas by, 41; wars of, with Prithwi Narayan, 46 ff., British aid requested by, 48; fate of, 50
Jhirdi, 186
Jhula Ghat, bridge at, 193, 196–7; Gurkhas colony near, 194
Jhunga, 74
Jibjibia massif, 4
Jibjibia or Dhaibung Mount, 25, 172
Jogbani, 29
Joodha Shumshere, Maharaja General Sir, Prime Minister, 177; status, functions and daily routine of, 87–8; and the earthquake, 178
Judha Pratap Jung, fate of, 80
Jung Bahadur, 55; career, murder and massacres in, 64, 65 ff., sudden rise of, to power as Prime Minister and Commander in-Chief, 66 ff.; characteristics of, 66 ff., 72, 74, 77–8; elephant prowess of, 67, 68, 119; friendship of, with Great Britain, and aid given during the Mutiny, 76, 78, 84, 85; honours offered to, and conferred on, 75, 78; internal reforms of, 77, built on by Sir Chandra Shumshere, 82; and the Massacre of the Kot, 65; and the murder of Matbar Sing, 64; plots against, 71, 73–4;

Jung Bahadur—*contd.*
residence of, earthquake damage at, 177; resignation of, and re-assumption of office, 75, 76; sporting prowess of, 67, 68, 119; stories concerning, 67, 68, 119, 145; visit of, to England, 72–3, 86
Jumla, 29
Jumla race, 194
Juwari Kheliako song, the, 123

Kabru, Mount, height of, 212
Kabul, British retreat from, 64
Kaiser Shumshere, General Sir, sportsmanship of, 89; library and garden of, 114; palace damaged in earthquake, 177
Kakani, Mount, 24
Kakani ridge and hamlet, 170; British envoy's residence at, 23, 173, views from, 170–1
Kakul, 145
Kal Bhairab Shrine, 189
Kali or Sarda river, 3, 17, 52, 59, 189, 193; as boundary, 192, 197; bridge over at Jhulaghat, 196; dug-outs on, 197–8; mountains on both sides of, 7; source and course of, 8
Kali Bahadur Regiment, 144
Kalimpong police circle, 209
Kamarupa, king and country of, 31, 32
Kangchenjunga, 18; height of, 13, 22, 211, 217; views of, 211, 212, 213, 217
Kanglachen Pass, 21
Kangra valley, 212; Sikh dominance in, 56
Karnali or Gogra division, 22
Karnali River, 3; source, course and tributaries of, 7, 22
Kasauli, camping at, 184–5
Kashmir, 38, 42, 136, 172
Asoka's rule over, 34, 147
Kashmir State Forces, Gurkhas in, 180
Kaski Pokhra, *see* Pokhra
Kasra, a royal shoot at, 118
Kathmandu, 2, 5, 11, 22, 27, 29, 38, 40, 44, 69, 123, 136, 152; atmosphere of, contrasts in, and people in, 142; and Benares, a link between, 153; British Legation at, 147, site of, 170; capital of Nepal, 45; capture of, by Prithwi Narayan, 48–9; college at, affiliation of, 83; Darbar Square in, 145, 176; the Basehra festival at, 165–6; the Diwali festival at, 174–5; earthquake damage at, 176; factions at, 61; Gurkha rule established at, 45, 56, 93; invaded by Harisinha Devi, 42; inscriptions in and near, 33; king of, *see* Jaya Prakasha; military seen in, 142, 143; Nepal-Tibet treaty signed at, 74–5; origin of the name, 146; Ochterlony's advance on, 58–9; Pagoda style of building in, 141; Palace at, 148; pensions paid at, 181; police force of, 143; the road to, 127 ff., refreshments along, 133; the Singha Darbar at, 148; statue of Bhairab at, 189; statues of Prime Ministers at, 132; temples in, 142, 146, 176; Thapa plots in, 79–80; the Thuni Khel (parade ground) in, 145, 176
Katrapura, King of, 31
Kaulia Peak, 24, 170
Kesavati river, 34
Khadga Shumshere, plot of, 81
Khas tribe, origin and language of, 38–9, *see also* Chetri
Khaskura, an Indo-Aryan dialect, the lingua franca of Nepal, 92
Khattri order, the, 39
Kheddah system of elephant-catching, 78, 118–19

Kilburn, Mrs., photographs lent by, 179
Kinloch, Captain, 48
Kiranti tribe, 13; lamaistic Buddhism of, 13–14
Kirkpatrick, Colonel, on Nepal in 1792, 53, 141
"Kirti Muka" in Newar decoration, 158
Kirtipur, sieges of, 45 ff.
Knox, Captain, 54
Kosi basin or Eastern division, 22
Kosi river, 25, 27; tributaries of, 12–13
Kosis, the seven, country of, 23, 25
Kot, the, the Massacre of, 65–6, 166–7; sacrifice in, to Durga, 166–7
Krishna Shumshere, Lieutenant-General, 176, 177, 179
Kshatriya or Rajput caste, 43
Kumaon, 17, 22; climate and soil of, 193, 197; dialect of, 94; Gurkha seizure of, 52, 53, 54, 194, and forced evacuation of, 58, 59, 194; hill stations of, 7; scenery beauty of, 197
Kumaon-Nepal borders, 192 ff.
Kumhara, Mount, 24
Kuraghat, 182
Kurseong, 202
Kusunda tribe, 16
Kuti Pass, 6, 8, 18, 74
Kuti-Lhasa route, travellers' accounts of, 19 ff.
Kyirong Pass, 6, 18, 19

Lahore, 67
Lahoriyas, 187, 190
Lakshmi, 167; festival of, 108
Lakshmi Devi, Maharani (the younger Queen), 61, murder by, 64; and the Massacre of the Kot, 65–6
Lalsing Gurung, 121, 137
Lamas, 134
Lamjung, Gurungs from, 190
Landon, Perceval, on the Vamshavali, 33, 34; 75, 132, 168
Lepchas, the, 205; at Darjeeling, 218, 219; appearance and characteristics of, 221, 222
Levi, Prof. Silvain, 19, 33; on the pagoda style of architecture, 141; on Patan and its beauty, 161–2
Lhasa, Illtreatment of Nepalese in, 74, and protection of, 75, 91; Nepalese influence on, 37; pass leading to, 18
Likhu river and valley, 171, 172, 173
Limbu tribe, 93, 94; harvesting songs of, 122; land of, 13, 217; religion of, 13–14
Limbuhang country, 13, 217
Little Nepal, 135
Lloyd, General, and Darjeeling, 204–5
Lucknow, Nepalese contingent sent to the relief of, 76

Maccha Pucchar, massif and peak, 3, 7, 170–1, 191
Machendra, image of, 163–4, temple of, 163
Machendrajatra festival, 163–4
Magar kingdom, *see* Palpa
Magarkura dialect, 190
Magars, military Mongolians, tribe of, 7, 8, 93, 172; country of, 9; language of, 109; in the Indian army, 94, in the Nepalese army, 144, 185; religion of, 109
Mahabharat, Mount, 25
Mahabharata, the, 32; songs from, 123
Mahadeo, boulder representing, 171; temple of, 146
Mahadeo Pokhri, Mount, 24, 25; shrine on, 154
Mahbu, 216
Mail-runner, the, 130
Maimajua village, 214, 216
Makalu, Mount, 13

Makaras, use of, 158, 159
Makwanpur, Gurkha defeat at, 59
District, 23
Malaria (Awal), in the Terai and elsewhere, 26, 27, 63, 129, 173, 185, 198
Malla dynasty, the, 33, 38, 45
Man lakes, rivers rising in, 7
Manibhanjang Pass, 173
Manichur, Mount, 24, 25, 170
Manjusri and the valley of Nepal, 32, 152
Manu, laws of, 14
Marakasur, Vishnu's victory over, 167
Markhu, road to, 135
Marsiangdi River, 8
Marwari traders, 198, 218
Massacre of the Kot, the, 65–6, 166–7
Massiang ridge, 185; associations of, 188 ff.
Matbar Sing, 61, 79; vengeance and fate of, 64
Mechi river, 25, 59
Milamchi river, 12, 23, 25
Mohammedan invasion of India, 39, 40, 42, 44
Mohan Shumshere, General Sir, Jangi Lat, 89
Mohindra Rai, 49–50
Monkeys at shrines, 150, 152
Monk travellers on difficulties in Himalayan passes, 5–6, 19–20
Morang district, 25, 26; annexation of, 40
Morris, Major C. J., 191, 214
Morek, custom house at, 187–8
Muktinath, shrine of, 18, 29, 189
Murmi or Tamang tribe, 13, 14, 93, 94, 134
Mustang district, 4, 8
Mustang Pass, 18
Mutiny rebels in Nepal, dispersed by Jung Bahadur, 76
NAGARJAN, Mount, 24, 158; woods on, game in, 160
Nagarkot, 170
Naini Tal, 7
Nairs of Malabar, the, 37, 44
Namguay, Mad Diwan of Sikkim, and the arrest of Hooker and Campbell, 206; trouble with, and flight of, 207–8
Nampa, Peak of, 3
Namri Srong Btsan, first king of Tibet, 36
Nanda Devi group, 3, 4, 22
Nanda Kote, 3
Nanya Deva, conqueror of Nepal, 37
Napier of Magdala, F.-M., Lord, road built by, 202
Napoleon the Great, tomb of, 73
Napoleon III and Jung Bahadur, 73
Narayan, festivals of, 163; shrines of, 158, 159
Narayani River, 8
Narbhupal Sah, King, defeated, 41
Narendra Deva, ruler, in Nepal, 36
Narsing, Mount, height of, 212
Naskatipur, 48
Nautanwa, railway extension to, 182, motor road near frontier, 28, 183
Nawakot, 46, 48; cairn at, 186; fruit at, 172; a visit to, 171 ff., 185
Valley, 23; malaria in, 173
Ne Muni, and the Gopala dynasty, 34
Nepal, administration of, 14, 89–90; ancient civilisation, 10 ff.; approaches into, from British India, 193; Asoka's visit to, 146–7; book on, by Levi, *cited*, 161–2; boundaries and frontiers of, 4, 17, 18, 25, 27, 53, 60, 183, 192, 193, 197, 201, 211, 213; Brahmans in, *see that head*; British resident accepted by, 54, position of, 59–60; Buddha's alleged visit to, 149; Central, 22, 180 ff.; charm of, 175, 217; Chinese invasions of, 6, 8, 52; Chinese missions to, 36; clans

in, 6; commercial treaty of, with Britain, fate of, 54; communications in, 3, 27 ff., 77, mail runners, 135, motor transport, 228, 230, porterage, human, 7, 15, 131, 132, rail, 27, 128, 182, river transport, 28, road, 5, 6, 10, 12, 27 ff., 127, 173, 183, 186, 202, 208; conquest of, by Harisinha Deva, 40; contributions from, in men and material during the Great War, 85, 87, 144–5, 185; currency in, 134; derivation of the word, 34; devotion in, ways of making, 151; divisions of, 6, 7, 10, 12, 22; early history of, 31 ff.; earthquake in, 89, 141 *n.*, 175 ff.; eastern, best known tribes in, 215, journeys in, 213 ff.; ethnology of, 93 ff.; fairs in, 15, 215–16; family feuds in, 55; feudal warfare in, 39; fertile soil of, 32; forests value of, and zones of, 27, 198–9; of the Terai, 25, 26, 198–9; four zones forming, 17–18; friendship of, for Great Britain, 69, 76–7, 84–5, 87, 144–5, 185; general survey of, by Brig.-Gen. the Hon. C. G. Bruce; geography of, 17 ff.; Gurkha invasion and conquest of, 5, 11–12, 40, 45, 55–6; hill country and its inhabitants, 3, 6 ff., 17, 22 Himalayas in, 2 ff. (*and see that head*), Hindu, sacred towns in, 189; hot weather resorts in, 170; hunting methods in, 116 ff.; inscriptions in, 35–6, 147; isolation policy of, Europeans excluded from, 19, 23, 30, 51, 127, 180, 186, 190, 213; King and Prime Minister, colloquial appellations of, 90; kingdom of, 5, 17–18; languages in, and the lingua franca, 9, 20, 92, 93, 190, 193; laws in, 14, 77, 84, 90; liquor trade in, 106; military stations in, 29; military tribes (*see also* Mongolian *and under names*), 6, 8, 9, 13, 56, 94, 109; mineral wealth of, 199; in modern days, 79; Mongolians in, 13, 43, 185, 219, 222 (*see also* military tribes); mountain scenery of, 190–1; natural divisions of, 22; physical conformation of, 17 ff.; Prime Minister of, 54; vast powers of, 75, 82, succession of, 75, 81, title and status of, 89, 147–8, councils advising, 89, residence of, 147–8; Rajput conquest of, 37; relations between all classes in, 15, with China and Tibet, 90–1, with India, 60; religions in, 9, 10, 11, 35, 43, 94, 109, 151, 163, 165, 166 (*see also* Buddhism *and* Hinduism); revenue of sources of, 90; rivers of (*see also under names*), 3, 4, 7, 8, 22, 23; ruling family and aristocracy of, religion of, 113, sportsmanship of, 113, homes of, 114; Sati abolished in, 84; slavery in, 205, abolition of, 81, 83; temples and shrines, 141–2, 149 ff.; the Terai (*see also that head*), 25; Tibetan influences on, 36 ff.; towns in, 29, plan of, 145; trade of, with Tibet and China, routes of, 5; treaty with China, 6; treaty with Tibet, 74–5; tribes, 93–4, Hinduising, 109, relative states of, 56 (*see also* military); war with (1814), 57 ff., and the Treaty of Segowli, 59, 194; weapons owned in, 181; Western races, religion and features of 194, 197

Valley of, 5, 10, 22, area, climate, physical features and beauty of, 23 ff., 135–6, 169–70; boundary of, 170; divisions of, 40, 41, 44; earthquake havoc in, 175 ff.;

Nepal, Valley of—*contd.*
geological origin of, 24, 32, 152; history of, 10 ff.; the key to, 174; mountains of, 17 ff., 25; Newars of (*q.v.*), 43; temples and idols in, 141–2; towns in, 29; valleys around, 23

Nepalese, the, amusements of, 15–16, 121 ff., 215–16; appearance of, Mongolian type of, 190, on the Western border, 193; architecture of, *see under* Newars; caste among, 42–3, 112–13, 124, 181, 225; characteristics of, 15, 35, 223, 224, 230; customs of, on birth, marriage, marital offence, burial, etc., 109 ff.; at Darjeeling, 218, 219; dress, of a general in full-dress, 103, of men, 215, of women, ornaments worn with, 221; festivals, the chief attraction of, 165; fishing methods of, 101, 215; folk-lore, proverbs and riddles, 15–16; folk-songs of, 122 ff.; as planters' servants, 224; postage stamps, 135; sports and diversions of, 102, 113, 115 ff.; as workers, 223, 230

Nepalese army, the, numbers, etc., of, 143–4; reorganisation of, 84
Regiments, bands of, 124, crack, 144, officers of, 143–4
Tribes in, 144, 185; tribes not enlisted in, 14

Nepalese escorts, 172, 197, 198, 216

Nepalese troops offered by Jung Bahadur to the Indian Government, 72, 76

Newars, the, 12, 43, architecture of, for houses, 157–8, 183; for temples, Chaitya or pagoda style, 41, 127, 149–50, 152, 172, finest examples of, 154–5, 168–9; carvings in wood by, 156, 157, 184; metal statues by, 156; artistic powers of, arts and crafts of, 43, 44, 91, 155 ff.; festivals of 163; grouped with Gurkhas, 93; Hindu nobles of, loss of power by, 51; history of, 43 ff.; increasing Hinduism of, 149; location of, 12, 43, 94; mode of worship of, 151; and the Nairs, 37, 44; at Nawakot, 173; resistance of, to Gurkhas, 45, eventually unavailing, 51; as traders, 142, 186, 187; women of, 142

Nilam, 8

North-West Frontier, Nepalese troops on, in 1915, 85

Nyatpola Deval, the, 168–9; damaged by earthquake, 176

Ochterlony, General, 58–9

O'Connor, Sir F., 91, 117

Oldfield, H. A., on the Khas tribes, 39; on the Massacre of the Kot, 66; on the sacred lake of Gosanthain, 171; on the use of the khukri, 39

Oliphant, Laurence on the looks of Gurkhas and others, 125

Oudh, kingdom of, 59, 76

Outcastes, 187

Pad elephant, an experience with, 120–1

Padma Shumshere, General Sir, 85, 89, 143

Palanquin-travel of the past, 128–9

Palpa, Magar kingdom of, 8

Palpa, province, 185; annexation of, 55; Raja of, schemes of, foiled, 54, 58

Palpa regiments, 184, 185

Palpa road, trade along, 186–7; types seen on, 190

Palpa town, 185

Palpa Tansen or Tansing, 29, 185

Panch Chulia, 3

Pandim, Mount, height of, 212

Panoni river, 133

Panre party dominance and downfall of, 63, 64, 69
Panre-Thapa feud, 55, 64
Paris, Jung Bahadur's visit to, 73
Pashupatinath, sanctity of, 50, 153, 189
Pashupati Parshad, badge of, 145
Pataliputra (Patna), 34
Patan or Devapatan, 29, 136; Asoka's stupas at, 11, 35, 162–3; the Darbar square in, 162; described by Levi, 161–2; earthquake devastation at, 175–6; fall of, 48; founding of, 147; greatest Newar festival held at, 163; Malla rulers at, 38, 40, 44, 46, 48–9; pilgrimage to, 163–4; a Rajput ruler of, 37; ravaged Prithwi Naryan, 48, 161; temples in, 41, 162
Patna, 34; university of, 83
Peking, 53
Phalut, Peak, height of, 213
Pharping Gorge, 24
Phatta, 169
Phewa Tal lake, unvisited, 4
Phulchok, Mount, 24
Pickersgill, Lieutenant, 59
Pilgrimages, objectives of, 4, 11, 29, 35, 36, 153, 159, 163, 165, 171, 172, 186
Pithoragarh, 193, 194; Gurkha settlement at, 194
Piyadasi, King, 147
Pokhra, town of, unvisited, 4, 8, 9, 29; lakes at, 30
Portrait figures in metal, 156
Prithwi Bir Vikram Sah, King of Nepal, 79, 80, 82; plots against, 79, 81
Prithwi Narayan Sah, King of Gurkha, accession of, 41, 43; character of, 46 ff.; conqueror of Nepal, 5, 11–12, 40, career of, 8, 10, 34, 40, 42, 43, 45, 55; as diplomatist, 46; at Nawakot, 172, 174; Patan ravaged by, 48, 161; successes and failures of, 45 ff.
Puns from Baglung, 190
Purano Gorakh Regiment, 144
Purnea, 184, 207

Rai tribe, 13, 93, 94, 215; harvesting songs of, 122
Raja Lachiman Sing, house of, 143, 145
Rajendra Vikram Sahi, King of Nepal, 60, 61; help offered by, to British, 64; banishment and final deposition of, 70–71; death of, 60
Rajput blood of the Gurkha, 42, 43, 126, 189
Rajput conquest of Nepal, 37
Ramayana, the, 32; songs of, used in Nepal, 123
Ramnagar district, Gurkha inroad into, 63
Rana Bahadur Sah, accession, reign, 51, 53 ff., murder of, 56
Rana Udip Sing, Prime Minister, plot against and murder of, 79, 80
Ranjang Panre and Bhim Sen Thapa, 61
Ranjit Malla, King of Bhatgaon, fate of, 50
Ranjit Singh, 67; Hodgson on, 62; victory of, over Amar Sing Thapa, 56
Rapti river, 120, 131
Raxaul, 29; rest house near, 127
Raxaul-Amlekhganj railway, the, 27, 128
Regmi, Lieut. Ganesh Bahadur, 183
Rhinoceros in Nepal, 115; hunting of, 117; magic associated with, 117–18
Rifle Regiment, Nepal, 124, 144
Rinchinpong, 207
Riri, fruit at, 189; inhabitants of, 189–90; shrine at, 29, sanctity of, 109

Rummindei, inscription by Asoka at, 147
Ruttledge, Hugh, Mr., and his wife, a stay with and help from, 194

SABUJ REGIMENT, 185
Sahi or Sah clan, head of, 93
Saila, a Nepalese servant, 224–5
Salyana, 29
Samudra Gupta, Emperor, 31
Sanak Sing, 71
Sandakphu, Mount, 214; view from, 213
Sandstone hills, boundary formed by, 17, 22, 27; forest of, 27; varying names of, 27
Santal Parganas, coolies from, 218, 223
Sapt Gandakis, the, 7, 23, 43
Sapt Kosi, 23; clans of, 12; mountains and rivers of, 12–13
Sarat Chandra Das and the passes into Tibet, 20–1
Sarda (Kali) river, 25, 197
Segowli, Treaty of, 59, 194
Seti River, 7, 8
Seti Gandaki river, 8
Seti Khola river, 8
Shekkar Dzong, 40
Sheopuri Mount, 23, 24, 170
Sherpa race, Everest porters drawn from, 21
Shiva, legend on, 153
Shivatri pilgrimage, the, 186
Shlesmantaka, sacred woods, 153
Sikkim, British Indian forces sent to, and subsequent treaty, 207ff.; cession of, to British, 204; Gurkha incursions into, 52, 204; Hooker and Campbell arrested in, 206; the Mad Diwan of, 206; Raja of, and British acquisition of Darjeeling, 204–5; slavery in, 205; valleys of, 15
Sikkim border, the, 4, 13, passes on, closed in 1854, 74, disputes on, 204
Sikkim Terai, annexation of, 206–7
Siklis, the Gurungs of, 9
Silgarhi, 29
Siliguri rail-head, 185, 201
Siliguri, 203
Simalghat, sport at, forest of, 198
Simbu, legend of, 152
Simla Hill States, once Nepalese, 53, 58
Simraun, 40
Singalila ridge, as boundary, 211; an expedition along, 213 ff.
Singha Darbar, earthquake-damaged, 177
Singha Pratap Sah, reign of, 51
Singhini, goddess, 169
Siniolchu or D2, 212
Sino-Nepalese treaty, a, 6
Sisagarhi pass, 128, fort on, 132; view from, 133
Sisnu Khola, river, 188
Siwalik range, 17
Slavery in Nepal, 205, abolition of, 81, 83; in other States, 205
Smith, Captain T., on camaraderie between Gurkhas and British soldiers, 97
Sohanpur, 76
Solajat division, Gurung tribe, 10
Solakhambu, Sherpa stronghold, 21
Someswar range, 27
Songs of various tribes, 122 ff.
Sorati, ceremonial songs, 123
Srong Btsan Sgam Po, the Alexander of Tibet, 36–7
Sthunko dynasty, the, 34
Sun Kosi river, 13
Sunars, the, 187
Sunwar tribe, 13, 93, 94
Surendra Vikram, and Jung Bahadur, 68, 69; Regent, 70, king, 71, death, 79
Sutlej river, 58; source, 7

Swayambhunath, temple in Chaitya style, 136, 150; sacred ever-burning flame at, 150; traditions on, 152; unharmed by earthquake, 176

TADI RIVER, 171, 172, 173
Takla Pass, 18
Taleju (royal shrine), Kathmandu, 146; earthquake damage to, 176
Tama Kosi river, 13
Tamang tribe, *see* Murmi
Tambar river, 13
Tanakpur, 193, 197
Tank of the Serpent, the, 152
Tansing, 29, 185, 189
Tashi-lumpo, looted by Gurkhas, 52
Tea industry, Darjeeling, 205, 206, 218, 222 ff., outlook of, 229–30
Tej Shumshere, General, 85
Tejnarsing, King of Patan, 46, 49
Terai, the, 17, 18, 22, 25 ff.; forests of, 25, 198, 199; game in, and shooting camps, 27, 78, 115 ff., 177; Gurkha annexations in, 57, war following, settlement after, 57–8, 59; cession and retrocession of, 77, 204; jungle of, 17, 25, 184; malaria in, 63, 129, 173, 183; Rajbansis in, 218; water in, a royal boon, 129–30
Thankot, 28, 139–40
Thakur tribe, high standing of, 93, 109
Thakuri dynasty, 33
Thapa-Panre feud, 55, 61, 64
Thapa party, 79
Thapathalli, earthquake damage at, 177
Tharu race, immune to Terai malaria, 26, 29, 173
Thuni Khel, the, 143, 145; at Dasehra Festival, 165; at Nawakot, 174
Tibet, or Bhot, 36 ff.; Chinese dominance over, 52; Gurkha invasion and looting in, 52; a second invasion repulsed, 36; Nepalese influence on, 37; Nepalese war with and treaty after, 74–5, 91; passes leading into, 2, 5–6, 7, 17 ff.
Tibetan form of worship, 151
Tibetan trade, first tapping of, 208
Tibetans, 190, 205, 218, 219, 222; characteristics of, 21; great mountains feared by, 15; rise of, and influence of, in Nepal, 36 ff.
Tibeto-Burman languages, 92, 93
Tigers in the Terai, 115, how hunted, 170
Tindho Khola, river, 184
Tirhut, 40, 42; Gurkha annexations in, 57
Tirsul, Tirsuli, or Tirsul Gandaki river, beauty of, 172–3
Tirsulganga, river, 23, 25
Tirsuli (Gandak) river, tributaries of, 3, 4, 7, 8, 12, 22
Tista river, 208, 209
Tongas, supersession of, 201
Tonglu, 213, 214
Tribeni, 120
Tribubhana Bir Vikram Shaha, H.M. Maharajdhiraja, 89
Tripura Sundra, Maharani, 54, 61; as co-regent, 56, 61; death of, 60, 63, 64; anti-British policy of, and invasion of India, 63
Tumlong, taken by Gawler, 208
Turner, Dr. R. L., on the origin and languages of the Gurkhas in Nepal, 92–3

VAMSHAVALI, the, 33–4
Vasubandu, 32
Victoria, Queen, and Jung Bahadur, 72–3
Vishnu, 32, 151; festival of, 167; incarnation of, 160; shrine of, 154, 155; vehicle of, 158

WALES, the Prince of (Duke of Windsor) in a shooting expedition in the Terai, 116, 118
Wallang or Wallanchen Pass, 18; crossed by Hooker, 20
Waziristan campaign, Nepalese troops in, 85
Wellington, the Duke of, 73

YAKSHA MALLA conquests of, disposal of, 40, 44
Yangma Pass and river, 20
Yassu Mount, 171

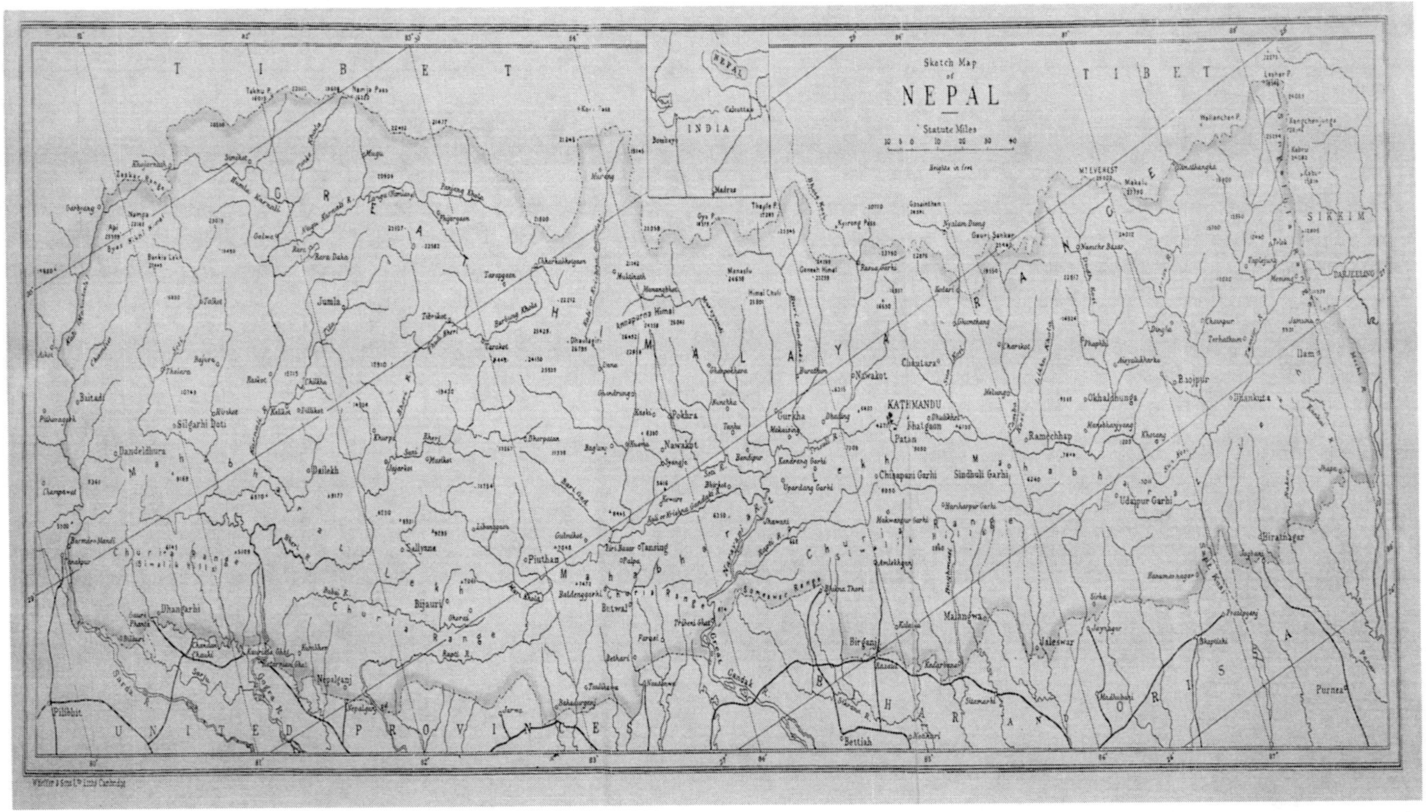
Sketch Map of NEPAL
Statute Miles
Heights in feet
TIBET
TIBET
INDIA
NEPAL
Bombay
Calcutta
Madras
SIKKIM
DARJEELING
MT. EVEREST
Makalu
KATHMANDU
Bhatgaon
Patan
Nawakot
Chautara
Gurkha
Pokhra
Nawakot
Jumla
Dailekh
Silgarhi Doti
Dandeldhura
Baitadi
Piuthan
Sallyana
Bijauri
Tansing
Palpa
Butwal
Chisapani Garhi
Sindhuli Garhi
Udaipur Garhi
Ramechhap
Okhaldhunga
Bhojpur
Dhankuta
Ilam
Biratnagar
Birganj
Jaleswar
Malangwa
Nepalganj
Dhangarhi
Pilibhit
Bettiah
Purnea
UNITED PROVINCES
BIHAR AND ORISSA
GREAT HIMALAYA RANGE
Mahabharat Lekh
Churia Range
Great Gandak
Wheeler & Sons Ltd. Litho Cambridge